SUFFOLK FEAST
ONE COUNTY, TWENTY CHEFS

cookbook & food lovers' guide

second edition

Tessa Allingham, Glyn Williams, Linda Duffin, Frances Hopewell-Smith

Foreword by Frankie Dettori

© Feast Publishing 2018

Text © Feast Publishing 2018

Photography © Feast Publishing – Phil Morley 2018
except for the following pages
As stock *(shutterstock.com unless stated)*:
3, 4, 5-6, 10, 11, 22a, 32a, 42a, 52a, 62a, 72a, 82a, 92a, 102a, 112a, 122a, 132a, 142a, 152a, 162a, 172a, 182a, 192a, 202a, 212a, 214a, 215a, 221, 225, 227, 233, 236
Supplied: (front cover, 236-237, back cover by Emma Kindred, eighty-one.co.uk), 9, 29, 50a, 51l, 53a, 63c, 63l, (73t, Keiko Oikawa), (73cl, Tony Bell), 73cr, 143t, 143bl, 143b, 177b, 177r, 183t, 183ml, 183bl, 183b
(Key: a - all; t - top; b - bottom; l - left; r - right; m - middle; c - centre)

Published by Feast Publishing
E: office@feastpublishing.co.uk
W: feastpublishing.co.uk

First published in paperback in 2018
ISBN (paperback): 978-0-9933601-3-8

Editorial: Tessa Allingham, Glyn Williams, Linda Duffin, Frances Hopewell-Smith
Design: Mark Shreeve
Photography: Phil Morley

All accolades or guide listings refer to 2018 unless otherwise stated.

Recipes listed in this book have been tested and provided to the publishers in good faith. Feast Publishing cannot be held responsible for any loss or damage caused by any omissions or errors therein. Occasionally, dish illustrations may feature elements for pictorial effect that are not included in the recipe methods due to the constraints of space.

All rights reserved. No part of this book may be reproduced, stored in a retrieval system or transmitted in any form or by any means electronic, mechanical, photocopying, recording or otherwise, without the written permission of Feast Publishing. Every effort has been made to clear all images with their respective copyright holders. If there are any errors or omissions, please contact the publishers, who will be pleased to make corrections in future editions.

Contents

Welcome	8
Cooking notes	10
Meet the chefs	12

The Bildeston Crown Bildeston *Chris Lee*	14	Hintlesham Hall Hintlesham *Alan Ford*	114
The Swan Hotel Southwold *Rory Whelan*	24	The Angel Hotel Bury St Edmunds *James Carn*	124
The Packhorse Inn Moulton *Greig Young*	34	The Unruly Pig Bromeswell *Dave Wall*	134
Mackenzie-David Events *Stephen David*	44	The Boarding House Dining Rooms Halesworth *Tyler Torrance*	144
Maison Bleue Bury St Edmunds *Pascal Canevet*	54	Lakes Restaurant, Stoke By Nayland Hotel, Golf & Spa *Alan Paton*	154
The Froize Chillesford *David Grimwood*	64	The Plough & Sail Snape *Oli Burnside*	164
Tuddenham Mill Tuddenham *Lee Bye*	74	The Weeping Willow Barrow *Nick Claxton-Webb*	174
The Anchor Walberswick *Sophie Dorber*	84	The Angel Inn Stoke By Nayland *Dan Russell*	184
Frederick's, The Ickworth Horringer *Iain Inman*	94	The Kitchen@Thorpeness *Cameron Marshall*	194
The Table Woodbridge *Pascal Pommier*	104	The Sail Loft Southwold *Jonathan Nicholson*	204

Food lovers' guide	214
Recipe index	238
Restaurant list	240

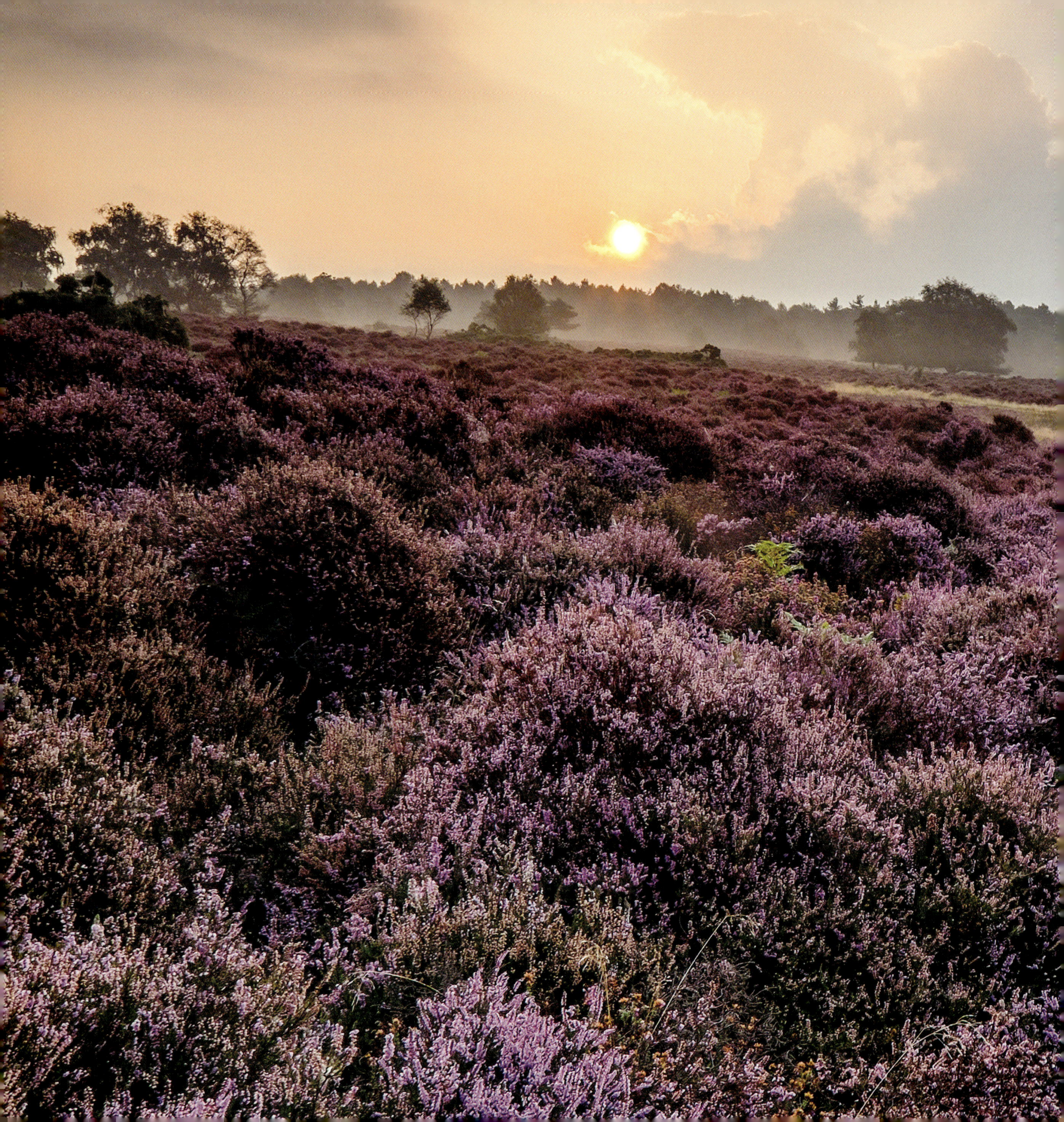

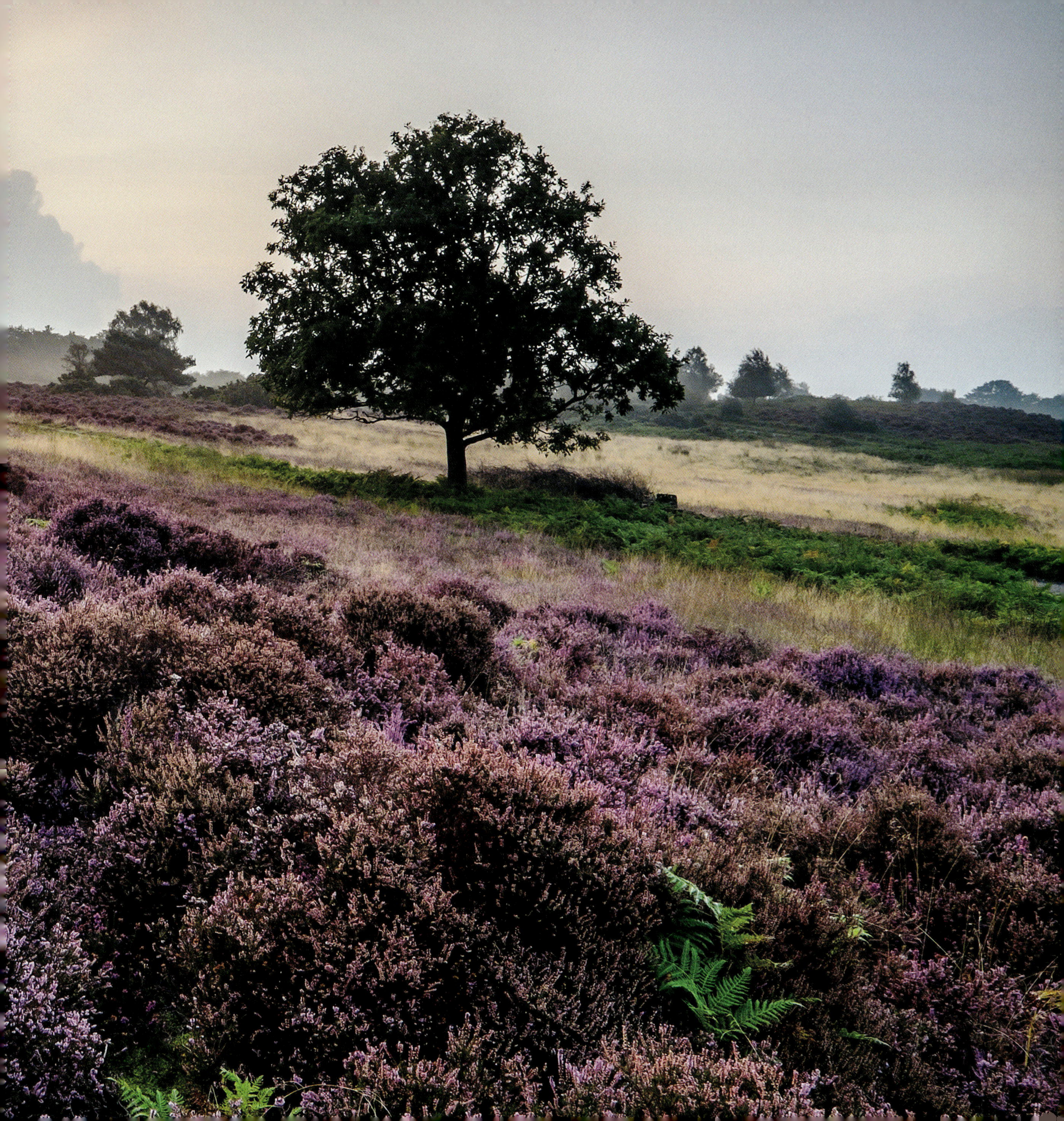

Foreword
Frankie Dettori

To look at me you wouldn't think I liked food that much. I'm 5'4 and during the season I have to get down to a racing weight of 54kg which means I am very disciplined about what I eat – that glass of red wine means an extra 15 minutes on the running machine the next day! But at the same time, I'm Italian aren't I, so food is in my blood and my bones. I love food… I can't stop thinking about it… You'll never meet a true Italian who doesn't like food, and I'm not about to change that!

My food memories are rooted in the beautiful island of Sardinia where as children my sister and I would spend long summers with my grandparents. My grandmother, my *nonna*, would use all the sun-ripened fruit and vegetables from her garden – figs, tomatoes, grapes, peaches drenched with flavour, fragrant herbs – to make simple, home-cooked food that we all loved. We'd stain our mouths and tops with pasta with a fresh tomato and basil *sugo*, suck every morsel from shellfish bought at market that morning, scoop up tangy fresh cheeses *fatt' in casa* (homemade) by the spoonful, and sweep fresh bread through salads seasoned with olive oil from my grandparents' trees. Everything was made with love and care, and using fantastic, simple, local ingredients. Happy times!

Eating for me is all about family and friends, about gathering around a table and catching up on everyone's news, sharing good times and enjoying good food that has been made with very little fuss but lots of heart.

I love cooking at home near Newmarket with my wife Catherine and our five children, and I am spoilt for choice when it comes to eating out too. Really, Suffolk is an incredible place for food. I'm always amazed at the quality of the pork and the beef, the vegetables and fruit, the fish and shellfish, the game, the cheeses… I could go on, but it's making me hungry! Put ingredients like these that have been grown or reared or made, often by small-scale producers, into the hands of chefs who burst with talent, and you have a recipe for a very delicious feast…

You've also got the recipe for a very delicious book, in particular this one, which shines a light on the food of this wonderful county we live in. I have been lucky enough over the years to have been fed by many of the chefs featured in these beautiful pages, and the ones I don't know are now definitely on my to-visit list.

> "I love food… I can't stop thinking about it… You'll never meet a true Italian who doesn't like food, and I'm not about to change that!"

I've lived in Suffolk since I came to Newmarket as an apprentice jockey aged 15, away from home for the first time. It's a place that has been good to me, and that I am delighted to celebrate by welcoming you to this stunning *Suffolk Feast* of a book. Enjoy the stories, try the recipes, and visit the twenty restaurants where you are assured of a warm Suffolk welcome and some delicious plates of food!

Salute!

9

Cooking notes

We want you to enjoy the exciting, original recipes from some of our favourite Suffolk chefs, that are included in this book. To ensure you get the best out of the dishes, please take time to read the following tips and the few words of caution. Much of it will be second nature to many home cooks, but if in doubt, do refer to these notes.

WELFARE IN THE KITCHEN

Sharp tools, high temperatures and close proximity to humans and pets make the kitchen a potentially dangerous place. Accidents can happen when cooking, so please minimise the risk by applying appropriate caution, care and common sense.

COOKING TEMPERATURES AND TIMINGS

Cookers, and especially ovens, can be fickle pieces of equipment. Please treat all temperatures and times as a general guide and adjust to suit your own cooker.

Temperatures and timings are based on the use of a domestic, electric, fan oven so please adjust to the appropriate equivalent level if you have a different cooker type.

MEASUREMENTS

- General cookery rules and common sense apply
- Spoonfuls are measured level
- Bunches for herbs are standard retail sizes
- Eggs are large and free range from a local, happy farm flock preferably
- Milk used is full fat unless otherwise stated

SEASONING

Recipe seasoning instructions refer to adding salt and pepper to taste. We choose to use local Maldon sea salt flakes, crushed between clean fingers or milled for fineness, and black peppercorns, freshly ground to order. Some dishes may taste or look better on the plate with the alternative use of white peppercorns, eg fish dishes and cream sauces.

GENERAL TIPS

- Rapeseed oil should be cold-pressed, good quality and local where possible.
- Keep warm plates to hand both for storing cooked elements of dishes hot while finishing recipes and then to serve on as required.
- Recipes call for standard preparation of ingredients ie the kitchen 'norm' such as all produce being washed before use and trimmed, peeled, cored, deseeded etc if need be. Any need to the contrary will be indicated. Meat and fish to be oven-ready and if required to be skinless or boneless, this will be stated accordingly.
- To rest food, leave somewhere hot on a warm plate, loosely covered with foil if your kitchen is cool or draughty, until required.

FOOD SAFETY

It goes without saying that ensuring the health and well-being of the people eating your food is vital! Use your common sense backed up with a bit of research and advice from reputable books and online sources.

Please do pay particular attention to:

- Quality and freshness of ingredients – check expiry and best-before dates
- Storage of produce and ingredients in the kitchen
- Use of raw and partly cooked eggs
- Allergen risks
- Cooling and refrigeration where dishes are stored mid-preparation before finishing
- Fridge temperature – is it low enough for safe storage?
- Oven temperature – is it hot enough before you start cooking?
- Core temperature of cooked dishes – has the food reached the right temperature before consumption?
- Finished dishes, not consumed immediately after preparation – are they stored at appropriate temperatures and consumed within safe time limits?

If in doubt, consult the Government's own online health and nutrition website for food safety advice at nhs.uk/livewell

SUFFOLK FEAST

1 THE BILDESTON CROWN
CHRIS LEE

2 THE SWAN HOTEL
RORY WHELAN

3 THE PACKHORSE INN
GREIG YOUNG

4 MACKENZIE-DAVID EVENTS
STEPHEN DAVID

Meet the chefs

Hungry? Let these chefs, twenty of Suffolk's finest, put that right.

Maybe you're feeling peckish after a brisk dip in the North Sea, or need to refuel after a walk in the achingly beautiful countryside of the south; maybe you'd like to drink in those expansive west Suffolk views over a bite to eat, or reboot your energy as you visit Suffolk's historic towns or captivating villages. Maybe it's simply lunchtime.

Whatever your reason for feeling hungry, the twenty chefs featured in this book are here to help. They are a talented lot, cooking delicious plates of food with originality, flair, and a deep-rooted connection with, and affection for, the fantastic ingredients that are grown, reared, fished or made on their Suffolk doorsteps.

We celebrate every one of them. They will all make you very welcome too – do pay them a visit to find out for yourself!

9 FREDERICK'S, THE ICKWORTH
IAIN INMAN

10 THE TABLE
PASCAL POMMIER

15 STOKE BY NAYLAND HOTEL
ALAN PATON

16 THE PLOUGH & SAIL
OLI BURNSIDE

5 MAISON BLEUE
PASCAL CANEVET

6 THE FROIZE
DAVID GRIMWOOD

7 TUDDENHAM MILL
LEE BYE

8 THE ANCHOR
SOPHIE DORBER

11 HINTLESHAM HALL
ALAN FORD

12 THE ANGEL HOTEL
JAMES CARN

13 THE UNRULY PIG
DAVE WALL

14 THE BOARDING HOUSE
TYLER TORRANCE

17 THE WEEPING WILLOW
NICK CLAXTON-WEBB

18 THE ANGEL INN
DAN RUSSELL

19 THE KITCHEN@THORPENESS
CAMERON MARSHALL

20 THE SAIL LOFT
JONATHAN NICHOLSON

Game on

The rich, earthy flavours of autumn and winter define Chris Lee's cooking. He is in his element working with locally shot partridge

THE BILDESTON CROWN, BILDESTON
CHRIS LEE

THE BILDESTON CROWN CHRIS LEE

It's February 1st, the last day of the shooting season. Keepers and beaters, dressed in their trademark sludgy green and brown, are gathered in the yard at Box Tree Farm for the traditional last outing. Assorted labradors and spaniels quiver and pace, eager to be done with the early formalities, and for the day to begin.

Our day begins differently, though Chris Lee also looks the part, every inch the shooting man in tweed waistcoat, shirt and tie, 12-bore hooked over a forearm. We head into the fields around the Wattisham farm with Elaine Rushbrook and Sandy her 12-year-old yellow lab. This is 4,000 acres of prime and picturesque Suffolk shooting land, the fields rolling in a gentle East Anglian way, and hedges, woodland, dips and valleys creating an ideal habitat for birds, and some challenging terrain for the guns.

While her father, Peter, runs the shoots, Elaine is the calm, unassuming force behind the food side of the Mallard Barn enterprise. She prepares and sells the feathered and furred game shot on three sites (Box Tree Farm where the Rushbrook family lives, and two estates where they run the shoots – Ampton, north of Bury St Edmunds, and Plashwood Hall near Haughley).

"In the season I'm most often covered head to toe in feathers!" says Elaine. "I prepare all the game myself – duck, pheasant, partridge, pigeon, hare, venison – so that it's ready for chefs like Chris."

"We've always got on really well," says Chris of the pair's 15-year professional partnership. "I even bought my gun from Elaine, and she always supplies top-class game." And that's the important thing, because when it comes to cooking, there is little that gets Chris' chef juices flowing more readily than game. He jokes – a day with Chris is sparky with banter – about the appeal of a 'meat and no two veg' menu. "Meat every time! I'm into food with gutsy flavour. I love using truffle, I like intense reductions, wintry slow-cooked casseroles." It tracks back to his mother. "Every morning when I was a kid, sausages, onions, carrots would go into the slow cooker and she'd make a classic 'one pot wonder' meal which I loved."

Back in his orderly kitchen – "yes, I am a bit OCD, I like my J-cloths stacked straight, and drawers must be organised" – he buttons himself into fresh whites. He has a loyal team here – sous chefs Stuart Darton and Steve Pattel have worked with Chris for 24 and eight years respectively – so it's not surprising to feel an easy atmosphere as he prepares a classic wellington using Mallard Barn partridge. It's a dish that works well with lean game, the wrapping of parma ham, spinach and pastry ensuring the breast meat stays succulent; it's helped further by a layer of rich duck liver through the middle.

Nothing is wasted, the legs confit'd for the accompanying terrine, the liver and heart kept for a sauce. He slices through the rested meat in its crisp, golden packaging, and arranges it with precision. It is a good-looking plate of food, but it's the flavours and textures, powerful and balanced thanks to a square of potato and turnip boulangère, and roasted, puréed and pickled turnips, that make it sing. And where some might be tempted to decorate with a fiddly flurry of micro herbs or a sneeze of foam, Chris leaves it as it is.

The Bildeston Crown menu is rich with top-notch ingredients. Many are local – Red Poll beef is from a nearby herd, Suffolk Blue cheese gives salty depth to a fondant served with sweet beetroot cannelloni, and the venison loin, simply pan-fried, is from Elaine – but Chris is known for an unabashed use of luxury ingredients. Lobster, ceps, hints of truffle, oysters, and caviar pop up on both the Classics line-up (his lobster Caesar salad is rarely off, and a baked camembert with truffle honey is an indulgent starter), or the Select menu (cep and truffle risotto with salsify and wild mushrooms packs a tasty punch). Even his burger becomes deluxe if you choose to add duck liver and truffle mayo.

"We used to be known for fine dining," says Chris, "but I'd rather be known for everyday good dining. There's so much competition these days. We can't assume people will choose us, so we have to offer a range of dishes, not just what we think customers should want. Some want the seven-course tasting and wine flight, others come for a sandwich and a pint, or fish and chips." 'Fish and Fizz' Fridays, and a midweek set lunch are part of a mission to offer the everyday alongside the special.

Kent-born Chris fell into cooking. "I wanted to be a banker but didn't get the maths grade so ended up as a kitchen porter at the Hilton in Northampton. I did a day-release catering course, realised I enjoyed food, and got a job at the Hilton Park Lane aged 16." From there, Chris went to Fawsley Hall near Daventry to work under the legendary Nico Ladenis, before he and his wife Hayley took on The Bildeston Crown for owner and local farmer, James Buckle. Hayley finishes the story. "In 2013 we left, but we came back in 2015, and it felt like coming home."

THE BILDESTON CROWN CHRIS LEE

Partridge and duck liver wellington and terrine, boulangère potato

There is nearly always a version of this main course classic on our menu. It works well with all types of wild game, and cooking game this way in a casing of parma ham and puff pastry ensures the meat stays juicy and tender. It can also be prepared almost entirely in advance, though you do need to do the final stages simultaneously. Pictured, it is served with turnips, prepared four ways, but other seasonal vegetables will equally complement it. (serves 4)

Jus
- **Carcasses from 4 oven-ready partridges, legs and breasts reserved**
- **100ml madeira**
- **1 litre of good game stock**

Chop up the carcasses and roast in a very hot oven until browned. Boil the madeira in the roasting tin, scraping it to deglaze. Add the stock and bring to a boil. Reduce to a syrup before sieving and adjusting the seasoning. Cool and refrigerate.

Terrine
- **8 partridge legs**
- **Duck fat**
- **200g horn of plenty or other wild mushrooms**
- **Unsalted butter**
- **Tiny fillets from the underside of the partridge breasts**
- **Seasoned game stock**

Place the partridge legs in a snug tin covered with duck fat and bake at 100c for about an hour until tender. Tear the mushrooms into bite-size pieces and sauté in foaming butter until softened. Gently simmer the fillets in a little stock until just cooked. Once cooled, remove the meat from the legs and combine with the fillets and mushrooms, adding a little duck fat to moisten the mixture. Press into a terrine dish, weigh down and chill for at least 24 hours.

Boulangère
- **2 large onions, thinly sliced**
- **Unsalted butter**
- **4 large turnips, thinly sliced**
- **8 large Maris Piper potatoes, thinly sliced**
- **100ml seasoned game stock**

Gently fry the onions in melted butter until softened and caramelised.

Layer the potatoes, turnips and onions in a deep, buttered tray or gratin dish, seasoning in between, finishing with a final layer of potato. Dot with butter and pour over the seasoned game stock. Bake at 160c until cooked and tender when skewered. Remove, cool and refrigerate overnight, weighted down.

Wellington
- **8 large leaves of spinach**
- **8 partridge breasts**
- **4 slices of parma ham**
- **4 thin slices of duck liver**
- **1 large block of rich puff pastry**

Blanch the spinach in boiling water and plunge into iced water to cool before draining well. Season the partridge breasts. Lay out a dinner plate-sized sheet of clingfilm, place a slice of the ham in the centre add a spinach leaf, a breast, a slice of liver, another breast and another leaf, before folding around the ham and by using the clingfilm, bring together into a tight ball. Chill for 12 hours to set.

Roll out the puff pastry and cut into four 10cm x 10cm squares. Unwrap the balls and encase in the pastry. Brush with egg yolk.

To serve
- **Unsalted butter**

Bake the wellingtons in a pre-heated 185c oven on a hot tray for 12 minutes till cooked through. Remove and rest for 10 minutes.

Portion the potato and reheat in the oven for a few minutes, dotted with butter. Slice the terrine onto a roasting tray, dot with butter and reheat briefly. Bring the jus to a simmer. Place the wellington, potato, and terrine on warmed plates and dress with the jus and vegetables of your choice.

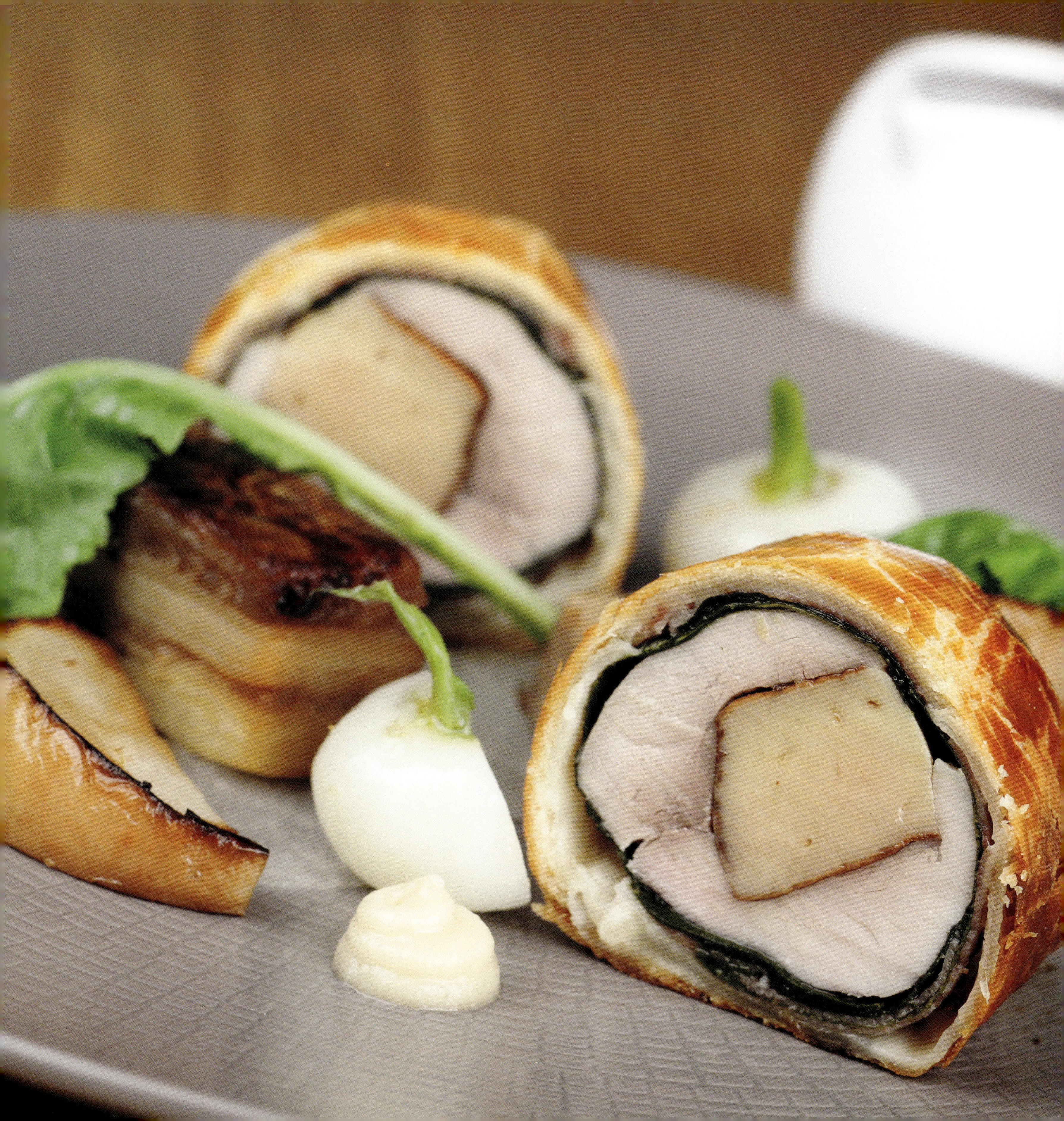

THE BILDESTON CROWN CHRIS LEE

Seared scallops and cauliflower

There's a delicious combination of unusual textures and flavours in this starter. We add apple slices, jelly and syrup for fruity contrast. Prepare the tempura and scallops at the same time. (serves 4)

1 each of white, romanesco and purple cauliflowers
Chicken stock
Unsalted butter
Plain flour and cornflour
Soda water, ice cold
Ground cumin
8 scallop meats, coral removed

Char thin slices of white cauliflower in a hot, dry griddle pan. Keep warm.

Blanch trimmed florets of the other two cauliflowers in salted water until just softened and remove. Simmer the cauliflower trimmings in hot chicken stock with a good knob of butter until soft, drain, season and purée. Keep warm.

Pre-heat a deep fat fryer to 180c. Mix equal parts of both flours with a little salt and whisk with enough soda water into a single cream texture. Coat the florets and deep-fry till golden. Drain and keep warm.

Arrange the cauliflower slices and florets on warmed plates.

Combine equal parts of cumin and salt and dust the scallops with the mix. Sear the scallops in a hot oiled pan till golden-brown on both sides, finally basting with a knob of butter. Add the scallops and purée to the cauliflower, arranging the plate attractively.

Smoked salmon with horseradish crème fraîche and beetroot

An elegantly simple yet rather stunning starter. The salmon is the hero of the dish, so use the best quality, locally smoked variety you can find. I like to serve this with warmed blinis or just wholemeal bread. (serves 4)

400g crème fraîche
2 tsp grated horseradish
Lemon half
Cayenne pepper
2 large beetroot
150ml white balsamic vinegar
150ml olive oil
8 slices of smoked salmon
8 hard-boiled quails' eggs
8 breakfast radishes, thinly sliced
1 cucumber, deseeded and diced
Flat leaf parsley

Beat the crème fraîche until thickened, before whisking in the horseradish, a squeeze of lemon and two pinches of cayenne with seasoning to taste. Chill to set.

Use a pastry cutter to cut a cylinder from both beetroot, reserving the trimmings. Slice the beet thinly into rounds and place in a bowl. Simmer the vinegar and oil before pouring over the beetroot slices. Simmer the trimmings in water until soft, season and purée.

On cold plates, assemble the salmon scattered with the halved eggs, beetroot slices, cucumber and radishes. Finish with the purée, crème fraîche and parsley.

Parsley risotto

This vibrant and herby risotto is a great base for a main course or a light starter on its own. Chef's secret: you can make a perfect risotto without having to be at your stove continually stirring for 20 minutes! To finish this, I fold in salsify root, braised in red wine, rosemary and garlic and wild mushrooms, sautéed in butter. (serves 4)

1.5 litres good vegetable stock
4 shallots, finely diced
Unsalted butter
450g arborio rice
125ml dry white wine
1 onion, finely sliced
Small bunch of curly parsley
Small bunch of flat leaf parsley
100g grated parmesan
Lemon

Simmer the stock. Separately, soften the shallots gently in a little butter without colouring in a deep sauté pan. Add the rice and cook for another minute over a medium heat. Pour in the wine, turn to high and stir while it dries out.

Add 1 litre of the stock gradually, stirring until all absorbed but the rice is still al dente. Season to taste before scraping out onto a flat tray.

Soften the onion in 50g of butter and add the parsley stalks and the remaining stock. Simmer until soft, then add the leaves, cooking for 4 minutes before blending smooth. Cool and chill.

Bring the purée to a boil and mix in the rice, simmering until tender. To finish, fold in the parmesan, a knob of butter, a squeeze of lemon and seasoning to taste before serving.

CHRIS ON HIS...

WHAT THREE QUALITIES DO YOU ADMIRE MOST IN PEOPLE?

I like people with ideas, people who buy me beer, and people who are on time. Even if a person is just two minutes late for something, I can't forget it!

INSPIRING SUFFOLK VIEW?

If I'm lucky enough to get a day's shooting with James Buckle, [owner of The Bildeston Crown] there are some fantastic views across his land. I love walking there on a crisp winter day.

WHICH OF YOUR HABITS WOULD YOU FIND HARDEST TO GIVE UP?

That sharpener at the end of service, a Bud in the back bar as I'm doing my orders.

A SPECIAL CHILDHOOD MEMORY?

My mum's cooking. Everything would go in one pot. Her spag bol was amazing and she still hasn't told me the secret to the recipe.

SIGNATURE DISHES

Starters

Lobster caesar salad, anchovies, bacon

Partridge 'all day breakfast'

Smoked haddock fishcake

Mains

Brixham sea bass, braised oxtail, rainbow chard

Local pheasant kiev, ceps, pancetta, kale, white beans

Tongue & cheek of Red Poll beef, watercress, shallots

Puddings

Lemon tart, crème fraîche sorbet

Banoffee soufflé, vanilla ice cream

Herring roes on toast, garlic butter, parsley

IF NOT A CHEF...

I'd have been a banker. I've got a thing about money! I got a D in GCSE maths so I retook the exam but got an E, so I got a job as a kitchen porter at the Northampton Hilton instead. The rest is history.

PERFECT DAY OFF?

Food would always be part of a day off, but sometimes I just want to sit on the sofa, put on a Ray Winstone movie or watch some cheffy programme, open a pack of Jelly Tots and chill with Hayley and Truffle.

IS THERE A FILM YOU NEVER TIRE OF WATCHING?

The Shawshank Redemption. Brilliant every time.

FAVOURITE COOKBOOKS?

I have hundreds — in fact the shelf collapsed last night it was so overloaded — but the one I'd save from a fire would be John Campbell's *Formulas for Flavour*. I buy cookbooks to read on holiday so I often come back with white knees! And when I took Heston's *Big Fat Duck Cookbook* with me it sent my case over the weight limit too.

QUICK SNACK OR MIDNIGHT FEAST?

Chicken and salad cream sandwich. Forget posh mayonnaise, salad cream goes with everything! Or maybe mac 'n' cheese with tomato ketchup. The ketchup mixes in and makes a lovely marie rose sauce.

SHARE SOMETHING ABOUT YOURSELF THAT NOBODY KNOWS

I do have feelings. Not a lot of people know that...

SUFFOLK FEAST

Inn our style

There may not be a straight wall or floor to be seen in The Bildeston Crown, but that all adds to the appeal of this beautiful 15th century former coaching inn. Unmissable with its mustard-yellow walls, The Bildeston Crown sits on the high street of pretty Bildeston – it's one of Suffolk's ancient wool towns – and draws people with the promise of top-notch food from Chris Lee and a warm welcome from his wife, Hayley. During their first ten years running the inn (2003-13) as chef and manager, the couple built a local and national food reputation, something they have restored since taking on the lease in 2015 to run the inn as their very own business. They were greeted with open arms when they returned, not least those of The Bildeston Crown's owner and local farmer, James Buckle.

Original beams and fireplaces, old paintings, shelves filled with leather-bound books, and comfortable wing-back armchairs by the fire make this a hard place to leave, a problem compounded if you stay overnight in one of the 12 beautiful rooms. There are contemporary touches, however: the inky blue of some walls is bold and enveloping, and the handmade wallpaper by designer Adam Calkin on others is striking.

And while open fires are stoked throughout the colder months, the inn is just as attractive in summer when the courtyards and terraces are perfect for pre-dinner drinks and maybe a few appetite-sharpening Colchester oysters or Chris' popular tandoori soft-shell crab and salsa.

The Bildeston Crown
104 High Street, Bildeston IP7 7EB
W: thebildestoncrown.com
T: 01449 740510
E: reception@thebildestoncrown.co.uk
- /BildestonCrown
- @BildestonCrown
- /cheflee01

Accolades and listings: Waitrose *Good Food Guide*; AA Two Rosettes; *Michelin*; *Harden's*; *Sawday's*; *Good Hotel Guide*; Charming Small Hotels; Cool Places

Food served: all week B 8-10; L 12-2.30; D 7-9.30 (9 Sun)

Cost: starters from £7; mains from £12; desserts £8; seven-course taster menu (pre-booked) £80 or £110 with wine flight; set lunch Mon-Thurs £15 (2 courses), £20 (3 courses); light bites from £7; afternoon tea (pre-booked) £15; wine from £17.50; beer from £3.75

Details: 120 seats; bar area with open fire; al fresco tables; private hire possible for weddings, parties or meetings in the Green Room (seats 16), Ingrams (seats 34), summer marquee (seats 150); 12 en suite bedrooms; accessible in parts with lift; dogs welcome in bar; parking

THE SWAN HOTEL, SOUTHWOLD
RORY WHELAN

Grain power

Rory Whelan celebrates the distinctive flavours of Adnams beer, brewed just yards from his kitchen door at The Swan Hotel

25

Maybe it's because he's a Dubliner, that Rory Whelan's sip of choice – after service or during time off, of course – is a pint of Adnams Blackshore Stout. Classically an Irish recipe, the beer is rich with the flavour of chocolate and coffee, heady with notes of liquorice and dark fruits (or so the tasting notes of head brewer Fergus Fitzgerald promise), and no doubt the perfect antidote to Rory's busy chef's life.

That busy life recently got a whole lot busier when Rory stepped up to become head chef at The Swan Hotel in Southwold in spring 2018, reaching the top of the culinary tree at Adnams after a loyal ten years with the company. "I was ready," he says in his quiet, direct, warmly Irish way. "It's an exciting opportunity and I wanted the challenge."

He has wasted no time in gathering menu ideas for the Still Room (The Swan's elegant dining room with its design nods to the Copper House distillery), and the more informal Tap Room where Adnams' brewing heritage is celebrated. There, regular beers – Ghost Ship pale ale, Broadside and Southwold Bitter – line up with seasonal ones, Dry Hopped Lager perhaps in the summer or Rory's favourite Blackshore in winter. "It makes sense for me to find creative ways to bring the flavours of Adnams beers and spirits into my food. How many chefs have a brewery like this in their back yard, and a distillery? It's unique!"

Beer doesn't take kindly to being heated though, so when we meet across the bench in his peaceful kitchen, he is rippling his fingers through a pile of grain. It's a few handfuls of the malting barley that is grown on contract by East Anglian farmers, Fergus tells us as we later walk along gantries and up and down myriad stairways, peer into mash tuns, and talk wort, yeast, hops, how beer tastes better nowadays, and how Adnams is a proudly sustainable and community-minded business. The brewery is a gleaming hive of modern industry, a place where Fergus and his team transform barley into some 85,000 barrels of beer every year.

"I've gone back a stage," Rory says. "For me as a chef it makes sense to work with the grain rather than the end product. It tells the Adnams 'grain to glass' story – and it doesn't undo all Fergus' good work on flavour!" We crush the husks, taste the unmistakable, nostalgia-laden, toasty malt. "It works well with these morels," he says, indicating some mushrooms waiting to be prepped. "They're earthy but they also have a fresh, spring taste."

He puts the dish together, moving easily between several pans on the stove. Plump breasts of free-range chicken have been gently cooked

THE SWAN HOTEL RORY WHELAN

in a water bath. He's a fan of the technique. "It's a brilliant way of keeping moisture in lean ingredients, retaining natural flavour, and having complete control." The meat is finished in butter, the breasts topped on the plate with a deep-fried nugget of leg meat, and a curling length of leek that has been blanched and griddled whole, its tufty edible roots intact. Pearl barley braised in stock enriched with malted barley extract references the beer and gives texture, while the toasted grain, infused into more stock, gives depth to a clear consommé. It's a plate of food that's in tune with the time of year and Rory's love of ingredient-led, rigorously seasonal cooking.

Adnams' spirits are arguably easier to work with. A dish of salmon cured in Rising Sun gin (made from rye grown on the Reydon farm belonging to chairman Jonathan Adnams OBE) is popular, and Triple Malt whisky is the star of Rory's take on a classic Scottish cranachan. He soaks the oats in the whisky and finishes them with honey, stirs more whisky into lightly whipped cream and crème fraîche, arranges the raspberries carefully. "I'm picky about my whisky," he says, waiting for one of his chefs to bring a shot from the bar.

"It used to have to be a 12-year-old single malt Jameson – an Irish whiskey of course! – but now I prefer this Triple Malt. I like its lingering, clean finish."

For all the nods to his Irish roots, Rory is very much at home in Suffolk. "I was on a flight to the UK seven days after I left school!" he recalls. "I was just 18." He left early jobs in London to work with Alan Ford for a formative decade at Hintlesham Hall, then Paul Whittome at the Hoste Arms in Burnham Market, Norfolk, before being lured back to Suffolk in 2008 to The Swan, Southwold. And here we are, ten years on, talking fresh ideas and fresh menus for both the Still Room and Tap Room restaurants, the importance of creating food that customers will come back for again and again, and of running a calm kitchen in which ego is irrelevant. "Adnams has changed so much in the years I've been here," Rory reflects, looking out at Southwold's timeless High Street. "The brewing has changed – Fergus said how much the quality of beer has improved, didn't he – The Swan has changed with the refurb, there's a real energy. I'm excited to be part of it." I make a note to come back to chat in another ten years.

THE SWAN HOTEL RORY WHELAN

Chicken breast, leg croquette, leek, morels, tarragon, malted barley broth

The nutty flavours of the malting barley really come out in this lovely dish which champions the grain that is at the root of all Adnams' beers. Choose the best quality chicken you can – a plump free-range bird is always my first choice. Best to make the broth, whizz the tarragon oil and cook the pearl barley in advance (serves 4)

Tarragon oil
- Small bunch of tarragon leaves (keep stalks for the broth)
- 150ml rapeseed oil

Cover the tarragon with boiling water, stir and drain after 30 seconds. Squeeze out any excess water, blitz in a food processor with the oil until smooth and green. Strain through clean muslin and set aside.

Broth
- 100g malted barley
- Rapeseed oil
- 2 shallots, finely diced
- 1 garlic clove
- Tarragon stalks
- 1 litre chicken stock
- 2 tbsp malted barley extract

Toast the malted barley until warmed to release the natural oils and aroma. Gently fry the the barley, shallot, garlic and tarragon stalks with a little oil until softened but without colouring. Add the stock and malt extract and bring to the boil. Reduce to a low simmer and cook for an hour. Strain through clean muslin and reserve the liquid, discarding the solids. Cool and chill the broth until required.

Leg croquettes
- 4 chicken legs
- 200ml chicken stock
- Seasoned flour, beaten eggs, breadcrumbs

Gently braise the legs in the stock until tender and flaking. When cooked, remove the legs and allow to cool before flaking off the meat. Meanwhile reduce stock to a quarter of its volume. Allow to cool. Mix the meat with the reduction and chill until cold. Prepare three separate bowls of the flour, eggwash and crumbs. Roll the meat into stubby sausage-shaped croquettes. Dip alternately in the flour, egg and crumbs, removing any excess at each stage before finally pressing in the crumb coating well. Store on a clingfilmed tray, not touching each other. Chill for another 20 minutes. Pre-heat the deep fryer to 180c. Deep fry a few croquettes at a time until golden-brown. Keep warm.

Braised barley
- 2 shallots, finely diced
- 1 carrot, finely diced
- Rapeseed oil
- 100g pearl barley
- 200ml chicken stock
- 1 tbsp malted barley extract

Gently fry the shallots and carrot slowly in a little oil. When softened, add the barley and continue cooking for another 2 minutes. Add the stock and malt extract before simmering for 45 minutes until the grains are tender.

Chicken
- 4 boneless chicken breasts
- Rapeseed oil
- 2 leeks, halved lengthways
- 12 morel mushrooms, halved lengthways
- Butter

Pre-heat the oven to 180c. Season the chicken breasts and seal skinside uppermost in a very hot, oiled frying pan. Turn over and roast in the oven for 15-20 minutes. Remove from the oven and keep warm.

Blanch the leeks in boiling water until softening but still firm. Pat the leeks dry, season and brush with oil. Finish by charring both sides on a very hot griddle plate and then remove to keep warm.

In a small frying pan, gently cook the morels with a little butter and seasoning for a few minutes. Remove and set aside.

To serve, cut the chicken breasts in half lengthways and place in a bowl. Spoon warmed barley on top, add a leg croquette and the leek before scattering the morels around. Drizzle over a little tarragon oil and finish with the broth.

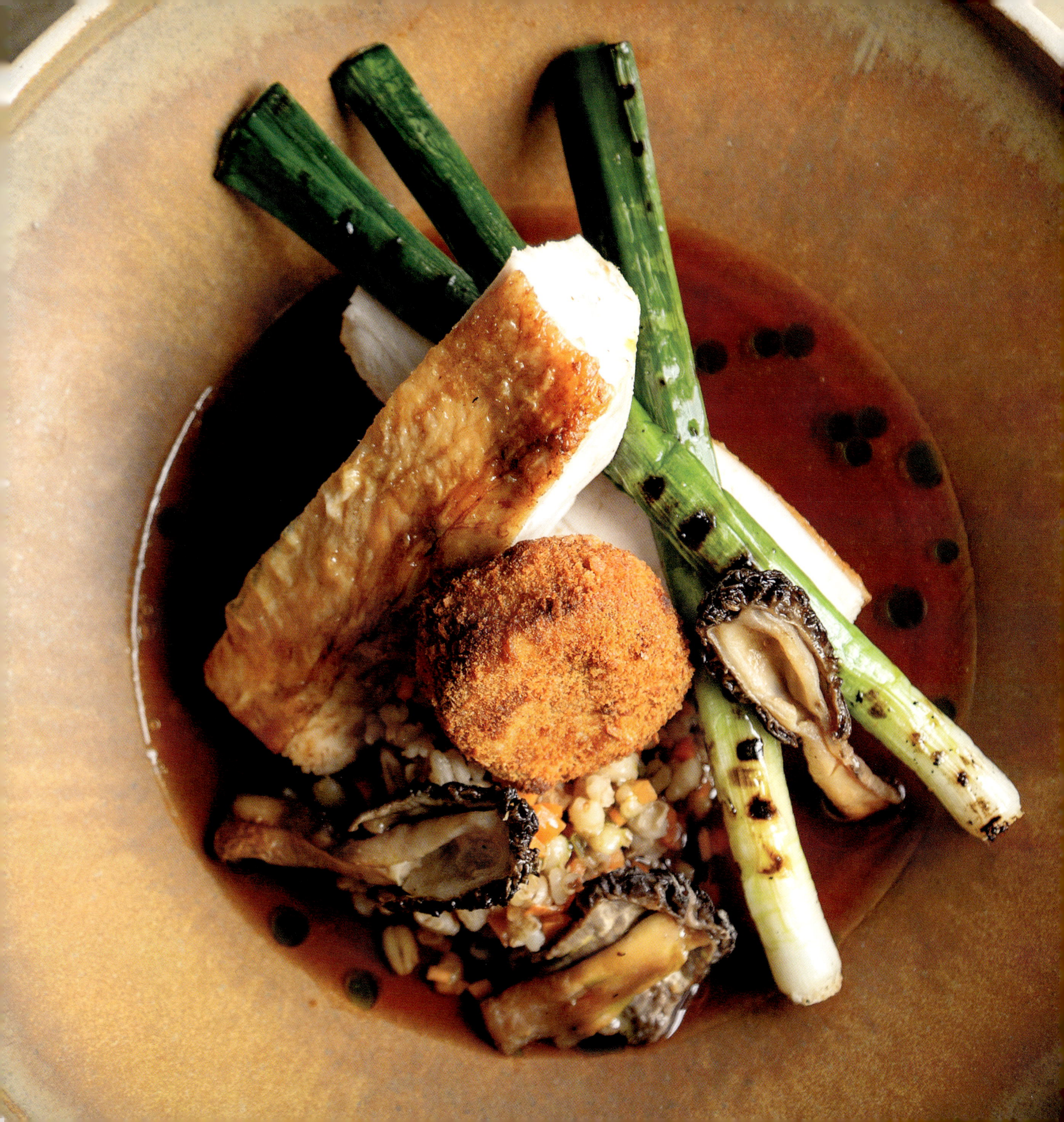

THE SWAN HOTEL RORY WHELAN

Sea trout tartare, horseradish crème fraîche

A colourful, light starter, full of flavour and punch. We add to the freshness with garnishes of a shallot, celery, cucumber and caper salsa, celery cress and pickled radish, as pictured. (serves 4)

400g sea trout fillets
500ml water
10g salt
Fresh horseradish root, peeled
150g crème fraîche
Juice of half a lemon
2 tsp olive oil

Boil the water and salt to make a brine. Cool completely. Soak the sea trout fillets in the brine for 30 minutes. Remove and pat dry. Cut fish into ¼cm dice and set aside.

Use a microplane grater to finely shred the fresh horseradish into the crème fraîche (a little at a time while mixing and tasting). Add seasoning before lightly whipping until thickened. Place into a piping bag and chill until required.

To serve, season the fish then add lemon juice and olive oil to taste. Arrange the tartare decoratively onto cold plates with a piping of the horseradish crème fraîche.

Elderflower gin pannacotta

A deliciously refreshing summer dessert with a lively kick of Adnams First Rate gin. It works well with the poached gooseberry flavour, enhanced by serving alongside, as pictured, a gooseberry tuile biscuit and sorbet, and lemon balm leaves. (serves 4)

142g whole milk
284g double cream
1 vanilla pod, split and seeds scraped
142g elderflower cordial
25g dry gin
3 gelatine leaves, softened
100ml fresh apple juice
100g sugar
200g gooseberries
4 scoops of gooseberry sorbet

Bring the milk, cream, vanilla pod and its seeds to a simmer, remove and whisk in the elderflower, gin and gelatine. Cool to infuse then remove the pod. Divide between 4 glasses and leave to set in fridge.

Over a gentle heat, dissolve the sugar in the apple juice. Add the gooseberries and poach for 5 minutes. Leave to cool. Serve the pannacotta topped with a spoonful of berries.

Oat and whisky cranachan with raspberry sorbet

I may be Irish, but Scottish cranachan is always a winner! It's such a simple dessert to make, perfect with the zing of our Adnams Triple Malt and a real crowd-pleaser in the local raspberry season. (serves 4)

160g organic rolled oats
95ml whisky
50g honey
15g unsalted butter
100ml crème fraîche
100ml double cream
25g icing sugar
2 punnets of raspberries
Raspberry sorbet

Soak the oats in 70ml of the whisky for 30 minutes. Pre-heat the oven to 140c. Warm the honey and butter and stir in the oats. Bake, spread out onto a baking sheet, until lightly coloured. Remove and allow to cool. Softly whip the cream, crème fraîche and sugar and stir in the remaining whisky. Fold one punnet of halved raspberries into the cream. Place a large pastry cutter onto a plate and arrange whole raspberries inside the edge. Fill with the cream mix, remove the cutter and top with the oat crumble and sorbet.

RORY ON HIS...

IF NOT A CHEF?
I'd be managing a carp and pike fishery. I love being outside in nature, and I especially enjoy fishing. How often do I go? Not enough. With two children (Tadgh is 5, Una is 2) I don't have the time. I'm trying to persuade Tadgh to come with me but he's not that keen – yet!

A FILM YOU NEVER TIRE OF WATCHING?
Heat with Al Pacino, Robert de Niro and Val Kilmer. It's a crime film about characters that get what they want, follow their principles to the end.

FAVOURITE SUFFOLK VIEW?
The rapeseed fields when they are in full flower. When you see the green turn yellow, that's the sign that spring has arrived in Suffolk. We're at the mercy of the eastern winds here, but to see the fields in flower means winter is over.

LAST THING YOU BOUGHT FOR YOURSELF?
A rocher spoon. They're expensive but I went into TK Maxx to buy a kettle and came out with rocher spoons for £5! No kettle though…

QUICK SNACK?
Chilli con carne, with half a baguette instead of the rice, or cheese and some cured sausage. My partner is Polish so we've always got kabanosy – dried sausages – in the house. Perfect for that post-service snack!

FOOD NOSTALGIA?
Rabbit stew! When I was in the Boy Scouts, aged about 14, we did an overnight hike and one of the leaders caught a couple of rabbits and made a stew. It was my first experience of wild food and I loved it. I think I was the only one who did, mind you!

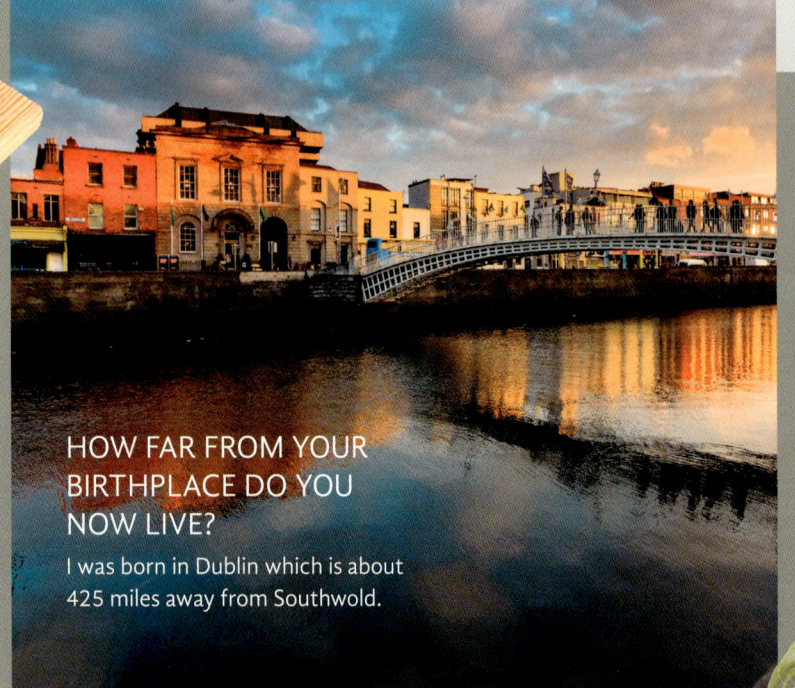

HOW FAR FROM YOUR BIRTHPLACE DO YOU NOW LIVE?
I was born in Dublin which is about 425 miles away from Southwold.

SIGNATURE DISHES

Starters

Wild sea bass sashimi, szechuan pepper, yoghurt sorbet

Sweet pea parfait, chalk stream trout, grapefruit, parmesan

Cocoa-cured venison, pear, pickled cauliflower, blue cheese

Mains

Breast of Gressingham duck, celeriac spaghetti, king oyster mushroom, sherry vinegar, maple syrup

Spiced monkfish, smoked cauliflower, lettuce, golden raisin, puffed rice

Grilled broccoli, almonds, saffron, almond milk

Puddings

Honey & saffron tart, caramelised pear, white wine sorbet

Apple tarte tatin, armagnac & date ice cream

Strawberry soup, lime sorbet, prosecco jelly

FAVOURITE TIME OF YEAR FOR FOOD?
I'm really into home grown produce. I've got six metres of drainpipe planted with tomatoes, courgettes, herbs, gherkins (from Polish seeds)… So spring-summer when things come alive in the garden is my favourite time.

SUFFOLK FEAST

There's nothing like a dame

It's hard to miss The Swan Hotel in Southwold, an imposing townhouse which dominates the market place. She is what Adnams' marketing manager Victoria Savory calls "a grand old dame".

In 2017 The Swan had a multi-million pound makeover that brought her flying into the 21st century. "We didn't want anchors on cushions, that slightly twee coastal look, because this is a heritage hotel," says Victoria. "It has grandeur, it has history, and we wanted to ensure the sense of place was represented in a more original way."

The result is a cool, contemporary, colourful decor that knits the story of brewery and hotel together, celebrating rather than hiding the connection. Design details reference the business – there are hints of copper throughout the property, and Adnams' trademark deep blue is frequently used – and The Swan's place at the heart of one of Suffolk's most popular coastal towns. "The Swan has already become that place people go to to treat themselves," says Victoria. "But we'd love local people to use it for coffees and catch-ups, lunches and dinners."

"People are leading increasingly complex and busy lives, and they're seeking new ways to chill out," she continues. "People don't just unwind by lying on a beach these days; they switch off by doing things." The Swan ticks this box with brewery and distillery tours, make-your-own-gin and cocktail-making experiences. "And if you look out to Southwold, there are fantastic yoga classes, great cycle routes, beautiful walks, places to go for runs or hire boats...you don't get bored here, that's for sure!"

The Swan Hotel
Market Place, Southwold IP18 6EG
W: theswansouthwold.co.uk
T: 01502 722186
E: swansouthwold@adnams.co.uk
- /SwanSouthwold
- @SwanSouthwold
- /swansouthwold

Food served: all week B 8-10.30; L 12-3; D 6-10 (Still Room); food served in Tap Room all week 12-10; lounge and room service menu; afternoon tea 3-5 (pre-booked)

Cost: starters from £5; mains from £12; desserts from £8; Sunday lunch £15 (1 course); £28 (3 courses); afternoon tea £21; wine from £18; pint from £3.80

Details: 52 covers in Still Room; 45 covers in Tap Room; al fresco tables seat 60; private dining in Reading Room (seats 24) and Juniper Room (seats 16); children's menu; bespoke menus; 35 en suite bedrooms; boardroom seats up to 19; wedding licence; brewery and distillery tours; Still Room accessible; parking

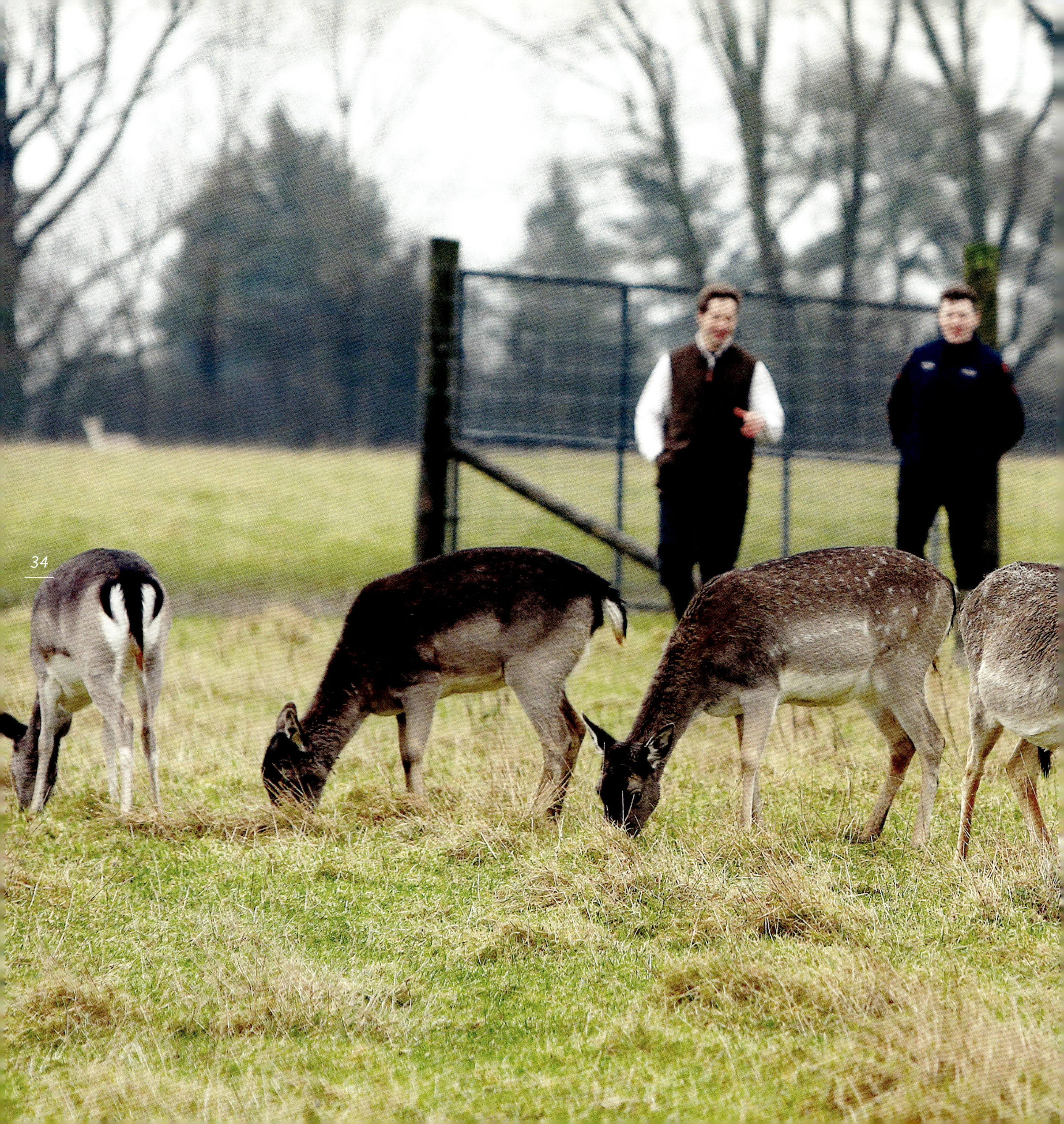

THE PACKHORSE INN, MOULTON
GREIG YOUNG

Fallow land

Denham Estate venison is a go-to ingredient for Greig Young — and it's not surprising when the deer have lived as well as these

THE PACKHORSE INN GREIG YOUNG

The Packhorse Inn kitchen clatters with pans, spits with butter, bubbles with stock. Four chefs, familiar with the small space, weave around each other, busy with lunch prep on their respective sections, peeling, chopping, stirring, tasting.

For all the noise of cooking, and despite the kitchen's diminutive size, this feels like an even-tempered place. The calm guiding hand is that of head chef Greig Young – "it's how I am, I've never been a shouty chef" – who is proof, were it needed, that it is possible to create delicious plates of food without the tension of raised voices.

The Scottish-born chef has been doing just that since arriving at The Packhorse in 2017, bringing his long-time sous chef, Sunny Win Lau, with him. "I want to create a Suffolk style of clean food using ordinary ingredients that I like," he says. "I'm not into dots or foams or gels; that's not my style. And I use turnip in this venison dish not because I'm Scottish and tight but because I like turnips!" He seasons a piece of venison haunch as he talks, pan-roasting it whole to get a dark crust before cooking it for a few minutes in the oven. Rested, the meat yields to the knife, pink-centred, and he places slices on a plate brushed with a treacle sauce. He adds turnip (roasted whole, cut, and tossed in butter), and a puck of fondant potato, finishing the plate with peppery watercress, crunchy salted walnuts, and spoonfuls of turnip cream.

It's a muscular plate of food, down to earth and downright tasty, but Greig's food is undeniably at the fine end of pub dining. Other dishes echo the style: classic beef tartar ("the godfather of starters and so easy!") uses local Red Poll beef, the finely diced meat topped with a free-range egg yolk, and plated up with chopped gherkin, shallot, capers and chives. "It's going on the menu," he says, "and I reckon it'll become a staple." An apple pudding combines roasted apples with aromatic tarragon oil and a sweet-tart Aspall cyder jelly. White chocolate ganache and vanilla ice cream remind that this is a pudding. "All my cooking is about clean flavours," says Greig. "Yes, there's some technique, but I'm more interested in the ingredient, the freshness, the taste."

We head to Denham Estate, a few miles from The Packhorse, and the source of Greig's venison. The fallow deer, a skittish group of last year's fawns, train their liquid-brown eyes on us as we approach in farm manager Matt Driver's 4x4, rocking and rolling along winter-wet tracks as inelegantly as the deer are elegant.

"We are converting to a parkland environment, giving the deer more space to roam in their social groups, just as wild fallow do," says owner Cecilia Gliksten who explains that the herd has been reduced from 1,000 to just 150, and that animals are no longer slaughtered in an abattoir, but shot in the field at about 18 months of age by Matt, an experienced stalker. "This approach is more natural, and it means I need to intervene less," says Matt. "There's less risk of disease so we don't need to vaccinate, and we don't use fertiliser on the land because the deer and clover replace nutrients." The impact? "A huge part of my job is conservation; already we're seeing wild orchids, barn owls, and great crested newts across the Estate." No doubt plantings of native woodland, and stretches of land sown with bee-friendly wildflowers, or plants to provide winter feed for wild birds, will see similar results.

For Greig this whole picture is important. "To see the respect for the animals and the environment is incredible," he says. "I can order meat over the phone easily, but to have a connection like this makes a huge difference." Back at The Packhorse, he insists that staff know about the venison so that they can explain its provenance to interested customers.

Fresh out of Glasgow college, Greig spent three years at the Airds hotel, Oban, and learnt fast. "I was working with saddles of venison, scallops in the shell, line-caught turbot. Menus changed daily; it was the best grounding." Time in Australia – "from a village in Scotland to the Quay restaurant on Sydney harbour, what a change!" – and New Zealand honed a light, antipodean style, one that renowned chef Daniel Galmiche helped fortify with a dose of classic French training when Greig returned to the UK and a job at the Vineyard at Stockcross in Berkshire. "Daniel was exec chef there at the time. I learnt a maturity in my cooking from him, about tasting food, really appreciating ingredients. He's my kitchen dad!"

From there, Suffolk beckoned. Greig and his fiancée Lizzie who is from the county, took on the Shepherd and Dog pub at Forward Green near Stowmarket, quickly building a weekend following, but struggling to tempt enough guests away from burgers and fish and chips at other times of the week. He accepted a job at the Wild Rabbit, the Michelin-starred pub in the Cotswolds, then a role with "a lovely big office and two kitchens" at The Gore Hotel in London, but the arrival of their daughter prompted a return to Suffolk for the couple. "And so here I am back at The Packhorse!" he smiles broadly, clearly happy. "The kitchen is small, but just look at the ingredients I get to cook."

SUFFOLK FEAST

THE PACKHORSE INN GREIG YOUNG

Skillet-roasted Denham Estate venison haunch with turnips, confit potato and salted walnuts

As we buy the whole legs, we tend to roast the haunch from a single muscle which makes it super tender. You are unlikely to be able to buy it like this from your local butcher, so just ask for it to be cut from a young animal. A heavy hobproof roasting tin or Le Creuset frying pan will be a fair substitute for an iron skillet. (serves 4)

Walnuts
- 100g walnuts
- 100g sugar
- 100ml water
- Sea salt flakes

Bring the nuts to the boil with the sugar and water and take off the heat. Leave for one hour and strain. Pre-heat the oven to 160c. Roast the nuts until golden and sprinkle with the salt.

Turnips
- Handful of hay
- 4 large turnips, whole
- Splash of double cream
- Salt

Preheat your oven to 180c. Place your seasoned turnips in a baking tray, lined with the hay, cover with tin foil and bake until tender (approx. 30-40 minutes). Remove, cool and peel the turnips. Cut four 1cm-thick rounds from the centre of each turnip and set aside.

Blend the remaining turnip into a smooth purée with the cream and set aside.

Confit potato
- 1 large starchy potato (eg King Edward or Maris Piper)
- 2 rosemary sprigs
- 2 garlic cloves, crushed
- Rapeseed oil
- Salt

Pre-heat your oven to 160c. Peel the potatoes and cut into four 1cm thick rounds. Lightly season the potatoes, add the garlic and rosemary, just cover with oil and then place foil snugly over the tin. Bake for around 30 minutes until tender. Keep warm.

Sweet and sour treacle
- 50g black treacle
- 50g malt vinegar
- Sprig of rosemary
- Black pepper

Simmer the treacle, vinegar, rosemary and a good grind of black pepper for 2 minutes and then set aside. When cool, strain and store at room temperature.

To serve
- 4 baby turnips, trimmed and halved
- 600g venison haunch (back leg)
- Vegetable oil

Pre-heat your oven to 160c. Put the baby turnips on to simmer in salted water until tender. Sear the oiled and seasoned venison in a very hot skillet until well-browned all over. Roast the venison in the skillet in the oven for around 6 minutes (looking for it to be quite pink in the middle when checked). Rest for 10 minutes somewhere warm while you reheat the turnip purée and the potatoes. Brush the treacle on your hot plates, lay on the drained turnip rounds, potatoes and drained baby turnips. Arrange the carved venison on top, spoon the sauce around before grating over the walnuts.

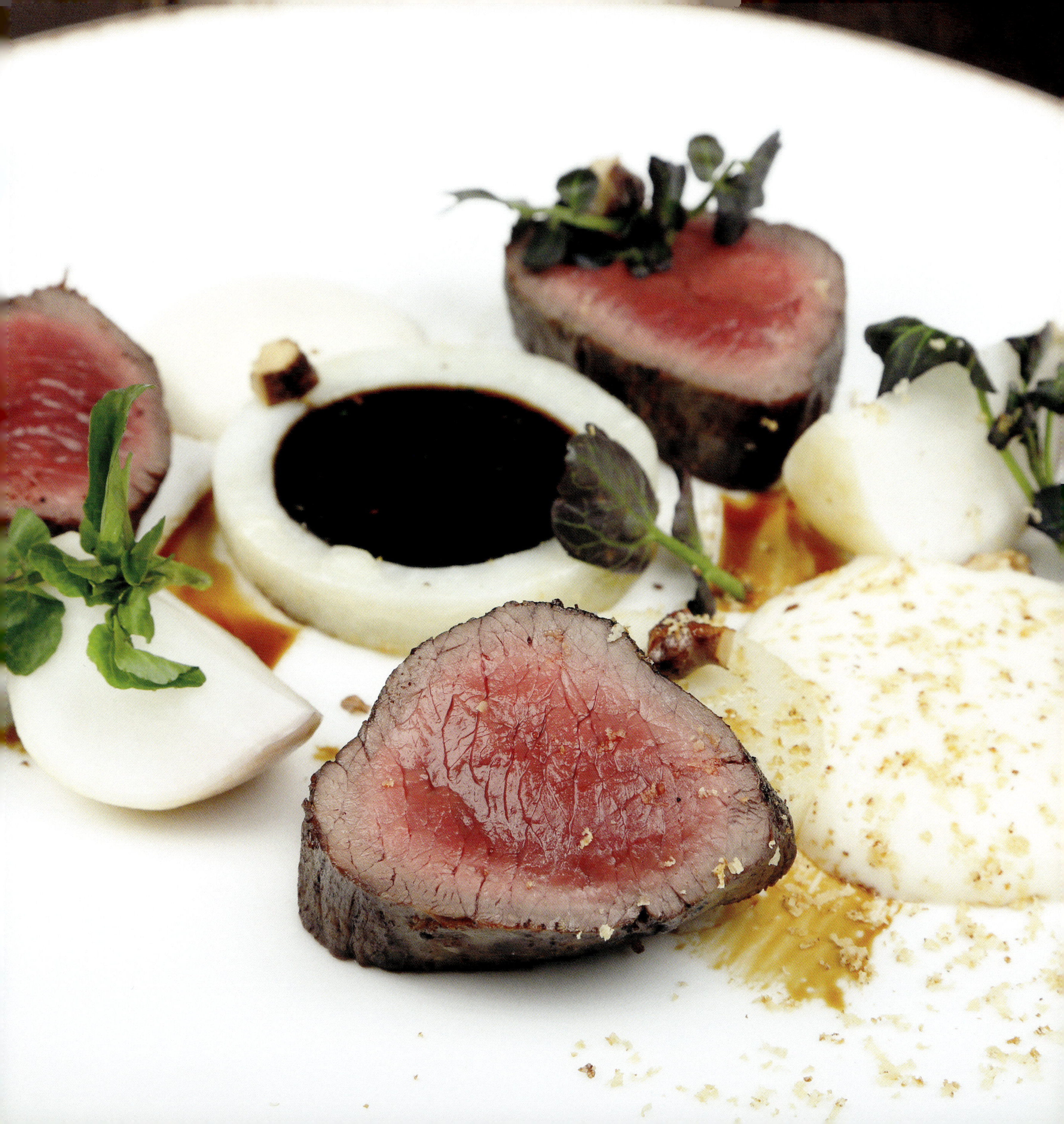

THE PACKHORSE INN GREIG YOUNG

Beef tartare

For this, the godfather of starters, I use the finest beef I can find, Suffolk Red Poll of course, properly trimmed by a good butcher. We serve this with thin toasts. Please note vulnerable diners are advised to avoid raw beef and raw egg. (serves 4)

400g beef fillet, trimmed
1 large shallot
1 large gherkin
1 tbsp capers
Chives
Tabasco
Worcestershire sauce
4 egg yolks

Finely dice the beef and add to a bowl, set over a larger bowl lined with ice. Beat the beef with a spatula for two minutes then season well before refrigerating. Dice the shallot and finely chop the gherkin, capers and chives before folding into the beef and adding seasoning, tabasco and worcestershire sauce to taste. Divide into four portions on chilled plates and top each with a yolk.

Salt-baked celeriac soup, smoked mackerel and English mustard

A lovely earthy soup for a light lunch, garnished with pickled shallot rings and soft herbs. (serves 2-4)

5 egg whites
500g white flour
100g salt
50ml water
1 medium celeriac
Splash of double cream
1 smoked mackerel fillet
1 tbsp English mustard

Pre-heat the oven to 180c. Whisk your egg whites until stiff. Mix your flour and salt and then stir in the egg whites and water to form a smooth dough. Refrigerate this for 30 minutes.

Encase the celeriac in the dough before baking for 1 hour or until tender. Peel off the pastry and the celeriac skin.

Cut off a slice, dice and set aside. Blend the remaining celeriac with the cream, season and keep hot.

Skin, bone and cut the mackerel into pieces. To serve, dot warm soup plates with the mustard and add the mackerel and diced celeriac before pouring in the soup.

SUFFOLK FEAST

Roast apples with white chocolate and tarragon

An unusual take on the farmhouse classic, one to impress your sceptical guests! Great with rich vanilla ice cream. (serves 4)

100ml dry cider, heated
1 gelatine leaf, softened
150g white chocolate, grated
200ml cream, heated
4 sweet red apples
75g caster sugar
20ml rapeseed oil
Tarragon sprigs

Dissolve the drained gelatine into the hot cider and pour into a shallow tray before refrigerating to set. Melt the chocolate in the cream, then cool and chill. Peel and ball your apples using a melon baller and set aside. Heat the sugar in a small saucepan over a medium heat and allow to melt without stirring, carefully agitating occasionally.

Once the sugar starts to colour, stir with a wooden spatula until it is melted into a golden caramel. Fold in the apples and cook over a gentle heat until caramelised and softened. Set aside.

Heat the oil to 70c, add the tarragon and set aside to infuse. When cool, strain the oil into a jug and discard the herbs. Whisk up the chocolate to a whipped texture. Serve the apples with a quenelle of the chocolate, cubes of the jelly and a drizzle of the herb oil.

GREIG ON HIS...

COOK'S CHEAT OR CHEF'S TIP?
I had a bit of a Yorkshire pudding breakthrough this year! This may be common knowledge but I was amazed by the results. Make your batter by volume not weight (equal quantities of strong flour, eggs, and a 50-50 milk-water mix). Make it before you go to bed the day before, and let it stand at room temperature. The next day pass the batter through a sieve, season with salt and cook the Yorkshires in searing hot fat at 210c. They are mega!

FAVOURITE BIT OF KITCHEN EQUIPMENT?
It has to be my digital quick-read thermometer. It takes all the guesswork out and makes my life a whole lot easier.

GUILTY FOOD PLEASURE?
Hands down, Turkish delight! Not that gross stuff covered in chocolate, but the traditional ones covered in icing sugar and cornflour.

WHAT GETS YOU UP IN THE MORNING?
I've got the best daughter in the world, she is a proper morning person. Spending all day at work means that mornings with my fiancée Lizzie and our daughter mean so much.

IF NOT A CHEF WHAT WOULD YOU HAVE BEEN?
I spent the best part of my childhood wanting to study music and play instruments. I am pretty glad to be honest that I ended up in the kitchen as there's much less luck involved in making a career in cooking than music.

HOW FAR FROM YOUR BIRTHPLACE DO YOU NOW LIVE?
I'm from Oban, Scotland, a small fishing town on the west coast. It's not a million miles away from Moulton, but it still feels far.

INSPIRING SUFFOLK VIEW?
I love it when the rapeseed flowers in Suffolk turn yellow! I have never seen anything quite like it.

SIGNATURE DISHES

Starters

Pan fried mackerel, marinated yoghurt, parsley purée, charred broccoli

Whipped goats' curd, roast salsify, black olive

Roast Norfolk quail, confit leg, butternut squash, pickled walnut

Mains

Glazed pigeon breast, mushroom, celeriac, turnip

Pan-fried hake, roast cauliflower, young leeks, crab sauce

Rib of beef, mushrooms, parsley, duck fat potato, roast shallots, confit carrots, peppercorn sauce (for two)

Puddings

Suffolk heritage apple tarte tatin, brown butter ice cream, custard (for two)

Marinated strawberries, bitters sorbet, sorrel ice cream, lime posset

Baked plums, white chocolate ganache, fennel, vanilla

FAVOURITE TIME OF THE YEAR FOR FOOD?
Definitely spring for me. It's a drastic change from winter and there is lots of crossover produce. Everything is just a bit lighter and fresher.

MOST THRILLING MOMENT IN YOUR CAREER TO DATE?
I cooked in the Manila Shangri-La hotel in the Philippines. Just being there was thrilling enough, the size of the operation was mind-blowing!

A good bet

Moulton is just three miles from the beating heart of UK horseracing, so it is not unusual to see village locals and visitors mix with Newmarket's jockeys, trainers and owners at The Packhorse Inn.

The pub with its happy mix of customers is owned by Moulton resident Philip Turner who, with his wife Amanda, bought his ailing local back in October 2013. With considerable personal investment and funds from several individual backers, he stripped the former King's Head right back, renovated the adjacent coach house to create more bedrooms, and redressed the whole place stylishly. The property became the first of the growing Chestnut Group collection.

The Packhorse feels like a relaxed, elegant country home, even when the bar is at its busiest. Leather armchairs have a tempting squishiness, the open fires make everything toasty in cooler months, and the rug-warmed wooden floors, mismatched furniture, and simply laid tables give a no-fuss atmosphere. The individually designed bedrooms, curated like the rest of the interior by Amanda, are comfortably glamorous – think fluffy throws, generous baths, and AV systems such as you wish you had at home.

Look out for special menus that mark the game season, celebrate English Wine Week, or recognise particular events in the racing calendar, or just come for well-earned refreshment after completing the seven-mile 'Three Church Walk' that takes in the pretty Suffolk villages of Moulton, Gazeley and Dalham. The front-of-house team will make you very welcome!

The Packhorse Inn
Bridge Street, Moulton CB8 8SP
W: thepackhorseinn.com
T: 01638 751818
E: info@thepackhorseinn.com
- /packhorseinn
- @moultopackhorse
- /thepackhorseinn

Accolades and listings: Waitrose *Good Food Guide*; AA Two Rosettes; *Michelin*; *Harden's*; AA Five Stars (Inn); *Sawday's*; *Inn Places*

Food served: Mon-Sat B 8-10; L 12-2.30; D 7-9.30; Sun L 12-3.30; D 7-8.30

Cost: starters from £7; mains from £15; desserts from £8; set lunch menu Mon-Sat from £16; five-course taster menu £45 (£25 wine flight) last Thu evening of month

Details: 60 covers; 8 bedrooms (4 accessible and dog-friendly); Club Room, with AV system and seating for 32, available for private hire; accessible; dogs welcome in pub and restaurant; parking

A cook on the wild side

Escaping the kitchen to forage and feast in the Suffolk countryside is Stephen David's favourite diversion

MACKENZIE-DAVID EVENTS
STEPHEN DAVID

Smoke wisps through the glade down a winding track deep in a Darsham wood. As the plumes part, chef Stephen David comes into view sitting on top of a fallen tree. He throws another bough on the fire, seemingly a world away from his busy events kitchen as he watches his spit-roast rabbit turning a perfect golden-brown.

"A campfire might be cooking at its simplest, but for me it's so expressive," he says. "It's about a few perfect ingredients, cooked caveman-style, and our appetites and senses being heightened by being outdoors." Juices hiss onto the coals from his inventive rotisserie, courtesy of hazel switches from a nearby coppice. "Sourcing as close to harvest in terms of distance and time is what I am all about, whether here or for my kitchen. Suffolk and East Anglia are so provident and the foodie community is so passionate – it makes my cook's life much rosier! Of course you can't find fresher or more local or seasonal than when you're foraging, and wild-grown food usually has more character and flavour too."

On cue, foraging expert, and Stephen's old friend and culinary like-mind, quietly appears. Jon Tyler from Wild for Woods leads hedgecraft and foraging courses and bangs the drum for localness in how we shop and eat, encouraging people to find nature's food for free on their doorsteps. "There is so much tasty produce locally which we can discover for ourselves, really common, sustainable things such as these alexanders; they're an invasive species, easy to find and identify, and so useful in the kitchen." He pulls out thick green shoots from his laden wicker basket; his first foray around farmer Jeremy Thickitt's farm was clearly a fruitful one. Chef and forager deep in conversation, we are soon seeking out more of nature's bounty, plucking jelly ears (some call them wood ears) from dying elder stumps. "You can eat them raw," says Jon cheerfully. "Mmmm, the texture of a mouse's ear," jokes Stephen. "They'll rehydrate well in the rabbit stew, though. And what about some early season nettle tips too?" suggests Jon, as they move onto a patch of disturbed earth by the cattle fence, lush green with this tasty if generally unwanted plant. "One person's weed is another's lunch", quips Stephen as he gingerly fills the trug.

Back in his woodland 'kitchen', Stephen is eager to try another old campfire recipe. Jeremy appears as if on cue, black labrador at heel, with a brace of rabbits in hand. "I'm going to stuff one with the nettles and another fleshy green called spring beauty, then wrap it in bacon for flavour and lots of cabbage leaves. That will keep the lean meat succulent in the firepit," he explains before burying the

MACKENZIE-DAVID EVENTS STEPHEN DAVID

parcel in the hot coals, covered over with thick soil and burning branches. "An hour or two at gas mark something should be perfect!"

"I hope you're going to stay around for our little wild feast, Jeremy?" asks Stephen. "About time I returned the favour!" Jeremy's butchers shop, Clarke's of Bramfield, has faithfully supplied Stephen for well over a decade. Jon throws incense-scented pine needles onto the embers and starts to whittle a hazel wood skewer for Stephen to 'kebab' the rabbit liver and kidneys as a little appetiser.

For the much-awaited country stew, Stephen browns Blythburgh pork pancetta and onions before pouring in Aspall cyder and chicken stock to reduce, then root vegetables and wild greens to soften in the now fragrant pot au feu. Out comes stoneground flour from Woodbridge Tide Mill and grated suet, ingredients that are quickly transformed into wild garlic dumplings which are then simmered to fluffy perfection. The remaining dough joins the frying pan on the red-hot coals and is sizzled in the bacon fat into an opportune flatbread. Savoury, smoky and herby, it's sampled with gusto and complements the delicious caramelised, juicy offal. "Don't tell the food police! We're only allowed to cook cardboard liver these days," mourns Stephen.

To finish the stew, Stephen takes the spitted rabbit and slices the perfectly pink loin with the shredded greens and jelly ears. He serves it up with the baked rabbit, dug up from the embers and unwrapped from its jacket of pancetta and cabbage leaves. "That rabbit leg tastes like a confit, it's so tender," declares Jon. The ability to pull a culinary rabbit out of the hat is something Jon admires in many chefs, and is one of the reasons he enjoys working with them. "They'll look at something, taste it and then they'll harness their experience of combining flavours and textures, and find a way to use it, pushing their own culinary barriers. I enjoy that passion."

The last word goes to Stephen, though. "It doesn't have to be the glitz and glamour of fine dining all the time. I haven't forgotten where cooking all started – over a fire. And I'd say that's been good food, wouldn't you?" And with that, everything packed away, they bury the fire and kick leaves over the site. It's as if they'd never been there, save for the wisps of woodsmoke lingering in the glade.

MACKENZIE-DAVID EVENTS STEPHEN DAVID

Rabbit and roots stew with herb dumplings, greens, wild mushrooms and Suffolk cyder

Cooking this rustic lunch fireside is optional! It's certainly much easier to put it in the oven, but not quite as much fun! The recipe works well with all manner of wild game and less savage farmyard poultry, guinea fowl for instance. In terms of vegetables and other ingredients, as the foraging season goes on, there will be lots of hedgerow greens and interesting edible fungi to glean. As always, ensure you are confident of what you are harvesting in the wild and consult a reliable reference book for safety first. Ultimately when out on a foray, if in any doubt about your find, just discard it. If you can't escape into the great outdoors with your basket, fill one in your local greengrocer or deli instead. Don't forget a warm, homemade granary loaf or soda bread alongside. Sear the offal skewer just as the dumplings are cooked through as it doesn't take to waiting around. (serves 4)

Rabbit
- **Handful wild garlic leaves**
- **Handful (careful!) of nettle tops**
- **Savoy cabbage leaves, destalked**
- **Unsalted butter**
- **Smoked streaky bacon rashers, flattened out**
- **1 whole rabbit, oven ready (liver and kidney reserved)**
- **Bay leaves**
- **250ml dry cyder**

Blanch the wild garlic and nettles quickly, and repeat for the cabbage until wilted.

Overlap several widths of baking foil to make a sheet and butter generously. Cover with sufficient cabbage leaves to generously encase your rabbit once it is rolled up later. Lay touching rashers of bacon on the cabbage and scatter over the wild garlic and nettles. Lay the rabbit on top, with a few bay leaves in the cavity. Season well inside and out before rolling up tightly, securing the ends of the foil well and tie with string.

Pre-heat the oven to 150c. Place the rabbit in a snug roasting tin and pour around 250ml of simmering cyder. Loosely cover with foil and bake for around 3 hours until tender and flaking. Cool, remove the rabbit meat and submerge in the strained cooking liquor. Shred the cabbage and bacon and reserve.

Dumplings
- **150g self-raising flour**
- **75g beef suet, grated**
- **1 handful soft herbs, chopped**

Make the dumplings by mixing the flour, suet, soft herbs and generous seasoning with enough cold water, about 4 or 5 tbsp, to just bring it together. You want a soft, sticky dough. Divide into 10-12 pieces and roll gently into balls.

Offal skewer
- **Reserved liver and kidney**

Cut the liver in pieces and thread with the kidneys onto a long skewer (soaking first if wood). Lightly oil and then sear in a hot, dry frying pan on all sides until cooked to your liking (it's now recommended to cook offal through, but I prefer to risk it pink).

Stew
- **4 rashers of smoked streaky bacon, cut into lardons**
- **1 large onion, peeled and chopped**
- **Rapeseed oil for frying**
- **250ml dry cyder**
- **1 litre good chicken or game stock**
- **2 good handfuls of root vegetables, peeled and diced**
- **Few sprigs of woody herbs such as rosemary or thyme**
- **Handful of wild mushrooms, sliced into pieces**
- **Good bunch of seasonal greens, shredded bite-size**

In a hot heavy saucepan, fry the bacon and onion over a medium heat with rapeseed oil until starting to brown. Add the cyder and boil hard until well reduced. Add the stock, root vegetables and herbs and simmer for 10 minutes. Add the dumplings, bring back to a good simmer and cook covered for 15 minutes whilst you cook the mushrooms, quickly stir-frying them in hot oil and seasoning for a few minutes.

Add the greens, cooked rabbit meat, cabbage and bacon, as well as the mushrooms, to the stew, bring back to a boil, adjust the seasoning and cook until the greens start to wilt. Serve in hot main course bowls with the offal skewer.

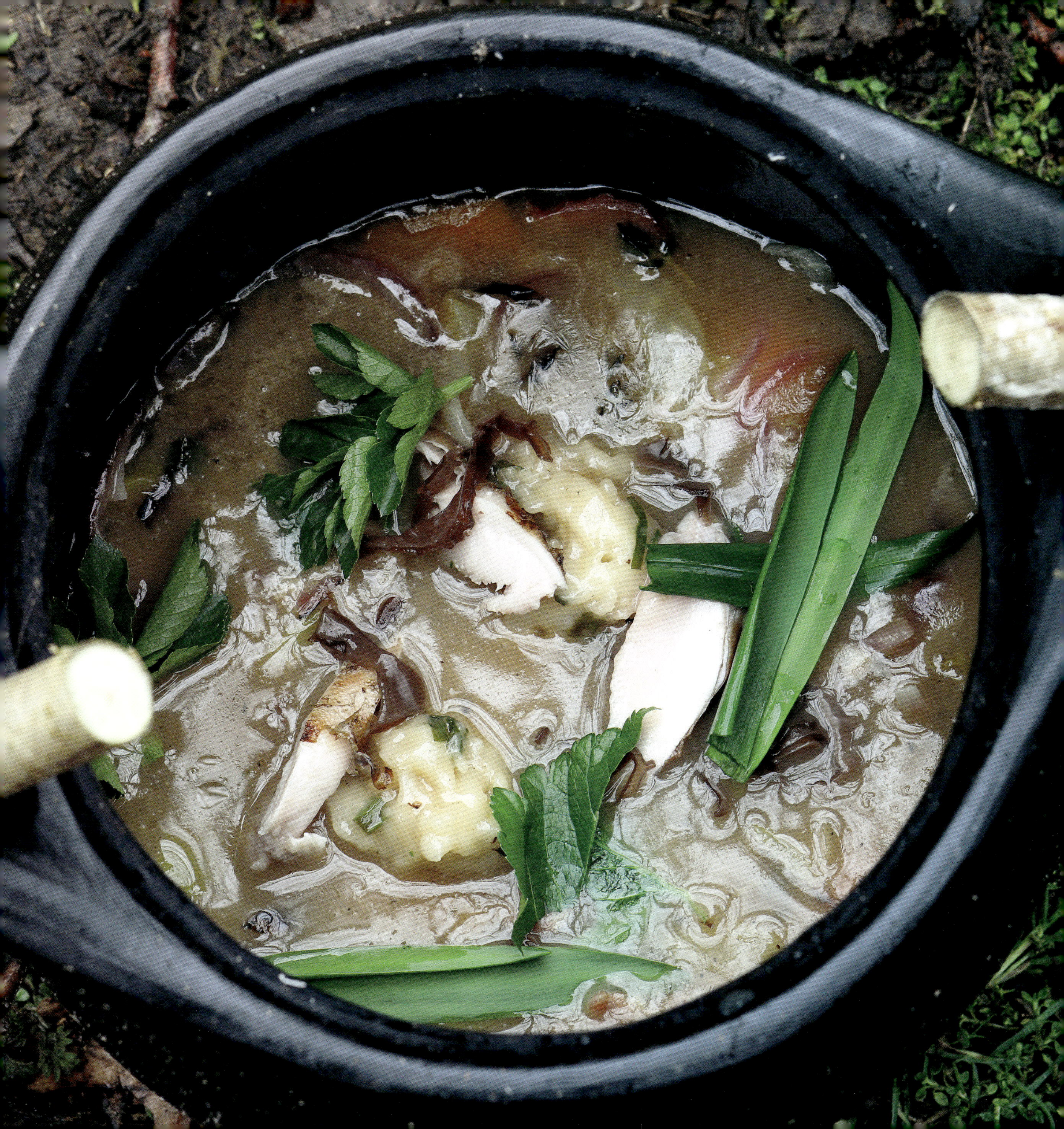

MACKENZIE-DAVID EVENTS STEPHEN DAVID

Crab risotto

Fresh peas, fennel and spring onions really complement the white flakes of local crabmeat in this light lunch rice recipe. It is best enjoyed alongside char-grilled seafood – here we've used griddled squid. (serves 4-6)

1 litre good, light chicken stock
Unsalted butter
Rapeseed oil
1 long shallot, peeled and finely chopped
1 garlic clove, peeled and finely chopped
300g risotto rice such as arborio
100ml dry white vermouth
150g peas, fresh (or defrosted)
1 head fennel, finely diced
300g white crabmeat, flaked
1 bunch thin spring onions, finely sliced
Parmesan shavings

Bring the stock to a simmer. Soften the shallot and garlic in a little melted butter and oil and season lightly. Stir through the rice and cook over a medium heat. As it dries up, add the vermouth and stir continually. Once absorbed, add a ladle of stock and turn heat down to low. Stir the risotto and add more stock as it is absorbed for 15-18 minutes. Meanwhile blanch the peas and fennel in simmering salted water until just softening.

At the end of cooking, fold in the drained vegetables and the crab. When hot and still al dente, mix in the spring onions and adjust the seasoning. Serve up with parmesan shavings on the side.

Salt cod tartare fishcakes

Crispy crusted and squidgy centred, this fishy starter works well with marinated cucumber, a chilli dressing and local dressed samphire. Salt down locally landed fish if you can, or buy ready-made salt cod to save time. Made smaller, the fishcakes are perfect canapés. (serves 4)

300g skinless salt cod, rehydrated
150g warm mashed potato
100g hard white cheese, grated
1 heaped tsp grated garlic
1 heaped tsp grated horseradish
2 spring onions, trimmed and finely chopped
1 heaped tbsp cornichons, finely diced
1 heaped tbsp baby capers
2 tbsp flat leaf parsley, shredded
Grated zest of half a lemon
Juice of half a lemon
Flour, eggs and breadcrumbs
Oil for frying

Mix the first 11 ingredients together. Divide into 8 parts and roll into balls before gently flattening. Chill for an hour.

In separate bowls, coat the cakes in seasoned flour, then beaten egg and finally breadcrumbs, knocking off any excess as you go. Chill again and then deep fry at 180c until hot and golden brown. Drain well and serve.

Strawberry cheesecake

A perennial favourite, this is an easy dessert to make in advance, which you can adapt it to suit any seasonal berries. I often bake this in individual tins and garnish them with a minted red chilli syrup and Pimms jelly. (serves 4+)

250g ginger biscuits in crumbs
80g butter, melted
150g hulled strawberries
4 large eggs, beaten
175g caster sugar
Grated zest of 1 lime
1 tbsp honey
2 tsp vanilla extract
500g mascarpone
200g crème fraîche

Combine the biscuits and butter and press into a buttered 18cm spring-form tin before refrigerating. Finely dice the strawberries and drain in a sieve. Whisk together the remaining ingredients until smooth and then gently fold in the berries. Spoon the mixture onto the set base. Bake for 45 minutes in a 170c oven until just golden. Cover with a tea towel to cool and then refrigerate in the tin. To serve, run a hot knife around the edge and unclip before slicing.

STEPHEN ON HIS...

FAVOURITE TIME OF YEAR FOR FOOD?

Has to be the autumn, a forager's dream, all that natural harvest plus the return of those root and green veggies and new season game of course, something like partridge, Suffolk pancetta, cep mushrooms, bread sauce, sweet parsnips and sprouts. Heaven!

FOOD HEROES?

I guess it all started with my great-grandad; he trained with Auguste Escoffier, and that must have something to do with why I am a chef...

GUILTY FOOD PLEASURES?

Oysters in the half-shell are a must-have in a good restaurant; my first and delicious al fresco lunch this year at Darsham Nurseries' lovely garden café near Yoxford started with a half-dozen plump ones with a rhubarb vinegar dressing, the perfect appetiser.

CAREER HIGHLIGHT?

Apart from cooking for childhood heroes and celebrities over the years, it must be one of my Halesworth Skills Academy's school student chefs being national runner-up in a Jamie Oliver Food Revolution competition (check out Jamie's Youtube feed) and some of them now being professional chefs. It's all about inspiring the next generation.

BIGGEST EXTRAVAGANCE AS A CHEF?

After three decades at the stove it's having an extra pair of hands in the kitchen so I can take it a bit easier.

BIRTHDAY CELEBRATION?

My last one was a milestone, the big 50, so I was whisked away on a surprise trip by Bec, Maddy and Seb to the delights of Dubai. There's nothing like it, spending a week in a tropical paradise, truly memorable and luxurious, and then back to the simple pleasures and coastal chic of Aldeburgh for a few more days.

FAVOURITE EVENT?

A real pleasure has been co-founding the Woodbridge Shuck seafood festival, held every year in September on the banks of the river Deben. It's one not to miss!

SIGNATURE DISHES

Starters

Charred mackerel, slow-baked beets, orange, courgette and flat leaf parsley salad

Balsamic-glazed asparagus spears, baked in Suffolk pancetta, poached duck egg, chervil béarnaise

Superfood salad of giant couscous, broccoli, roast peppers, marinated feta, toasted almonds and pomegranate yoghurt

Mains

Crispy slow-braised pork belly, crushed Jersey Royals, braised lettuce and peas, caramelised shallots and Aspall reduction

Wood-roasted hake, warm salad of chorizo, heritage tomato, butterbeans and cockles, gribiche dressing

Cromer crab arancini fritters, shaved fennel and cucumber, pickled apple, wild garlic

Puddings

Rhubarb and ginger tarte tatin, elderflower syrup and clotted cream gelato

Summer berry and white chocolate cheesecake, hazelnut crumb, minted red chilli caramel

Chargrilled figs, honey and lavender-soaked ricotta, bellini sabayon

COOKING FOR ONE FAMOUS PERSON...?

Discretion is our middle name, but publicly we looked after HRH Prince Charles at the launch of a Houghton Hall art exhibition; it would be lovely to cook for him again, showcasing the best of Suffolk produce of course!

The little black book

Mackenzie-David Events, or quite simply Rebecca and Stephen, are often the first to be called when there is a society occasion in the offing, whether it's a grand wedding, charity gala, house party or simply a smart dinner. Being on first-name terms with their clients helps – and it's not surprising that they are, given that the pair have spent 20 years creating memorable bespoke occasions. They have been the creative force behind celebrations at some of the region's finest addresses – the likes of Holkham Hall, Wilderness Reserve at Sibton Park, Kimberley Hall, and Sennowe Park – pouring flair, professionalism, and of course restaurant-standard cooking, into events that often take them far from their base at Aldeburgh Yacht Club.

Every event is treated as one-of-a-kind and they love catering for the weird and the wonderful: a tapas party on horseback; a ten-course gourmet dinner prepared without cooking facilities on a Broads paddle steamer; being flown to a Scottish castle to look after a celebrity wedding; a Russian princess' marquee wedding in a remote Suffolk field, surrounded by doormen, but without a spectator – let alone paparazzi – in sight; it all comes as second nature to them. Discretion their 'middle name', their lips are sealed when it comes to the subject of the famous faces they have looked after.

Stephen and Rebecca's is a tried-and-tested partnership, not just working side-by-side as head chef and general manager respectively but also as a couple and family. They met in the late 1980s at Hintlesham Hall and moved on together to head up some of East Anglia's most stylish destinations, including the renowned Hoste Arms (as it was then called) in Burnham Market, Norfolk, which they ran for Paul Whittome for several years. Stephen was subsequently chef patron at The Crown at Woodbridge, overseeing its relaunch as a contemporary inn and restaurant in 2009.

However, outside catering has been Stephen and Rebecca's passion since earlier days when they ran the Earsham Street Café and deli in Bungay. There, they turned faded tearooms into a foodie destination with a reputation that went far beyond the county borders, and took on the catering for guests' private events, as and when time allowed, alongside running the business. They came to love running events more and more, and the rest, as they say, is history.

Mackenzie-David Events
Aldeburgh Yacht Club, Slaughden Road, Aldeburgh IP15 5NA
W: mackenzie-david.co.uk
T: 01986 893991   07460 400276
E: rebecca@mackenzie-david.co.uk

MAISON BLEUE, BURY ST EDMUNDS
PASCAL CANEVET

Lambs in clover

Organic lamb from Shimpling Park Farm travels a scant few miles to reach Pascal Canevet's kitchen at Maison Bleue

55

In August 2016, Pascal Canevet posted a picture on social media. It was a lamb dish, new on the menu at Maison Bleue that week. The fillet was pink, the pieces of confit belly and shoulder promised melting tenderness, the delicate baby carrots gave pops of colour, and the shiny sauce spoke sweet-savouriness in volumes. The food looked tasty, modern, the plate was thoughtfully arranged.

Alice Pawsey can hardly contain her excitement. "That's it! That's the first dish you did with our lamb! It's incredible to think that that lamb was reared on our fields here, and ended up just a few miles down the road on your menu." She stops, composes herself a little, before the party – she, her husband John, Pascal and his sous chef Vincent Gross – launches into lively talk of field-to-fork eating, food miles and sustainability. She tells the story too of the chance conversation with Pascal after a birthday dinner at Maison Bleue when Alice suggested he might like to try their organic, grass- and clover-fed lamb. "As farmers, we're often removed from what we do," she says. "Our wheat goes off in 29-tonne lorries and even though we always grow for traceable markets because that's a good organic business model, you do feel a bit removed from the end product. It's different with the lamb; we can see it right there on the plate."

Its route, to be precise, is from the Pawseys' organic Shimpling Park Farm, just outside Bury St Edmunds, to the Long Melford butcher, Ruse & Sons, less than five miles away, where it is slaughtered. Pascal buys the whole carcass, and uses his ingenuity to do justice to every part of the animal. The belly might be slow-cooked for 48 hours and served as a tender carpaccio, or he might confit the legs (skin and fat removed) then serve the boned, butterflied meat rolled and stuffed with a black olive paste. In early summer, a simple rack of spring lamb with rosemary, cumin, carrot, celery and courgette is popular.

Today, however, Pascal's focus is on a stuffed saddle. Working closely with Vincent and junior sous chef, Laurent Deloutre, he cuts the joint lengthways, keeping the fat covering to maximise flavour, and spreads the centre with a mixture of the trimmings, herbs and egg. He rolls it up, seasons the fat and scores it so that it renders more easily, then knots the saddle tightly before cooking it gently sous vide. Portions are finished in a hot pan to order, as Pascal demonstrates, filling the small kitchen with buttery, herby, sizzling smells. Two evenly pink rounds are plated up carefully on an orderly pile of shredded cabbage with baby carrots and parsnips, a puck of fondant potato, and a glistening pool of jus. "The potatoes are from Andrew Long at Hall Farm in Fornham St. Martin," Pascal says as the

MAISON BLEUE PASCAL CANEVET

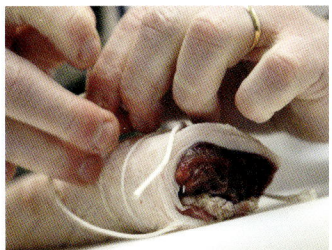

plate is captured on camera. "They grow onions, broccoli, and a range of potatoes for us. It's a fantastic arrangement."

The dish chimes with Pascal's cooking which is undeniably refined, artistically presented. He makes no bones about liking the consistency he can achieve by using a water bath, but insists that the focus is always on taste. No doubt this tracks back to growing up with his three siblings in the family home in Brittany where food was central. "I think I learned from my mother the pleasure in feeding people well, and the importance of using good fresh ingredients. Every lunch time there was a meal made from produce from our smallholding, and of course we had crêpes! Every family in Brittany would have a crêpe day – ours was Saturday – and even now when I go home it's the first thing we do together. These days my niece cooks for everyone from the end of the big family table."

Pascal's Breton roots (and he does describe himself as Breton first, French second) pervade his cooking. The rice pudding [see recipe] is a memory-trigger dish – "there'd always be a tray of rice and milk in the oven at home, and the milk would be from the farm next door" – and there are hints of home elsewhere: maybe roast langoustine tail in a langoustine broth, or oyster tartare with shallots and parsley, or buckwheat (the gluten-free Breton flour used in traditional crêpes) used in the crust on a fillet of halibut.

Back at Shimpling Park Farm, we walk under a rippling sky across fields wet with recent rain. Ewes, heavily pregnant, graze in welcome winter sunshine. The flock of 1,000 or so New Zealand Romneys are never fed concentrates, John Pawsey explains, and are fully part of the organic rotation. "They do the weeding very effectively, and they raise the nutrient content of the soil naturally. They're easier to manage than cattle because they can be outside year-round, and they are great mothers." This is vital in the organic system – the ewes give birth in the fields, and although they are constantly checked, intervention only happens if absolutely necessary.

Pascal is delighted to see this for himself. "When we first arrived in England 20 years ago, British food was still all about scampi and chips and prawn cocktails. Things have changed so much, there's so much more interest now in where food has come from. It's fantastic to understand the care that goes into this flock, and to make the connection with the dish that I will put on my menu."

SUFFOLK FEAST

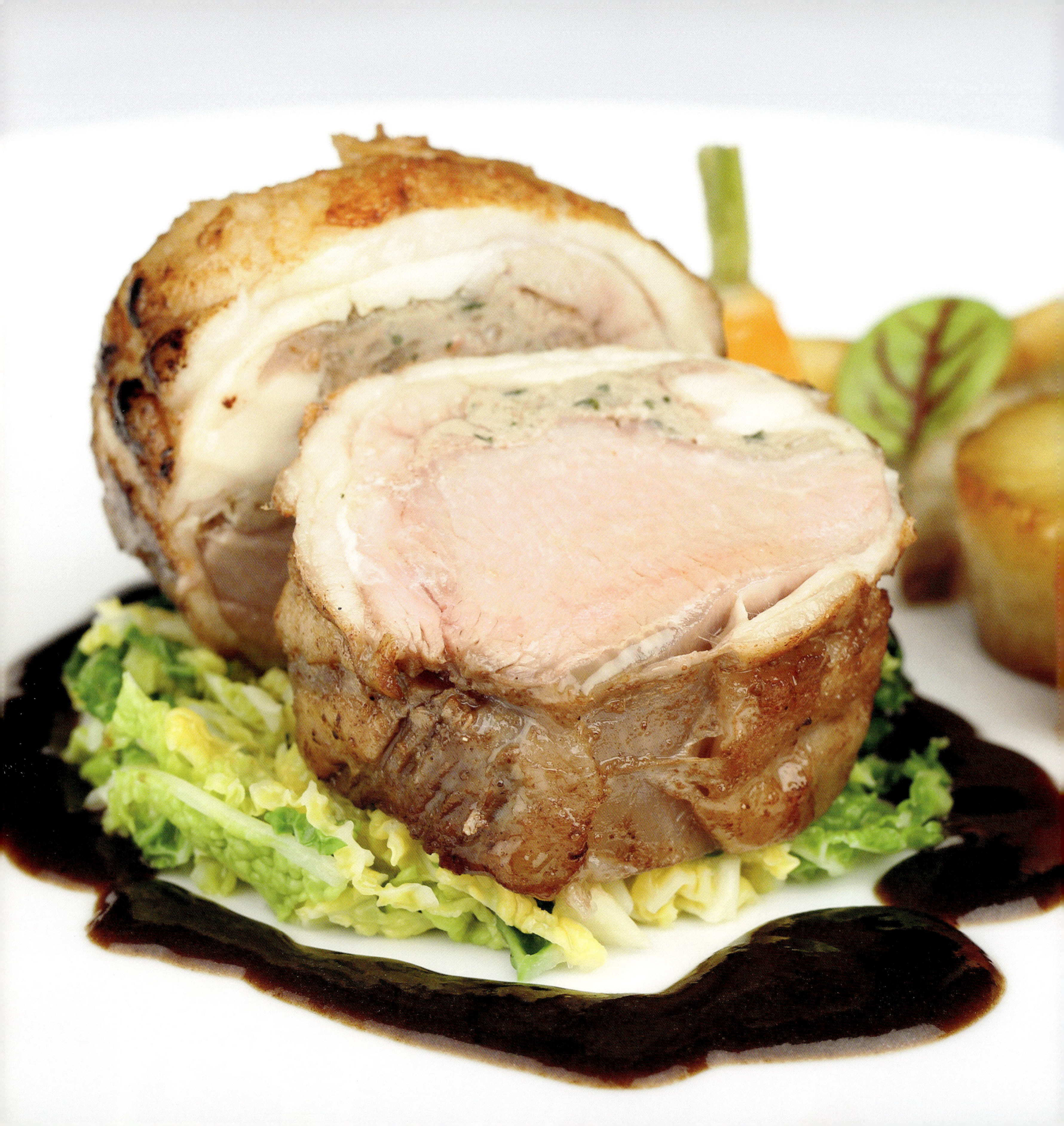

MAISON BLEUE PASCAL CANEVET

Stuffed saddle of lamb, savoy cabbage and fondant potato

The finest, most tender cut, the saddle is the mid-section of the lamb carcass cut as a whole, incorporating the two loins. Buy the best local meat you can – mine is organically reared from Shimpling Park Farm. Once boned out but still one piece held together by the skin, it is ready for stuffing and tying into a perfect boneless roasting joint (your butcher can do the boning for you but ask to have the bones to make the stock). This hearty but elegant recipe suits a family Sunday lunch. (serves 4)

Saddle
- **1 saddle of lamb**
- **1 egg white**
- **100g lamb trimmings, coarsely minced**
- **100ml whipping cream**

The saddle needs to be boned out while keeping the joint whole with the twin loins and belly flaps joined as one piece. Reserve any trimmings and bones for the stuffing and gravy respectively.

Whisk the egg white to soft peaks and mix well with the lamb trimmings, cream and seasoning.

Unfold the boneless saddle skinside down, place the lamb stuffing along the centre. Bring over the flaps and overlap tightly into a roll, tying securely every 2 cm with butcher's string. Chill for 30 minutes to set.

Gravy
- **Lamb bones**
- **2 sprigs of rosemary**
- **500ml well-reduced lamb or chicken stock**
- **Balsamic vinegar**

Preheat the oven to 180c. Chop the lamb bones and roast for 1 hour until golden-brown.

Simmer the bones with the rosemary and stock for 30 minutes before sieving. Add a good dash of balsamic vinegar before tasting and adjusting the seasoning. Set aside.

Garnishes
- **4 large potatoes, peeled**
- **Unsalted butter**
- **Sprig of rosemary**
- **8 baby carrots, trimmed**
- **1 small savoy cabbage, destalked and shredded**

Cut cylinders from the potatoes, approx. 6cm wide and 4cm deep, and then simmer with a good knob of butter and the rosemary until almost tender. Drain and set aside.

Gently pan fry the potatoes in melted butter until golden brown on all sides. Simmer the carrots with a knob of butter until tender. Drain and keep warm. Repeat for the cabbage.

To serve
Pre-heat the oven to 200c. Seal the saddle joint all over in a hot, dry ovenproof pan until light golden-brown all over. Put in the oven and after 5 minutes, reduce the heat to 180c and continue cooking for a total of 15-20 minutes or more if you like your lamb well done. Place the lamb on a hot plate, cover with foil and allow to rest for 15 minutes.

Put a bed of savoy cabbage onto warmed plates. Slice the lamb thickly and place on top of the cabbage, with the carrots and potatoes around. Drizzle with the gravy.

MAISON BLEUE PASCAL CANEVET

Citrus-marinated salmon mi-cuit

Mi-cuit means half-cooked in French and is a favourite starter of mine, served at room temperature. It keeps the fish moist and the citrus juice marinade adds a fruity touch, complemented by the rich avocado mayonnaise. (serves 4)

6 very fresh salmon portions
Juice of an orange
Juice of a lime
2 avocados
15g spinach
20ml olive oil

Toss the salmon in the fruit juices with seasoning. Wrap up tightly in several sheets of clingfilm into a parcel. Refrigerate for 2 hours.

Halve, stone and peel the avocados. Blanch the spinach in boiling water, transfer with tongs into iced water and then remove. Process the avocado flesh, spinach, olive oil and seasoning together until combined. Decant and chill.

Pre-heat the oven to 50c. Place the salmon, still wrapped, in a snug deep roasting tin and then create a bain marie with a larger, deep roasting tin. Add boiling water into the larger tin avoiding the smaller tin to make a water bath (up to 5cm of water).

Carefully transfer to the oven and bake for 7 minutes. You want it to be part-cooked and warm in the centre (45c on a digital thermometer is perfect). Allow to rest for 1 hour. Unwrap the salmon gently from the clingfilm and place on warmed plates before dotting with the mayonnaise.

Risotto rice pudding and lemon ice cream

A refreshing take on this classic British dessert, with a creamy texture from the Italian rice and a citrussy zing. Pictured is our elegant version with the addition of crisp biscuit and other lemon garnishes. (serves 4)

Zest of a lemon, plus some to garnish
125g of full fat milk
125g whipping cream
120g caster sugar
1 egg yolk
200ml full fat milk
100g arborio rice
75g caster sugar
1 vanilla pod, split and scraped
200ml whipping cream

Heat the zest, milk and cream until blood temperature and remove from the heat. Beat the sugar and yolk together and then gradually whisk this into the milk mixture. Cook gently stirring constantly until thickened to coat the back of a spoon.

Cool and set in an ice cream machine before freezing.

Meanwhile, make the rice pudding. Pre-heat the oven to 140c. Stir the milk, rice and sugar in a heavy saucepan, add the vanilla pod and seeds, then bring to a very gentle simmer. Stir regularly until it starts to dry out and the rice is completely soft. Fold in the cream and transfer to a buttered, snug gratin dish before baking for 1 hour.

To serve, divide the rice pudding between 4 bowls, adding the lemon ice cream on top and a pinch of lemon zest to garnish.

Buckwheat-crusted halibut steaks

A light delicious main course with a beautiful texture and indulgent sauce. We serve this with broccoli and cauliflower. (serves 4)

50ml good fish stock
50ml dry white riesling wine
75g whipped cream
Unsalted butter
30g clarified unsalted butter
20g breadcrumbs
10g buckwheat
Salt and black pepper
4 line-caught halibut steaks

Simmer the stock and wine until reduced by half. Mix in the cream and continue reducing until a spoonable, rich texture. Stir in a knob of butter, sieve, season to taste and set aside.

Process the crumbs, buckwheat, clarified butter and seasoning into a dough. Place between silicon paper sheets and chill for an hour, Roll out the crust thinly between the paper and cut to suit the size of your fish steaks.

Pre-heat the oven to 100c. Pan fry the halibut steaks in melted butter until browned on one side. Place on a deep baking tray, cooked side down. Top the fish with the crust slices. Bake until browned, for approx. 5 minutes. Spoon the sauce onto warmed plates and place the halibut steaks on top.

PASCAL ON HIS...

QUICK SNACK OR MIDNIGHT FEAST?
It has to be a good glass of full-bodied red wine, French of course!

WHAT CHARITY DO YOU FEEL DESERVES SUPPORT?
GeeWizz Charitable Foundation is a Suffolk charity that supports our community and raises money for local people who really need it. We are committed supporters. GeeWizz prides itself on 100% transparent giving, where every £1 donated or raised is carefully spent, helping change the lives of many.

PERFECT DAY OFF?
I love spending time with my family, and a summer's day enjoying a relaxed coastal walk at Aldeburgh with Karine and our dog, followed by fish and chips as the sun sets, is perfect!

FAVOURITE BIT OF KITCHEN EQUIPMENT?
My Thermomix! Every kitchen should have one (in fact I have two). It's not just the texture of soups and purées that it makes so good, it's also the taste somehow.

FOOD NOSTALGIA?
My grandmother's carrot soup still conjures up memories of my French childhood and happy family times. I can recall the taste and smell so vividly, yet my mother and I have never been able to re-create the recipe.

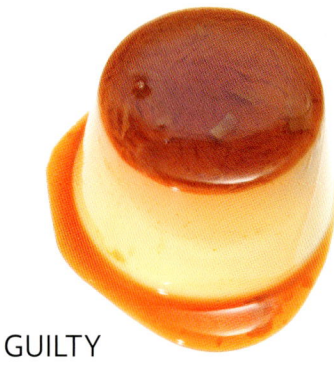

SPECIAL CHILDHOOD MEMORY?
Long summer days with my family eating endless fresh crêpes cooked by my mother in our garden in Quimper, Brittany. We had a long, rustic weather-worn table and my mother would take centre stage; it was magical. My mother taught me how to prepare food with love.

GUILTY FOOD PLEASURE?
Delicious crème caramel. I love the silky texture with just the right balance of sweetness.

I CAN'T WAIT TO EAT AT...
Jean-François Piège's two-star Le Grand Restaurant in Paris. Piège's food balances modernity with classic traditions. It's somewhere I'd love to go.

SIGNATURE DISHES

Starters

King scallop, clams, garlic rouille, kohlrabi, fish soup emulsion

Buttered confit and crunchy fennel, Granny Smith apple, fennel purée, tuile, toasted buckwheat, orange dressing

Roasted breast & slow-cooked leg of Norfolk quail, aged balsamic vinegar sauce, chicken liver mousse, parsnip pannacotta

Mains

Roasted saddle of Breckland venison, butternut squash, Jamaican pepper reduction sauce, savoy cabbage, fondant potato

Roasted fillet of line-caught cod, chervil & courgette gel, lemon confit, glazed turnips, chervil & parsley sauce

Fillet of Norfolk-reared Aberdeen Angus beef, roast salsify, baby parsnip, sage sauce

Puddings

Almond biscuit, William's pear, tonka bean crémeux, white chocolate, pecan nuts

Orange sphere, date crumble, saffron ice cream, orange coulis

'Pain perdu' brioche, custard, roasted pineapple

FAVOURITE TIME OF YEAR FOR FOOD?
Autumn is my absolute favourite. I love creating heart-warming dishes using local root vegetables, game and shellfish that celebrate the abundance of our Suffolk harvest.

SUFFOLK FEAST

Hospitality à la française

This modern French restaurant occupies that sweet spot where sleek service meets relaxed neighbourhood informality and friendliness.

Pale walls, white cloths, gleaming tableware, and gentle lighting are a foil for centuries-old beams and exposed brickwork that give the interior a unique character. This is a place that combines old and new with easy elegance – the art is contemporary and mirrors cast light cleverly – and where the modern menu created by chef patron Pascal Canevet is in tune not only with the immediate decor, but also the surrounding history of the town. The restaurant is in the heart of Bury St Edmunds' medieval grid with its cobbled lanes and ancient buildings, a stone's throw from the magnificent St. Edmundsbury Cathedral and Abbey Gardens.

Maison Bleue is owned by Pascal and Karine Canevet and has been run by them for the past 20 years. All their staff are francophone, and the hospitality they deliver is warm, professional and knowledgeable whether they're welcoming guests, explaining the menu, or advising on drinks from the wide-ranging wine list which champions, *naturellement*, French vintages.

Ask for one of the window tables to watch the comings and goings of Churchgate Street, or tuck yourself away at the back of the restaurant for a tête-à-tête meal – it's a romantic spot after all. Wherever you sit and whatever you eat, leave room for the incredible cheeseboard; nobody will mind if you have it before or after your dessert.

Maison Bleue
Churchgate Street, Bury St Edmunds IP33 1RG
W: maisonbleue.co.uk
T: 01284 760623
E: info@maisonbleue.co.uk
/MaisonBleueRestaurant
@Maison_Bleue
/pascalcanevet1309

Accolades and listings: Waitrose *Good Food Guide*; AA; *Michelin; Harden's; Tatler* 'Best of Britain' Restaurant Guide 2018; award winner, World Luxury Restaurants Awards; 'Good France' participant

Food served: Tue-Sat L 12-2; D 7-9

Cost: starters from £10.50; mains from £20.95; desserts from £7.95; set lunch £19.50 (2 courses), £26 (3 courses); wine from £19.50

Details: 55 seats; private hire of restaurant by negotiation

THE FROIZE, CHILLESFORD
DAVID GRIMWOOD

Top of the game

Mythologised and a little bit magical, woodcock have long been prized for their flavour. David Grimwood pays his abundant respects

65

THE FROIZE DAVID GRIMWOOD

Lined up on a board in The Froize kitchen are six woodcock. They've been plucked, but – as tradition dictates – the heads, beaks and feet are intact. David Grimwood handles them with care, talks in reverential tones as he describes how he's going to cook them.

It'll be simple, he says, the better to enjoy the exquisite flavour (it's gamey, rich) of this most prized of birds. He decides against using the beak as a skewer as chefs to the gentry would have done, and he removes the feet, but leaves the guts inside before browning the birds in Suffolk rapeseed oil, and oven-roasting them briefly. David lets them rest – "as a rule of thumb, rest any meat for the same amount of time that it's been in the oven" – before he removes the breasts and arranges them on a mound of creamy risotto. The flavour is matched with earthy mushrooms (this time a mix of shiitake, mousserons, chanterelles, ceps), and given a sweet dimension from caramelised red onions and roasted carrots, pumpkin and celeriac. It is indeed a simple, and simply delicious plate of food, homage to one of David's favourite game birds.

"I love to watch woodcock," he says as we bump over farm tracks at Glemham Hall towards a spot favoured by this elusive bird. "Sometimes at dusk you get just the briefest glimpse before they disappear into the woodland. Magical! I have immense respect for them, and I always shoot, collect, prepare, cook and eat them with great reverence." He drifts off into his own thoughts. "Very special birds..." he murmurs to nobody in particular.

There's been a 'fall' of woodcock recently, and it's only when that happens – when the birds arrive in numbers on our eastern seaboard from their native Scandinavia or Russia – that David (like any responsible gun) will shoot them. Tracking technology reveals that the birds haven't dropped from the sky as folklore and the word 'fall' suggest, but have travelled in search of insects and worms when home is too icily inhospitable. "It's a truly wild bird, not reared like partridge or pheasant," he says. "You have to gauge the population, understand their migration and how weather affects their behaviour."

It's a bird tangled up in countless mysteries. Small, boggle-eyed, long-billed, it wades on short legs, picking and probing for food, yet takes cover and breeds in woodland, where mottled feathers make its ground-level nests all but undetectable. It is famously difficult to shoot, flying a fast, weaving path on eerily silent wings. Females have been seen carrying chicks to safety between their thighs if they feel threatened; and the pin-feather from the leading edge of a woodcock's wing is prized by artists.

It seems right that talk on the rough shoot (we're guests of gamekeeper Mark Howard and in the company of Glemham Hall's Tom Hope-Cobbold) is as much about the surroundings as it is the sport. "Isn't this wonderful," David says, as we walk over the tussocky, marshy terrain. He's in his element, identifying birds by their call or flight, shotgun hooked over his arm. "I'm an armed birdwatcher really. It's not just about pulling the trigger. It's about being out in this incredible environment and respecting it."

Mark manages the 3,000-acre estate with his underkeeper Robert Alden, and daughter Kimberly, a qualified deerstalker. "My job is about looking after the habitat," Mark explains as we stop for sausage rolls, still oven-warm, jam tarts, and a nip of something fortifying, "keeping a balance so that songbirds and native species thrive. It's about conservation, not preservation; there's an important difference between the two."

He manages us too, instructing the guns, setting the pace. Beaters knock on trees, whistling gently to put up birds. Hares bound away, snipe launch themselves like rockets from almost under our feet, partridge whirr past, pheasant heave themselves, squawking, into flight. The occasional woodcock darts, weaves, disappears. The smell of cordite pricks and lingers. David's labradors, Ruby, Imp, and Robert's spaniel, Carrot, search and retrieve through maize, woodland and water.

Back at the Froize, David reflects. "I like cooking with a story. I like being able to tell guests where their meat has come from, or who grew the vegetables. The provenance thing is not a trend for me; it's how I've always cooked, instinctively." It goes without saying that all his feathered game comes from Glemham Hall while a passion for wildfowling means he shoots the duck he needs from flight ponds and the foreshore. Closer to home, his allotment is laden in season with raspberries and other soft fruit, as well as squash, courgettes, beans, tomatoes.

He calls himself a "restaurateur who can cook" rather than a chef. "I've made a living from cooking for 45 years, and my style has been in and out of fashion countless times. I've been through the melon boat years, the times when a starter meant tomato soup or a piece of pâté, or when black forest gateau was the height of elegance..." David has seen it all, it would seem, but whatever the current food fashion he always welcomes guests with genial hospitality, and serves them from his trademark hot table. "It is sociable and relaxed, and it makes absolute sense to me: I love talking to my guests, and I love giving them food that has heart and soul."

THE FROIZE DAVID GRIMWOOD

Roast woodcock, wild mushroom risotto, root vegetables and balsamic onions

There's something very special about this main course because we cook it so infrequently. Risotto is another dish to be made with care, stirring it constantly while you sip something delicious. Mushrooms are the perfect partner – any mix of fresh or rehydrated dried varieties will work, especially edible, foraged fungi (do try to find penny buns/ceps if possible, or buy dried porcini which are very special). For the roots, I tend to use carrot, parsnip and celeriac. (serves 4)

Woodcock
**4 oven-ready woodcock
Rapeseed oil
Unsalted butter**

Pre-heat the oven to 200c. In an hobproof shallow casserole, brown the birds, seasoned inside and out, in a little hot oil and melted butter, basting regularly for 2 minutes. Transfer to the oven and roast for 10-15 minutes. Remove and rest somewhere warm.

Root vegetables
2 handfuls of root vegetables, diced

Oil and season the vegetables before roasting in a hot, deep baking tray until caramelised and tender. Remove and keep warm.

Balsamic onions
**2 red onions, thinly sliced
Oil for frying
Balsamic vinegar
100g soft dark brown sugar**

Soften the onions slowly in a little oil, covered, until tender, add a good glug of balsamic vinegar and the sugar and continue to cook for as long and slow as you dare, uncovered and stirring regularly, until the onions are crisp but not burnt. Set aside somewhere warm.

Mushrooms
**1 small onion or 2 long shallots, diced
Oil and butter for frying
2 large handfuls of mushrooms, thickly sliced
1 clove of garlic, chopped
Generous glug of white wine**

Soften the onion or shallot in a little oil and butter. Take care not to let the onion burn or it will be bitter. Add any fresh mushrooms, fry over a medium-high heat (do not allow them to stew). Add the garlic and stir for a few seconds just to warm through. Add the wine, turn up high and allow the alcohol to evaporate. Add any rehydrated mushrooms with their sieved soaking water – you really can't have too many! Allow the liquid to quickly reduce down while the mushrooms soften. Keep warm while you make the risotto.

Risotto
**500g arborio rice (this is generous, but it doesn't hurt to have leftovers – think arancini balls!)
2 litres good chicken stock
125ml double cream
Handful parmesan, grated**

Heat a heavy-based pan on a low-medium heat and add a thin layer of oil. Add the rice to the pan and keep stirring until it almost changes colour and crackles. Start adding stock little by little, cooking the rice over a low heat, stirring after each addition until the liquid is completely absorbed (I use a figure of eight motion so everything is mixed in). It should take about four or five additions before you see the grains of rice filling out as they absorb the stock. Be careful not to allow the risotto to boil madly; it should be just simmering.

When the risotto is just about dropping off a spoon and just cooked through (not porridge-like), remove from the heat, season to taste, and stir in the cream and parmesan. Add the mushroom mixture. Don't stir too much because the colour will bleed from the mushrooms and make it grey. Adjust seasoning if necessary. Cover with a lid and leave for five minutes.

To serve
Curly parsley, freshly chopped

While the risotto is resting, remove the breasts from the woodcock using a sharp knife. Put a good portion of risotto on each warmed plate, add the balsamic onions and root vegetables, before topping with the woodcock. Finish with a little sprinkling of parsley.

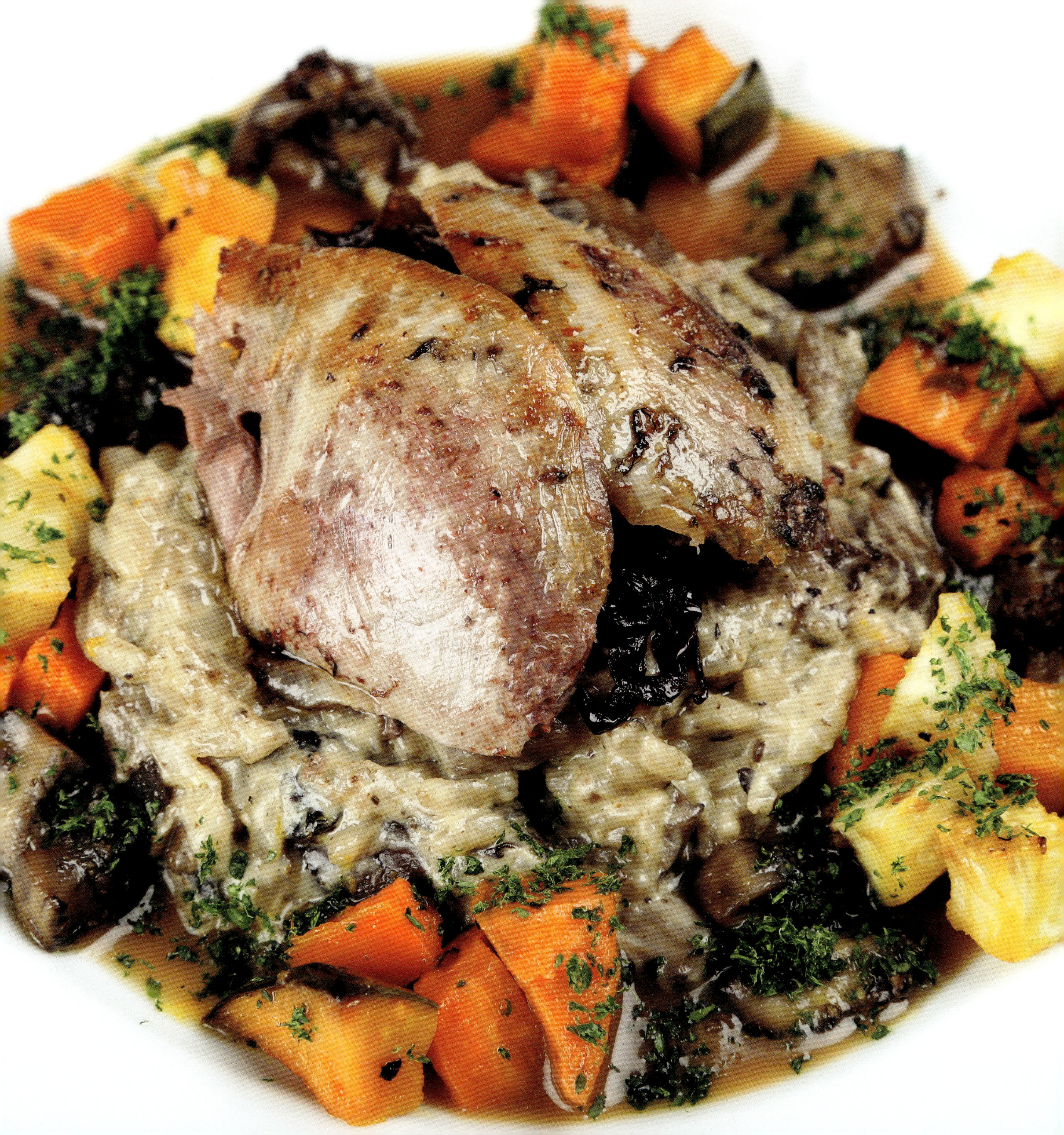

THE FROIZE DAVID GRIMWOOD

Finger lickin' partridge

You can't just remove the legs from a partridge, coat them and deep fry – you'd be chewing for hours! We cook them sous vide, a Froize homage to modern techniques, putting orange zest, rosemary, peppercorns, and garlic into a vac-bag with the legs, sealing, and cooking them at 65c for three hours. You can buy domestic sous vide equipment quite easily, or simply follow the instructions below. We make our own chilli jam to dip them in, but you can use a good quality shop-bought one. (serves 4 as a starter)

12-16 whole partridge legs
Flavourings to suit
Seasoned flour
Beaten egg
Panko bread crumbs

Place the legs in a pan that accommodates them comfortably. Add your flavourings and cover with water. Poach very gently for a few hours on the lowest heat until completely cooked and tender (you may prefer to slow braise them foil-covered in a low oven).

Allow legs to cool completely in the liquor. Drain and pat dry. Pre-heat the deep fryer to 180c. Dip each leg alternately in separate bowls of flour, egg and crumbs (pressing the latter on well). Deep fry until golden and heated through.

Pan-fried partridge breasts, parsnips three ways, English truffle oil

I 'stole' this wonderful starter from Madalene Bonvini Hamel, a chef friend who used to run the British Larder in Bromeswell. It's all about the perfect balance of flavours, fragrance and textures. (serves 4)

6 good-sized parsnips
Single cream
Rapeseed oil
8 partridge breasts, skin on
300ml game stock, hot
English truffle oil to serve

Pre-heat the oven to 200c. Dice four of the parsnips and simmer until soft. Drain and leave to dry a little on the switched-off hob. Liquidise half of them into a silky purée with a little cream and seasoning to taste. Keep warm. Toss the remaining cooked parsnips in a little hot rapeseed oil and bake until golden-brown. Slice the other 2 parsnips very thinly. Pre-heat your fryer to 180c and cook until golden and crisp. Drain and lay on kitchen paper, sprinkling with a little salt.

Pan-fry the seasoned breasts on both sides in a hot oven-proof pan, then roast for a few minutes till cooked. Remove from the pan and rest somewhere warm.

To make the gravy, heat the same pan, scrape round the roasting juices and stir in the stock. Boil to reduce by half and season to taste. Place the purée on hot plates, top with the carved breasts and roast parsnips, adding some gravy, a drizzle of truffle oil and the parsnip crisps.

Cinnamon pannacotta with blackberry and apple

We have this classic pudding on the menu year-round, but in the game season it's nice to give it an earthy, wintry warmth from fragrant cinnamon. To flavour the sugar, just bury a stick of cinnamon into the jar and leave it there for a while. Defrosted blackberries work fine. This dish is best made the day before if possible. (serves 4)

435ml whipping cream
3 tbsp cinnamon sugar
Half a vanilla pod, split and scraped
1 gelatine leaf, softened
2 Cox apples (or 1 Bramley for a sharper flavour)
Handful of blackberries
2 tbsp brown sugar
Unsalted butter

In a small pan, gently heat the cream, sugar and vanilla, stirring until melted. Whisk in the drained gelatine. Once dissolved, sieve into a jug and fill four lightly oiled moulds. Refrigerate for a few hours until set.

Pre-heat the oven to 160c. Dice the apples into cm dice (peeled if using Bramley). Place on a baking tray with the blackberries, scatter with the brown sugar and dot with butter. Bake for about 10 minutes until softened. Cool and chill. To serve, dip the pannacotta moulds in hot water to release, then turn them carefully onto a plate. Spoon the fruit on the side.

DAVID ON HIS...

FAVOURITE BIT OF KITCHEN EQUIPMENT?

Can I have two? My Thermomix for its versatility. I prefer my old one to the new one, but they both produce beautiful results. Then there is the kitchen temperature probe. I believe every kitchen (domestic ones too) should have one, not only for safety but also for getting those internal temperatures of food spot on. Just make sure you buy a decent SuperFast Thermapen.

FOOD HEROES?

Fergus Henderson for the simplicity of his menus and depths of his flavours, and my grandmother Anna Rosetta Turner who was the most wonderful farmhouse cook. She was like my own Mrs Beeton. I learnt about complementing flavours and textures from her, how 'threes' are good – what use is a profiterole filled with cream if there is no chocolate sauce! She had an amazing kitchen with a larder but no fridge. She cooked one day a week, a Monday, and as a child I would make something with the leftovers. Nothing was wasted.

WHAT'S ON YOUR KITCHEN PLAYLIST?

If I had to choose one band to play nice and loud it would be something from [folk-rock band] Merry Hell, and if I had to choose one of their tracks it would be *Come On England!* which I think is rather apt for today.

SPECIAL TIME OF YEAR FOR FOOD?

I love all the changing seasons, but I suppose it must be autumn and the start of the shooting season.

WHAT IS YOUR BIGGEST EXTRAVAGANCE AS A CHEF?

Wild mushrooms are my passion! When I don't have time to forage, then I will buy! Truffles, ceps, chanterelles – you name it, I will cook with it. Those I do forage usually get dehydrated and blitzed to a powder. What an addition to soups and stews that is!

MIDNIGHT FEAST?

What I call a three-course meal! – ie the holy trinity that is chocolate (a good milk chocolate for preference), big salted cashew nuts, and quaffable red wine!

WHAT THREE QUALITIES DO YOU MOST LIKE IN PEOPLE?

Honesty, sincerity, and most definitely humour

SIGNATURE DISHES

Starters

Glorious, smooth dark mushroom (field and penny bun) soup

Pan-fried pigeon breasts, garden salad, balsamic & blackcurrant dressing

Locally sourced game terrine with our own runner bean chutney

Mains

Baked Orford cod with home-grown spinach and asparagus

Local venison (fallow deer), Adnams ale & field mushroom pie

Devilled lambs' kidneys with Mr Revett's little chipolata sausages

(all served with sides from the hot table)

Puddings

My Grandmother's original recipe sherry trifle (hic!)

Warm sunken chocolate and almond pudding, locally made ice cream

Lemon posset, our raspberries and very short bread

WHICH OF YOUR VICES WOULD YOU FIND HARDEST TO GIVE UP?

Red wine! I like a good claret, a nice rioja, or something gorgeous from Australia such as Penfolds Grange if anyone's buying!

SUFFOLK FEAST

Do come in...

There is a well-trodden path to David Grimwood's restaurant – and it's not surprising. The welcome at The Froize, a place rooted in its rural east Suffolk community, is as warm as the food is abundant and the beer well-kept, guests travelling to enjoy David's determinedly traditional cooking and his genuine hospitality.

Formerly two gamekeepers' cottages that were knocked together, the roadside building is David and Louise's home as well as the beating heart of their business. It's comfortable, unpretentious, with oak beams and low ceilings in the bar area, and a lighter, more modern feel in the dining room where the hot table means that guests' plates are inevitably piled satisfyingly high. This is not a place that you will leave feeling hungry.

During the summer months, look out for Gloria!, David's street food truck that pops up at food and music events in the region (the pigeon burgers are legendary!), or book a seat at one of his 'Folk at the Froize' gigs that have established the restaurant firmly on the national live folk music circuit. The more recent 'Froize Uncovered' talks and workshops, meanwhile, attract guests keen to understand more about the countryside in this corner of Suffolk, learning from local experts. Otherwise, just settle happily into a squashy sofa with a pint or a coffee and observe the wildlife activity that's fed back to a screen from nest box and wildlife cameras set up in the grounds.

The Froize
Chillesford, Woodbridge IP12 3PU
W: froize.co.uk
T: 01394 450282
E: dine@froize.co.uk
/The-Froize-Freehouse-Restaurant
@Froizesuffolk
/the-froize-freehouse-restaurant

Food served: Tue-Sun L from 12; Fri, Sat D from 7

Cost: starters £6.75; mains £18.50; puddings £6.50; wine from £22.50

Details: 40 seats main restaurant; 24 seats al fresco; comfortable bar area; regular 'Folk at the Froize' music and food gigs, booking essential (folkatthefroize.co.uk); wildlife cameras in garden provide content for 'Froize Uncovered' special interest talks and masterclasses (froizeuncovered.co.uk); pub and garden available for private hire by negotiation; accessible; dogs welcome outside; parking

TUDDENHAM MILL, TUDDENHAM
LEE BYE

A prize catch

Abundant but still very special, lobster is a seasonal favourite of Lee Bye, chef patron of Tuddenham Mill. He heads as far east as you can in Suffolk to find the freshest

TUDDENHAM MILL LEE BYE

When he was 18, Lee Bye cooked a lobster for his grandad. The rookie chef, a junior in the Tuddenham Mill kitchen then led by Gordon McNeill, served it with buttery new potatoes, wedges of lemon, a hollandaise sauce "and a dodgy sunblush tomato salad", and his grandad loved it.

Fourteen years on, Lee tells the story as if it had happened last week, as if his grandad had popped into Tuddenham Mill – as he occasionally does – for a bite to eat and a catch-up. "He scrunched a tenner into my hand saying 'I can pay for my own lobster, boy'. I didn't tell him I had actually spent a day's wages on it. It was very special."

It still is, of course. Lobster is a regular feature of summer menus at the Mill, most often served classically, more or less as Lee did all those years ago. "I love it best like this," he says. "Maybe not with sunblush tomatoes – asparagus would have been better – but simple, not crowded with different flavours. I'll never forget the 200-dollar fruits de mer platter I had when I was working in Australia in 2008 – lobster, Moreton Bay bugs, king prawns (and my first pink champagne!) at Doyles [Watsons Bay, Sydney]. Just fresh and simple. That was an important food moment for me."

Sitting – carefully – on sleepers that separate the shingly edged, mist-shrouded river Deben from the collection of upturned tenders, lobster pots, buckets and nets that are the paraphernalia of fishing at Felixstowe Ferry, Lee shares his food ethos with Mike Warner, fisheries expert and advocate for small fishing communities. He's clearly glad to have time away from the pressures of the day job, and talks – a lot – about what matters to him as a chef. "I'm about real ingredients, sometimes humble ones, sometimes less humble. Carrots that still have Fenland soil sticking to them, lobster straight from the pots, pork from pigs that have lived well… I don't want manipulation in my food, I don't want it fiddled with." He pauses to lift the makeshift polystyrene lid on his stockpot; no, the water – freshwater with a scoop of sea – is not yet boiling.

So he continues. "The flavours of my rum baba [see recipe] are vanilla, rhubarb and rum, the carrot dish is just beautiful carrots, buttermilk, dill oil and chives. Food doesn't need every micro herb under the sun to make it taste better. It doesn't need to be complex. Flowers? Why?"

Mike picks up the lobster, taken from one of the keep pots that morning, from the box of seaweed. Its dark blue, orange-flecked carapace shines, antennae switch, pincers powerful enough to break a finger strain in bands. It smells of the sea, a beautiful, if somewhat alien, creature. Lee kills it humanely and after very few minutes in the bubbling water the lobster is resting, coral-pink, on a makeshift board. "Got to rest it. Otherwise the texture is like a wet sports sock."

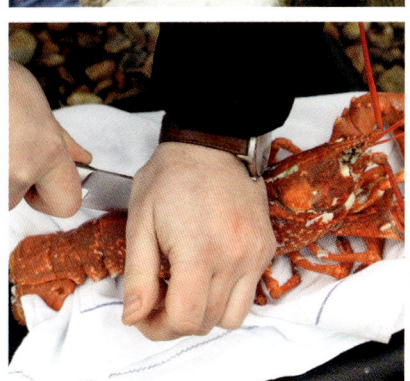

The spot at Felixstowe Ferry where Lee has balanced his camping stove is a real, unadorned, working stretch of the Suffolk coast, where day-boat fishermen (there are about ten full-timers at the Ferry), unglamorous in their oilskins, strive to make a living. There's no landing stage so boats are hauled onto the shingle before boxes are offloaded. "These fishermen have a precarious existence," says Mike. "And the job is incredibly dangerous in the dark. With the tide running, it requires real skill to bring the catch in." This place was Mike's playground as a child. His father fished, and Mike has his own boat and several lobster pots here; it's a place with which he feels a powerful connection.

"We need to show people just what we have in our seas, and that it is fantastic value, tasty, simple to cook, and healthy," he says. "The thing is, you should always buy fish seasonally. With the distribution channels what they are, anywhere in the UK is effectively local. Even cod fished from Shetland waters can be with us within 24 hours." The North Sea catch is abundant, however, the warmer months bringing financially important lobster, brown crab, Dover sole and bass, the colder ones cod, skate and less commonly used whiting, dab and flounder. Most is sold at wholesale markets, though enough stays just a stone's throw from us at Springtide Fish where gleaming-eyed, shiny-skinned catches are displayed for sale to local chefs and the general public. "We need to tell people!" Mike says. "It's madness that our whelks, pretty much all of them, are sold to export markets."

He watches as Lee tips the water from the stockpot, replaces it with generous amounts of butter and freshly chopped alexanders stems, leaves and the 'broccoli' (the plant's young unopened flower). The alexanders, ubiquitous in spring hedgerows, are fresh, citrussy, and the warm butter coaxes the flavour out deliciously.

Lee serves the lobster on a paper plate – as you do when you're a chef with three AA Rosettes. Without ceremony, we use our fingers to pick pieces of the sweet, pink-tinged flesh, scooping it through the alexanders butter that drips down our hands. It tastes none the worse for its off-the-cuff presentation; in fact it probably tastes a tiny bit better.

SUFFOLK FEAST

TUDDENHAM MILL LEE BYE

Lobster, oyster mayonnaise, alexanders butter, sea greens

Lobster is the king of the crustaceans, and its delicate-tasting flesh goes perfectly with a lovely fresh aioli and some lemon wedges. It's a classic combination and we often serve it at Tuddenham Mill like that, but here I've paired it with a simple alexanders butter and oyster emulsion (using two fresh oysters rather than egg yolks) for a really coastal taste. You can ask your fishmonger to cook and prepare a lobster for you. The shell and claw make a fantastic shellfish stock for risotto or other seafood dishes. Celery works well as a tame and quite different alternative to alexanders. (serves 2)

To cook the lobster
>   1 lobster, about 350g – the smaller ones are sweeter

Bring a large stockpot of water to a rolling boil. If you have bought a live lobster, render it unconscious in the freezer for two hours first, then kill it humanely just before cooking by putting a sharp knife quickly through the cross point in the shell behind the eyes where the head meets the body.

As soon as the lobster is killed, put it into the boiling water. Bring the water back to the boil and then immediately remove from the heat and leave the lobster in the water to come back to room temperature. This will take a few hours, but it's important – it's like resting a piece of meat and ensures the flesh is succulent rather than tight.

Unshelling the lobster
Place the lobster on a chopping board with a tray beneath it to catch any juices (it can get messy). Twist off the claws and separate into sections at the joints. Pull off the bottom pincer and remove the feathery bone and any flesh inside it. Holding the top of each claw firmly on the board with one hand use the back of a heavy knife or rolling pin to break the shell, tap sharply to crack it but don't crush it. Remove the flesh which should come away easily (a lobster pick is useful here). Repeat with the other claw and set aside the meat.

Lay the lobster on its belly and flatten out the tail. Put the tip of a sharp knife into the point where the head meets the body and cut firmly through the shell towards the tail. Turn the lobster round and do the same through the head so that you end up with two halves.

Scoop out the stomach sac behind the eyes and discard. Remove the soft green tomalley (liver) and coral-coloured roe if it's there. Both are edible and can be used in separate dishes if you wish. Carefully take the tail meat out of the shell in one piece and remove the digestive tract which runs the length of the tail. Replace the meat in the shell and set aside.

Alexanders butter
>   Two good lengths of alexanders stems or celery
>   Handful of unripe alexanders flowers or celery leaves
>   60g butter

Remove the fibrous outer layer of the stems using a sharp knife or potato peeler and chop finely. Melt about 20g of the butter in a small pan over a medium heat, increasing the heat till the butter turns light brown, then add the alexanders stems to warm through. Strain, discarding the butter. Using the same pan melt the rest of the butter and stir through the alexanders flowers (or celery leaves), then add the softened stems. Keep warm.

Oyster emulsion
>   2 fresh oysters, shucked
>   Squeeze lemon juice
>   50ml sunflower oil

Pat the oysters dry and roughly chop them on pulse in a food processor with a good squeeze of lemon juice. With the motor running, drizzle the oil in very slowly to combine with the oysters. Once it reaches the consistency of mayonnaise, pass it through a sieve, check the seasoning (it will naturally be quite salty) and adjust. Stir in more lemon juice if needed.

To serve
>   Coastal greens of your choice

Place half a lobster on each plate with the claw meat on top. Spoon or pipe the emulsion along the tail meat and dress with the alexanders butter. Finish with sea vegetables.

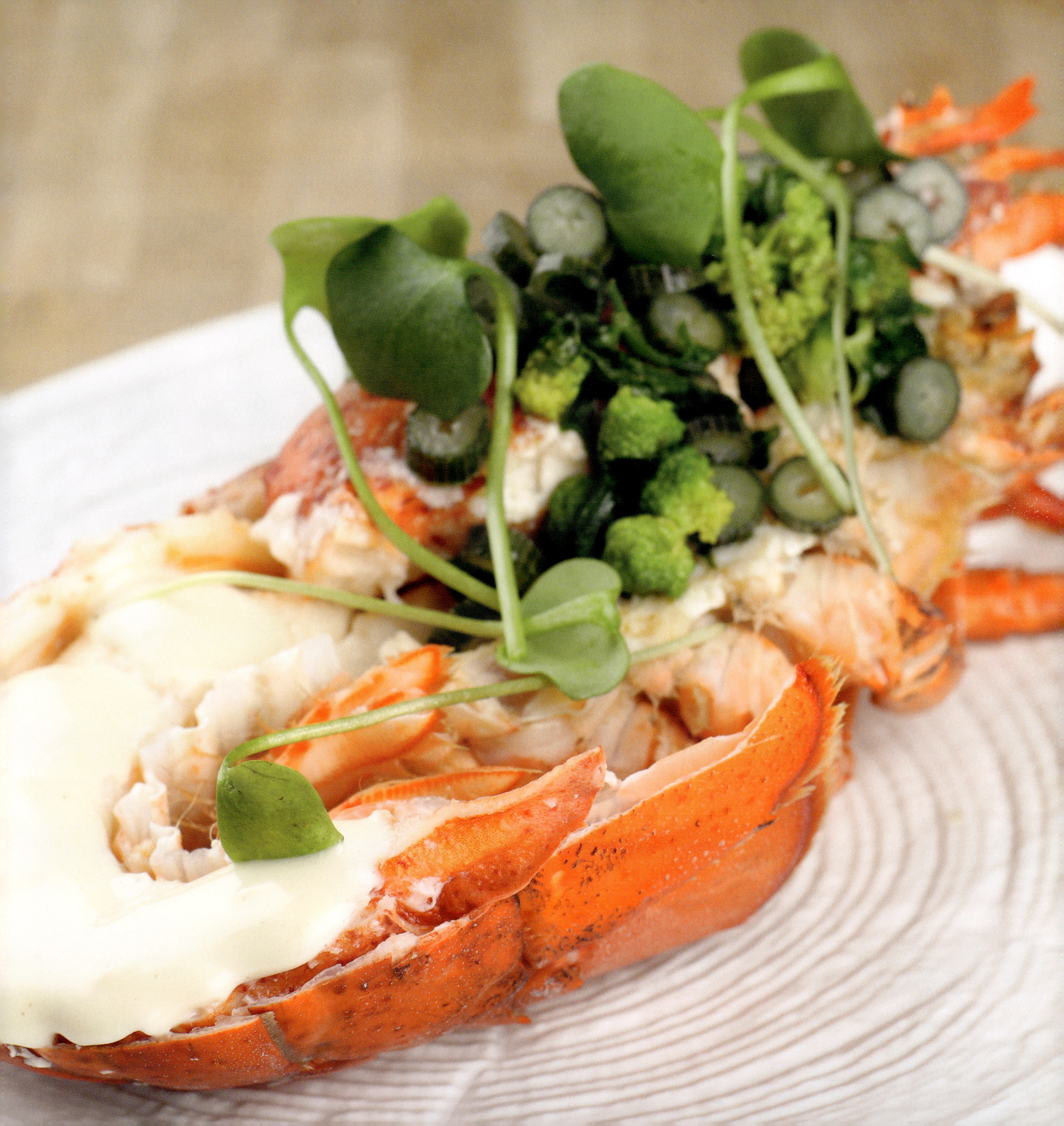

TUDDENHAM MILL LEE BYE

Pork jowl, oyster mushroom and artichoke broth, cavolo nero

Pork jowl is deliciously melt-in-the-mouth when cooked long and slow, and has an incredible flavour from the deep layer of fat. Here, I've used Blythburgh pork and served it with agretti (monks beard) poached in a butter emulsion, and a scatter of onion seeds for contrast. If you can't get jowl, buy pigs' cheeks instead. (serves 4)

250g pork jowl or pigs' cheeks
Salt to cure
100g dried mixed mushrooms
2 artichoke hearts, poached
Malt extract to glaze
Handful cavolo nero, shredded
Handful agretti, lightly poached
Onion seeds

Rub the pork all over in salt and refrigerate overnight.

The next day, rinse off the salt and pat dry. Roast for 12 hours in an oven pre-heated to 160c.

While the pork is resting, make the broth. Rehydrate the mushrooms until soft. Drain, reserving the liquor in a pan. Dice the artichokes and mushrooms and add to the pan.

Portion the pork and sear in a dry, very hot pan until golden-brown all over. Brush with the malt extract and set aside.

Warm the broth gently, adding the cavolo nero for just a few seconds. Serve on to hot plates and top with the meat, agretti and onion seeds.

Carrots with honey, buttermilk and herbs

Buy the freshest carrots you can – this dish is all about taste and treating a humble root vegetable with as much love as if it were a lobster. Where I'm from in Fordham, everyone buys Peter Canham's carrots from his roadside stall, but these are from Clem Tompsett, another legendary East Anglian carrot grower. This dish makes a delicious vegetable accompaniment, but we also offer it as a main course on our vegetarian menu and (without the honey) on our vegan menu too. (serves 4)

8 whole carrots
20g butter, plus more to finish
½ tbsp honey
Few sprigs of thyme
4 tbsp buttermilk
Chives, snipped
Dill oil
Sea vegetables or dandelion leaves

Wash the carrots thoroughly, peel them, then polish them using a clean scouring sponge. Melt the butter and honey with 200ml water and a pinch of salt in a pan to fit the carrots. Add the roots and the thyme and simmer on a very low heat till they are just cooked. Remove from the pan and set aside.

Melt a knob of butter in a pan and warm the carrots before sprinkling with sea salt. Put a spoonful of buttermilk onto hot plates, top with the carrots, scatter with the chives and drizzle with the dill oil before finishing with the greens.

Baba au rhum

At the Mill, I often serve rum babas as pictured with our own demerara ice cream, candied walnuts and a rhubarb compote (though any other slightly tart fruit will also work well). (serves 4)

3 eggs
5g fresh yeast
1 tbsp runny honey
125g plain flour
75g melted butter, at room temperature
175ml dark rum
75g caster sugar
Rind of a lemon or orange, or vanilla pod (optional)
Ice cream, fruit compote and candied nuts

Combine the eggs, yeast, honey and a pinch of salt in a large mixing bowl. Slowly mix in the flour and beat to create a smooth batter before mixing in the melted butter. Use to half-fill four greased metal ring moulds. Prove at room temperature for about an hour till the batter reaches the top of the moulds.

Pre-heat the oven to 180c. Bake the babas for 10-12 minutes until firm to the touch and golden-brown. Remove and rest for a few minutes before turning out onto a wire rack.

In a small pan, simmer the rum, sugar and a splash of water (with the citrus rind or vanilla if desired) and reduce to a syrup. Remove from the heat and place each baba one at a time in the pan for 30 seconds to soak up the syrup, turning once. Place on a cold plate, fill with fruit compote and top with ice cream and nuts.

LEE ON HIS...

WHAT CHARITY OR CAUSE DO YOU SUPPORT?
I love mentoring Level 1 students at the West Suffolk College. I give it as much time as I can because anything chefs can do to encourage young people into the industry, and give them a taste of what working in a real kitchen is like, has got to be worthwhile.

LAST FILM YOU WATCHED?
The Darkest Hour. I loved it. I'm interested in successful people in any field, and how they fight to achieve success.

MOST THRILLING MOMENT IN YOUR CAREER TO DATE?
Cooking jowl for Matthew Fort, food editor of *The Guardian* when he came for lunch on his way to Norwich a few weeks ago. It was a real honour to cook for him and to get his great feedback afterwards.

LAST THING YOU BOUGHT FOR YOURSELF?
A pint of Guinness last night.

I CAN'T WAIT TO EAT AT...
Moor Hall [Aughton, Lancashire]. The chef patron is Mark Birchall who used to be Simon Rogan's head chef at L'Enclume in Cartmel. Mark was cooking when I ate at L'Enclume for the first time a few years ago, so to taste his food in his own restaurant would be amazing.

WHAT GETS YOU UP IN THE MORNING?
The desire to succeed. I'm competitive and driven. I have to have goals, I need the bar to be set high and to be challenged.

FAVOURITE SUFFOLK VIEW?
West Stow is a beautiful place to walk. I enjoy the stillness. It's thinking time, I suppose - not that I get much of that! But when I need it, that's where I find myself going.

SOMETHING ABOUT YOU THAT NOBODY KNOWS?
I cried last week when I watched *Call the Midwife*.

TELL US YOUR NICKNAME
Which one? Lugs, Pasta, Soap (from the film *Lock, Stock and Two Smoking Barrels*), Lee-thal

SIGNATURE DISHES

Starters

Sea trout gravlax, Cornish oysters, French dandelion stems, dill

Jacob's ladder, wild celery, marrow, land cress

Cullen skink, brown hen yolk, three-cornered garlic, apple

Mains

Dingley Dell pork jowl, trotter sauce, roots, wild honey

Roasted halibut, rock samphire, beurre blanc, escabeche oil

Wild red deer, Robuchon mash, brambles, hispi cabbage

Puddings

Sea buckthorn posset, rum-soaked apricots, brown butter shortbread

Bitter chocolate pot, morello cherry sorbet, hazelnut oil

English raspberries, toasted oat cream, meadowsweet

LAST BELLY LAUGH?
This interview! Cringe...

IF NOT A CHEF...
I've wanted to be a chef since I was 15 but all my family are in construction, so if I hadn't found cooking as a teenager I'd probably be on a building site somewhere. I had a job as a scaffolder briefly and I was a scaffolding flop!

The mill's tale

Mix picturesque natural meadows, peaceful millpond waters with a loyal swan family in residence, an historic building and delicious food, and you have an intoxicating combination. Tuddenham Mill is a place that draws on the Brecks and the Fens for its identity, but brings a bit of urban dash to an otherwise deeply rural part of East Anglia.

There's been a mill on this West Suffolk site for some 1,000 years, but times they change, and what was a place of industry until the waterwheel ground to a halt in 1954, is now one of contemporary comfort, style and country luxury. Renovations have been done sympathetically and gradually over the years so that memories of the Mill's working past linger, most notably in the bar and first-floor dining room where the vast cast-iron waterwheel is illuminated colourfully as evening falls.

Stay in one of the spacious bedrooms in the main building, or a luxurious Loft Suite, or push back the glass doors onto your very own terrace from one of the Mill Stream or Water Meadow rooms. Meadow Nooks are cosy boltholes that despite their hobbit-like size offer king-size comfort – one even has a private hot tub – and uninterrupted views of the Suffolk countryside.

Tuddenham Mill
High Street, Tuddenham, Newmarket IP28 6SQ
W: tuddenhammill.co.uk
T: 01638 713552
E: info@tuddenhammill.co.uk
/tuddenhammill   @tuddenhammill   /tuddenhammill

Accolades and listings: Waitrose *Good Food Guide*; AA Three Rosettes; winner, Chef of the Year, *EADT* Suffolk Food and Drink Awards 2015 (Lee Bye); winner, Restaurant of the Year, *EADT* Suffolk Food and Drink Awards 2016; *Michelin*; *Harden's*; AA Four Silver Stars (accommodation); *Mr & Mrs Smith*; *Sawday's*; *Good Hotel Guide*

Food served: all week B 7.30-10.30; L 12-2.15; D 6.30-9.15

Cost: starters from £7.50; mains from £19; puddings from £8.50; children's menu; vegetarian menu; vegan menu; early dining 6.30-7.30 Sun-Fri £19.95 (three courses); set lunch £20.95 (two courses), £25.95 (three courses); five-course taster menu £65 with optional £40 wine flight; Sunday lunch £24.50 (two courses), £28.95 (three courses); afternoon tea (pre-booked) from £20.50; wine from £19.95

Details: 60 seats in main restaurant; up to 20 in bar; al fresco tables on terrace and lawn; private dining seats 36; 15 bedrooms plus 6 Meadow Nooks (one with hot tub); wedding licence; accessible in parts; dog-friendly; parking

THE ANCHOR, WALBERSWICK
SOPHIE DORBER

All hail, kale

Sophie Dorber bangs the drum for kale, the leafy green that has shed a poor image to become a star of the vegetable firmament

85

THE ANCHOR SOPHIE DORBER

Once, there was a green vegetable called kale. For years – generations – it faced up to the onslaught of the British winter, rooted sturdily in many an East Anglian field. It accepted rain runnelling like mercury through its curly head, it cared nothing for January frosts nipping its crimped edges, and stood strong against stalk-buckling snow – only to be cut, boiled to unrecognisable sludgy greyness, rejected by horrified children and just about tolerated by adults.

Then, sometime in the noughties, this ugly duckling of a vegetable underwent a PR transformation. Glossy people started juicing, steaming, stir-frying it, declaring their new-found adoration on t-shirts even; they would eat its young leaves raw, or toss them with similarly hailed ingredients such as garlic and extra-virgin olive oil, chillies, herbs and spices in a breathless love-in that elevated this ordinary brassica to 'superfood' status.

Sophie Dorber didn't need the hype to convince her of kale's (and its cousins') qualities; she was on board already. Kale, grown in coastal fields minutes from The Anchor at Walberswick is a go-to ingredient for her, a natural vegetable accompaniment throughout the year. "I love the abundance of kale, that it grows easily and close to the pub, that it's got texture and flavour and colour, and that it's so good for you." She's on a kale roll. "People use the word 'humble' with kale. But to me it's rather bumptious, funky, it's got personality, attitude. Maligned and misunderstood, maybe – but not humble!"

Sophie buys her kale – and most of her fresh fruit and vegetables – from Wangford Farm Shop. The weather-boarded huddle of farm buildings just a short drive from the Anchor is where the Miller family have been selling their own onions, potatoes and brassicas along with other produce bought from Lincolnshire farmers, since 1975. Roy Miller's parents ran the business at first from a lean-to shack, but the operation that he now runs with his wife, Linda, and Linda's brother Kevin has grown to fill a whole barn not only with produce, but pet and wild bird food, logs, coal, and plants brought on in an adjacent greenhouse.

"It's a fantastic business, and Kev is always on the lookout for interesting new things for me," Sophie says as we walk through the densely planted field of kale, wet with recent rain. She picks an armful of the purple sprouting broccoli growing between firm-hearted celtic cabbage, dark swathes of cavolo nero, and stalks of kalettes, the hybrid cross between brussel sprout and kale. "The produce is grown with care and real respect for the land," she says, "and they work so hard. I buy what they have and build my menu around that."

Sophie's ingredient-led cooking is fixed in simplicity and seasonality. Back in her busy kitchen she swirls heaps of kale through cold water, quickly removing tough ribs and cooking portions to order maybe to accompany grilled sea bass, or roasted pheasant crown, or the Persian rice that she prepares for our visit. She turns deep orange cubes of roasted butternut squash through sesame oil, herbs and spices, and into a mix of nutty brown rice, lentils and soft raisins, adding curls of kale, and a dollop of pungent, garlicky turmeric aioli. It's a plate of comfort food with a punch of flavour.

Her cooking is also wrapped up in a deep desire to nourish and nurture. As if on cue (teenage children being too old for this sort of thing) the family's eight-week old maltipoo, Poppy, burrows into Sophie's sweater, tucking herself into a bauble of café-au-lait fluff. "It tracks back to my grandmother and my mother who were both really good home cooks," Sophie says, distractedly stroking the puppy. "I grew up with thrifty food – fish pies made with scraps of fish, treacle tarts that are of course made with stale bread. My grandparents lived in rural Essex, and experienced the farming depression and the wars. Nothing was ever wasted."

The minimal-waste ethos pervades The Anchor: allotment soil is enriched with compost made from vegetable waste, old umbrellas have been upcycled as bean poles, butts made from sherry and whisky barrels collect rain water, and the glass recycling bins are available for village use. Gluts of rhubarb, beetroot, beans, tomatoes are pickled or preserved as jams and chutneys. No doubt new plantings of sea buckthorn, mixed with hops along a perimeter hedge, will find a similar use.

The arrival from Romania of Ana and Doru Avarvarei has further expanded The Anchor's food horizons, the couple sharing the richness of their homeland's food culture. "Romanian cooking is an incredible mesh of familiar Mediterranean flavours, and central European food with its culture of preserving," Sophie says. As Ana adds, no Romanian home would be without a jar of zacuscă [see recipe], the mix of preserved aubergine, red pepper and onions that will be used throughout the year on jacket potatoes or stirred through pasta, soups or stews.

Sophie encourages her team to listen, observe, to share experience and cook instinctively. "Cooking over fire as we do with our Bertha charcoal oven [steaks, ash-roast vegetables and slow-cooked braises all emerge deliciously] is about understanding ingredients, it's not about precise temperatures or exact methods. It's difficult to teach, but when you see a chef get it, it reminds me why I love this job!"

THE ANCHOR SOPHIE DORBER

Persian rice with kale, butternut squash, pumpkin seeds and turmeric aioli

This versatile spicy rice dish makes a fantastic main course. I love to serve it with kale, but any leafy green will work. Use any dried fruit you have in the cupboard, and change the flavour by adding preserved lemons, smoked paprika, sumac, little pimento peppers, chilli or herbs of your choosing. Any rice left over is perfect to stuff mushrooms or peppers before roasting them, or to serve as an accompaniment to grilled salmon or chicken. If you like, choose a good shop-bought aioli and stir in the turmeric. (serves 4+)

Rice and lentil base
- 100g brown rice
- 100g lentils

In separate pans, cook the rice and lentils in plenty of simmering water until tender. Drain well and set aside.

Turmeric aioli
- One head garlic
- 3 egg yolks
- 4 tbsp white wine vinegar
- 290ml good quality olive oil
- 1 heaped tsp turmeric

Roast the garlic in foil until soft. Squeeze the pulp into a food processor and add the egg yolks, vinegar and seasoning before blending to a paste. With the motor running, add the oil slowly to make a thick emulsified sauce. Remove, add in 1 tbsp of boiling water and the turmeric, stir to combine and adjust seasoning to taste. Refrigerate until needed.

Roasted squash
- 1 butternut squash, peeled and deseeded
- Good olive oil

Cut the squash into large cubes. Oil, season and roast in a medium-hot oven until softened. Set aside.

Spiced onions
- Olive oil and butter for frying
- 3 large onions, peeled and sliced into thin slivers
- Half head garlic, crushed
- 2 tbsp red wine vinegar
- 200g dried apricots
- 1 level tsp each of nutmeg, cinnamon, allspice

Fry the onions and garlic in a hot sauté pan with a little oil and butter over a medium heat until softened and slightly caramelised. Stir in 2 tbsp of vinegar, the apricots and spices and cook on a low heat for a few minutes. Set aside.

Wilted kale
- Large handful of kale per person
- Unsalted butter

Wash the kale in plenty of cold water, drain and remove the tough ribs. Add the kale to a large pan of boiling salted water, bring back to the boil and blanch for one minute. Drain well. Heat a large frying pan with a few knobs of butter, add the kale and stir to coat the leaves. Heat through, season to taste and set aside somewhere warm.

Roasted seeds
- Pumpkin seeds
- Sumac
- Good honey
- Olive oil

Combine a few handfuls of pumpkin seeds in a hot pan with a pinch of sumac, a drizzle of honey and olive oil and cook over a low-medium heat until roasted. Season and set aside.

To serve
- 1 tsp red wine vinegar
- Zest of 1 lemon
- Small bunch of coriander, chopped

Mix the rice and lentil base with the onion mixture and stir in the vinegar, lemon zest and coriander before seasoning to taste. Put a generous amount of rice onto warm plates. Add the squash, kale and a spoonful of aioli and scatter with the seeds.

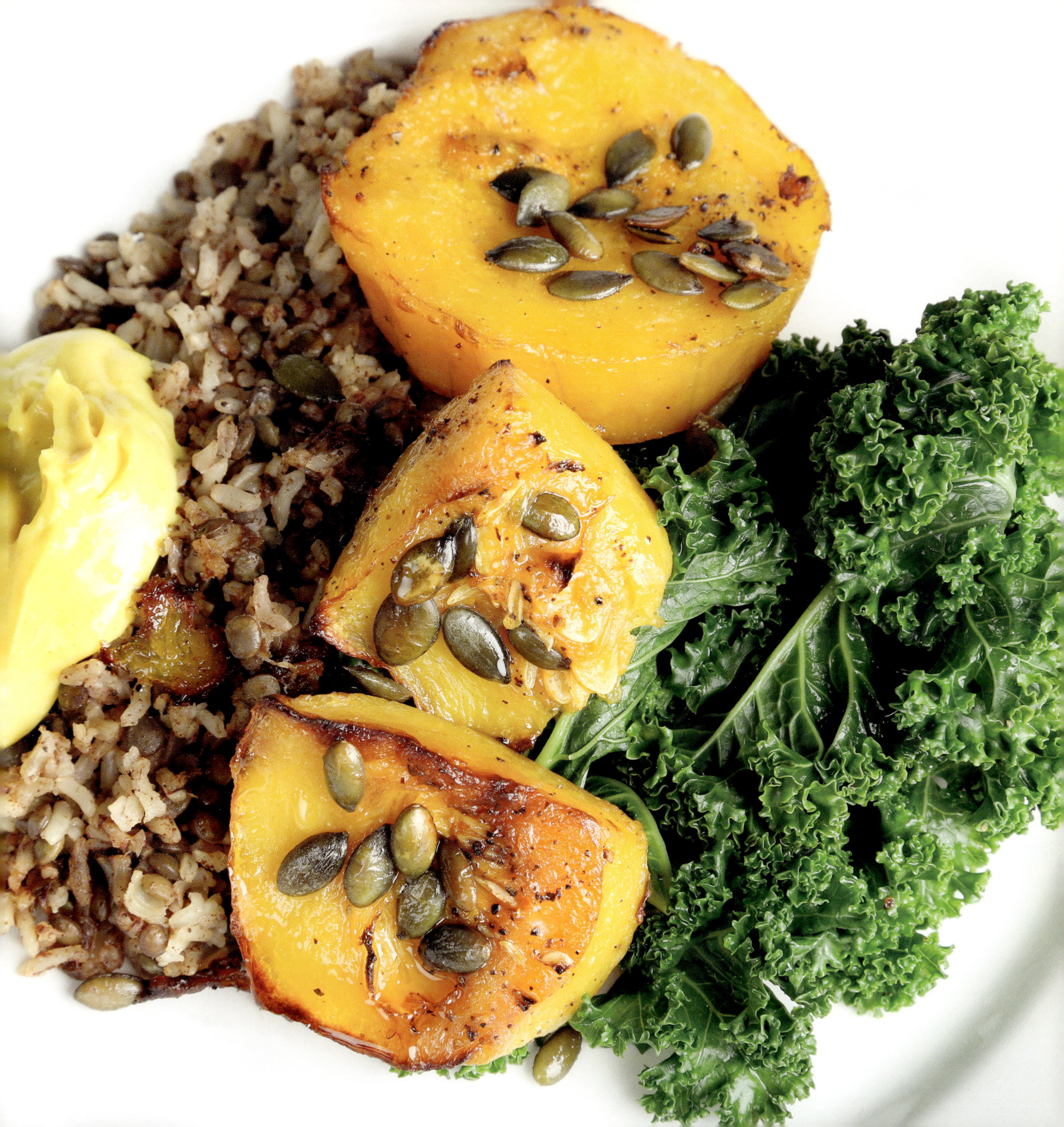

THE ANCHOR SOPHIE DORBER

Zacuscă

A preserved vegetable staple from Romania, zacuscă makes a fabulous base for a quick pasta sauce or is a great addition to soups, stews or curries. We make it in batches during quieter times at the pub, using produce from the allotment or our local farm shop. (makes about 3 jars).

1kg aubergines
1kg romano red peppers
500g onions, finely diced
Light olive oil
250g carrots, grated
1 bay leaf
A small bunch of thyme, leaves only
Caster sugar (optional)

Roast the whole aubergines and peppers in a hot oven until completely soft. Cool in a sealed container. Peel the aubergine and peel and deseed the peppers before straining overnight in a colander set over a pan (keep the juices – they are good in soups).

The next day, sweat the onions on a very low heat for about 45 minutes in the olive oil. Add the carrots, bay leaf and thyme. Chop the pepper and aubergine and add these to the pan. Simmer gently for a further 45 minutes. Season, taste and season again, adding sugar if liked. Cool and refrigerate or store in sterilised, sealed glass jars.

Courgette carpaccio

This simple starter is all about the quality of the ingredients. Use the freshest courgettes you can find, only when in season locally. Best of all, grow your own – it's easy! (serves 1)

1 very fresh courgette
5 green olives, sliced
Parmesan shavings
Good handful of rocket leaves
1 tbsp toasted pine nuts
Extra virgin olive oil

Carefully use a mandolin cutter to finely slice the courgette straight into a wide serving dish. Season well. Scatter on the olives, parmesan, rocket leaves and pine nuts before drizzling with the oil.

Hummus

A failsafe recipe for this ever-popular mezze starter. Serve it at room temperature with crunchy vegetable crudités and flatbreads for dipping. It's healthy too, packed with protein and fibre. We garnish this with olive oil, chopped coriander, paprika and sumac, and sometimes jalapeño chillies. Zacuscă works well too! (serves 4+)

1 whole head of garlic
1 400g tin of chickpeas, lightly drained
3 heaped tsp light tahini
Juice and zest of one lemon
4 ice cubes

Heat the oven to 220c. Remove the papery layers around the garlic but keep the head whole. Place on a piece of foil, drizzle with olive oil, and wrap loosely. Roast for about 40 minutes or until very soft.

Remove and cool before squeezing out the flesh into a food processor. Add the other ingredients with seasoning to taste, before blending on full power. Leave for 5 minutes to become really thick and creamy. Serve communally in a central dipping bowl.

SOPHIE ON HER...

GUILTY FOOD PLEASURE?
Crisps, cheese and bacon. I must have a need for salt! Any flavour of crisps will do, and I love all cheeses.

BEST DISH EVER EATEN?
Nettle and ricotta ravioli at the Slow Food Festival in Turin, with some beautiful wines, Mark my husband and our three-month old baby, Harry. It was almost 20 years ago, and it was as much about the place and that moment in time as the food. A great food experience is invariably bound up with the place and the people.

RECENT FOODIE DISCOVERY?
I've been learning so much about fermentation and preserving from our wonderful Romanian chef, Anna. Preserving the abundance of summer crops to use through the long winter is at the heart of Romanian cooking, and I'm so lucky to have learnt about it from someone who has always cooked that way.

FAVOURITE LOCAL FOODIE PLACES?
I love Darsham Nuseries, and Aldeburgh Food Market. Focus Organic café and deli in Halesworth is a real favourite too – Juan Suarez and Pippa Bergson who run it are amazing!

FOOD NOSTALGIA?
Nearly all my mother's cooking. She made comforting, beautiful-tasting food from next to nothing. Her cooking gave me a respect for food and ingredients that I've never lost.

CHEF'S TIP?
I use coffee in stews to enhance and give depth to the flavour. It's another of my mother's secrets and works in the same way that chocolate does, gives an umami savouriness and richness.

FAVOURITE KITCHEN EQUIPMENT?
My Victorinox tomato knife; it's small, lethal, and versatile!

SIGNATURE DISHES

Starters

Six Mersea oysters, shallot & sherry vinegar

Anchor fish soup, rouille, croutons

Wood-roasted local mackerel fillet, Asian slaw

Mains

Smoked haddock & salmon fishcake, creamed leeks, hand-cut chips

Crab gratin, new potatoes, roasted Romano peppers, allotment green beans

Pheasant 'au vin', confit legs, fermented red cabbage, roasted root vegetables

Puddings

Boozy orange pancakes, blood orange sorbet

Bay and tonka bean pannacotta, cherry compote

Danish apple and almond cake, toffee sauce, Mirabelle plum crème fraîche

CHERISHED COOKBOOKS?
Constance Spry's cookbook is a well-used favourite, and I love the recipes in Thomas Keller's *Bouchon Bakery*. I buy a cookbook every month on the basis of conversations and recommendations from friends, and I read them all. I don't generally follow recipes but I get ideas which percolate through my cooking. I bought Tony Kitous' book, *Comptoir Libanais* recently after having lunch there: his soul food, the home cooking, the pickles, all feed my current food interests.

A pub for all seasons

You can't miss The Anchor as you drive into Walberswick: the 1920s Arts and Crafts building is painted boldly blue and on warm days the outside tables are busy with families, locals, walkers and holidaymakers.

The Beer & Oyster Festival draws crowds in early August, as do Sophie's summer weekend roadside barbecues – she'll invariably be tongs in hand, filling homemade brioche buns with Blythburgh pork sausages or burgers and urging customers to pile their plates with salads and slaws. But come on cooler days too, when an open fire keeps the bar area cosy, and there are regular curry nights or wine/beer and food pairing evenings. This is a pub to enjoy however squally the coastal weather may be outside.

Mark and Sophie Dorber have built an enviable reputation for good food and an adventurous drinks list since taking on the Adnams pub in 2004. And whether you're in the mood for half a dozen Mersea oysters, beer-battered fish and chips (it comes with Sophie's own fiery jalapeño sauce), a crisp-based pizza from the outdoor wood-fired oven, or the ever-popular chocolate fondant, you know it will have been prepared with care. Despite the Adnams tie, there's an exceptional line-up of alternative beers, including Mark's own, Harvest Ale, brewed with hops grown at The Anchor's sister pub, The Swan at Stratford St. Mary. An Enomatic wine dispenser means that several fine wines are available by the glass, and Mark is always happy to share his drinks knowledge with interested guests.

Stay in one of the four house bedrooms or six family-friendly cedar-clad garden chalets to enjoy an evening to the full.

The Anchor
The Street, Walberswick IP18 6UA
W: anchoratwalberswick.com
T: 01502 722112   E: info@anchoratwalberswick.com
- /TheAnchorWalberswick
- @anchoratwalbers
- /the-anchor-at-walberswick

Accolades and listings: *The Publican Morning Advertiser* Top 50 Gastropubs 2014; *Michelin*; *Harden's*; *Sawday's*; *Inn Places*

Food served: all week B 8.30-10; L 12-3; D 6-9

Cost: starters from £6.75; mains from £14.75; puddings from £6; wine from £19.75; pint from £3.50

Details: 60 inside; al fresco tables; large garden; 10 en suite bedrooms in main building and garden chalets; pop-up food events; storytelling evenings; flint barn with AV system, available for private hire, seats up to 28; accessible; dogs welcome; parking

Castles on the hill

Iain Inman has long been a fan of Denham Castle lamb, reared on beautiful Suffolk pasture just minutes from his hotel kitchen

FREDERICK'S, THE ICKWORTH, HORRINGER
IAIN INMAN

Back in the 12th century, when Britain had a king called Stephen, the Earl of Clare built Denham Castle, a motte and bailey fortification designed to resist Fenland rebels during the civil wars that raged at the time. Today, if you stand on the grassy mound where the keep would have been, you can see why the Earl built here: for Suffolk, the spot is elevated, a place with views that would give ample warning of marauders.

In 21st century peacetime, however, the views from this English Heritage site are enjoyed — who knows? — by sheep, the flock of Denham Castle and Denham Horns reared on the 800-acre Denham Estate just outside Bury St Edmunds. They graze the pasture, shelter under ancient oak trees, or drink from the moat that would have surrounded the Castle.

It's an attractive sight, one that Iain Inman, head chef at The Ickworth hotel, is glad to see. "The lamb from here is incredible," he says. "I've been a fan of it for years." He's referring to the London kitchens he's worked in, first as a commis at the Mandarin Oriental, Hyde Park, under Hywel Jones ("I learnt more from him than anyone"), and later for "two tough years" with Philip Howard, then at The Square. In both kitchens, Denham Castle lamb was a regular feature. "It's about consistency," Iain continues, "as well as flavour and texture. It's probably the best lamb I've ever worked with."

The quality tracks back to the origins of the breed, developed by Michael Gliksten who crossed Soay sheep (the indigenous breed is small, highly regarded for its dark, gamey meat) with hardy Wiltshire Horn rams, prized partly because they shed their own fleece come summer. The resulting Denham Horn ewes are crossed with commercial breeds to create the Denham Castle lamb which retains the flavour and ease of management bestowed by its ancestry, but is a viable size.

Michael's widow, Cecilia, runs the business, supplying local restaurants not only with the lamb but also venison and (in season) other game shot on the Estate. The 300-strong flock grazes grass, clover and herbs, supplemented by silage if it's particularly cold, and salt licks to ensure sufficient minerals. Ewes give birth outdoors and lambs stay with the mother for four months. "This system and breed make sense financially and in terms of stock management," explains farm manager, Matt Driver. "It also benefits the environment. We use no fertilisers or pesticides, and the sheep manage the land naturally."

FREDERICK'S, THE ICKWORTH IAIN INMAN

Back in Iain's kitchen, it's hard to miss the whole lamb carcass on the stainless steel bench. "Alan [Plume, the Denham Estate butcher] delivered it a couple of days ago, and we've let it dry out a bit," Iain says, drawing his knife expertly through the fat and muscle, taking off the legs, shoulders, belly, breaking the animal down till he's left with bones for stock.

Iain cooks the saddle to pink tenderness, the fine-grained flesh cutting like butter alongside leg meat roasted slowly till it falls in satisfying flakes. The taste is balanced by a spring green purée, charred onion, earthy ceps (morels, come spring), bright broad beans, and punchy dandelion leaves. Robust dishes like this are Iain's love, and he looks forward to the first grouse from Scotland, pheasant and partridge from Denham Estate, and to cooking muscular dishes with venison, rabbit and wild duck. His is a classic style, pared back to fit modern tastes and to focus on the ingredient rather than technique. "I learnt from Phil [Howard] the importance of using the best ingredients possible, but not doing too much to them."

The Ickworth brigade is busy with deliveries when we arrive. Forced rhubarb, fresh and pink, will be used for a sorbet or poached to go with a tonka bean crème brûlée; there are trays of carefully prepped carrots, and a box of crinkly leaved savoy cabbages. At certain times produce will come from the allotments behind the National Trust-owned Ickworth House (the House has an arrangement with the local primary school whereby the children grow fruit and vegetables for school meals, but during holidays the supply is diverted to the hotel kitchen).

London-born Iain joined the hotel in September 2017 after six years as head chef at the Parc Hotel, Cardiff. "To be honest, the Welsh weather was getting to us!" he says with typical candour, and referring to his wife Monika and their two children, Freddy (8) and Alexa (5). "We wanted to move closer to London, and we have family in East Anglia; it's nice for our kids to see their grandparents without spending hours in the car."

It's a non-stop kitchen, the demands of a 24/7 operation intensified because of the hotel's position as a family-friendly property. Frederick's, the hotel's adult-only restaurant, is where guests can relax with candlelight and conversation, while the less formal Conservatory offers the same creative menu. However the needs of younger guests are never far from the kitchen's thoughts: High Tea at 5pm offers macaroni cheese and boiled eggs and soldiers, then there's junior Afternoon Tea, and even baby purée made to order. "It's nothing if not varied!" says Iain. "I never get bored, that's for sure!"

FREDERICK'S, THE ICKWORTH IAIN INMAN

Pink-poached loin and slow-roast leg of lamb, sweetbreads, roast onion and spring greens

Late summer is a great time for new season lamb and this elegant assiette uses three cuts of our lovely locally reared meat. We garnish it with wild mushrooms and broad beans, roast onion and spring green purée in the recipe. Herb-wise, mint, flat leaf parsley, chives, summer savory, tarragon and similar soft varieties work well together in the marinade for the leg. You will need to juggle pan-frying the sweetbreads, poaching the loin and reheating the leg at the same time as the final preparations of the garnishes. (serves 4)

Slow-roast leg
Small leg of lamb, boned
6 garlic cloves, peeled and chopped
Handful of soft herbs, shredded
Rapeseed oil
Plain yogurt
A few thyme sprigs
1 garlic bulb, cloves crushed in their skins
175ml dry white wine

The day before, rub the lamb with the chopped garlic, herbs and oil, along with generous black pepper and yoghurt. Cover and refrigerate to marinate for at least 6 hours. Pre-heat the oven to 130c. Wipe off the marinade and seal the meat all over in a hot, ovenproof oiled pan. Scatter over the thyme and crushed garlic, add the wine and bring to a simmer. Cover tightly with foil and bake for 6-8 hours until very tender. Sieve the liquor and set aside to cool. Carefully roll the meat in clingfilm tightly before cooling and refrigerating along with the liquor overnight.

Burnt onion
1 white onion
Butter
Good lamb stock

Slice the onion thickly (about ¾ cm wide) and cook in a hot, wide, dry pan over a high heat to char the cut edges.

Add the butter and enough lamb stock to cover, before simmering until tender. Set aside.

Spring green purée
100g unsalted butter, cubed at room temperature
Squeeze of lemon
200g spring greens, trimmed and shredded

Heat a heavy, sauté pan, add the butter and heat, gently moving, until it turns a nut-brown colour. Add a squeeze of lemon, then remove from the heat and set aside. In a large saucepan of salted, boiling water, blanch the greens for 30 seconds, then drain quickly. Liquidise the greens and warm (not hot) butter together until smooth, cool quickly and refrigerate.

Poached loin
300g lamb loin, trimmed
Lamb or chicken stock, hot

Bring the lamb to a simmer in the stock, turn down very low and gently cook for 8-10 minutes or until cooked to your liking. Remove and rest somewhere warm for 5 minutes.

Sweetbreads
1 large handful of lamb sweetbreads, trimmed and skinned
Rapeseed oil
Unsalted butter

Pan-fry the seasoned sweetbreads in a hot, oiled frying pan on both sides, adding a good knob of butter and basting until golden. Remove and keep warm.

To serve
Reserved liquor from the leg

Pre-heat the oven to 190c. Gently warm the spring green purée and the burnt onion separately in saucepans. Reduce the leg liquor down to a jus, season to taste and keep hot. Meanwhile, unwrap and slice the leg thickly and reheat on a baking tray, loosely covered with foil, in the oven.

Carve the loin and place on hot plates around the slow-roast lamb, topped with burnt onion in the centre. Garnish with the sweetbreads, purée and jus.

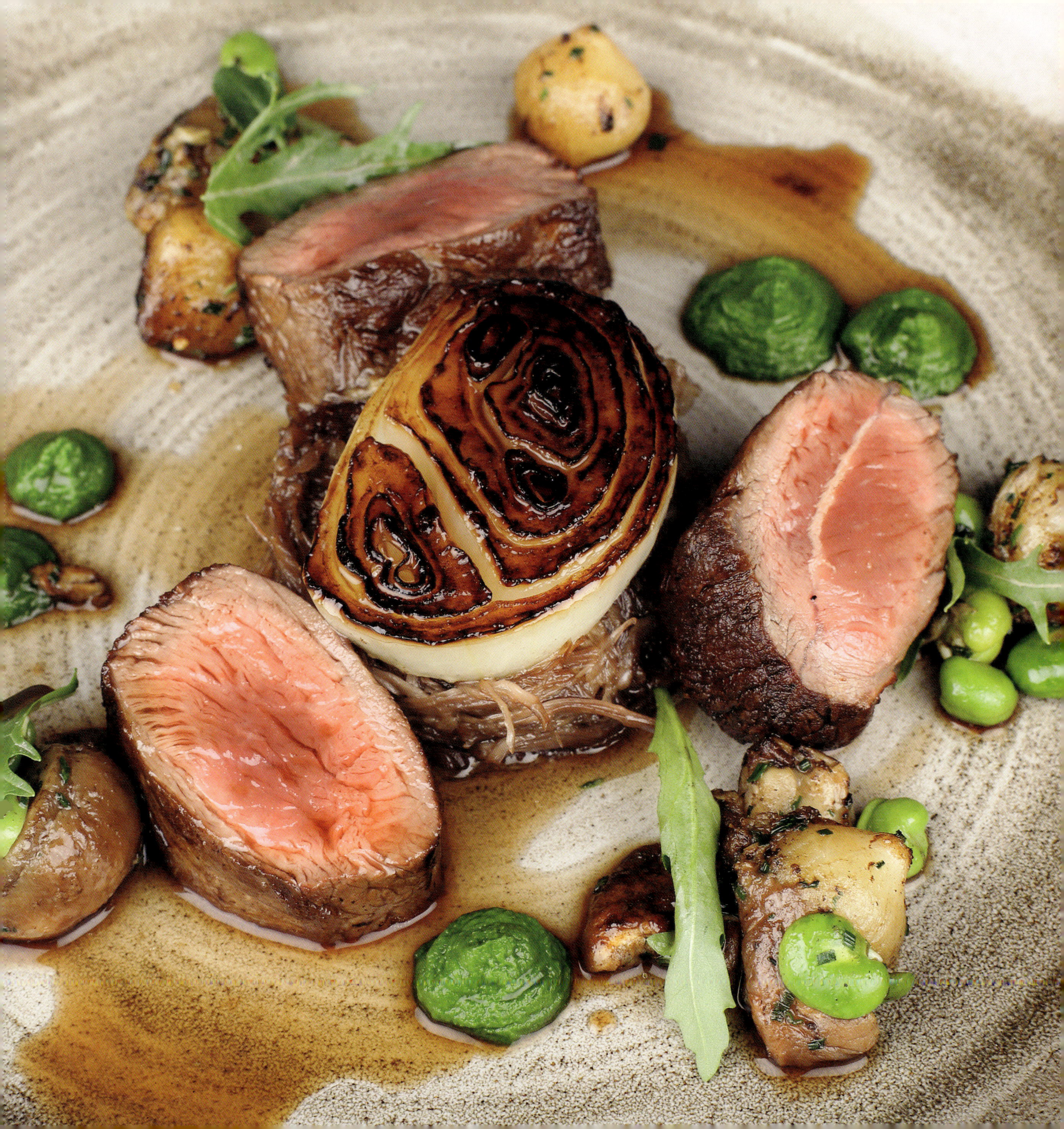

Pheasant three ways

A versatile, flavoursome alternative for chicken in most poultry recipes, some pheasant dishes may need the addition of fatty pork to keep the meat succulent – like all wild game, pheasant is very lean. It's pictured here with braised spelt and millet grains, rainbow carrots and a madeira cream (serves 2)

1 large, hen pheasant, oven ready
1 coarse pork sausage, skinned
Good pinch of oregano
Game or chicken stock
Oil and butter for frying

Cut the pheasant into a crown (a joint of both breasts on the ribcage), the thighs and the drumsticks.

Bone out the thighs and pulse the meat in a processor with the pork sausage, oregano and generous seasoning. Fashion into a sausage shape and clingfilm tightly, knotting the ends. Poach in simmering water until cooked through. Cool and unwrap. Dry on a clean cloth.

Pre-heat the oven to 190c. Gently simmer the drumsticks in stock until tender for about 30-45 minutes. Meanwhile, oil and season the crown and seal all over in a very hot pan. Roast for 10-12 minutes until cooked through. Pan-fry the thigh sausage in foaming oil and butter until golden-brown.

Carve the breasts and serve on warm plates with the thigh and drumsticks alongside vegetables of your choice.

FREDERICK'S, THE ICKWORTH IAIN INMAN

Lamb roly poly

A charming, rustic classic which we finish elegantly with pickled vegetables and textures of apple (as pictured). It calls for a slow-braised lamb shoulder – we cook ours for up to 6 hours in a low oven, covered with stock, cyder, garlic and herbs. Use the cooking liquor for a good gravy. (serves 4)

1 cooked lamb shoulder
2 tbsp onion marmalade
2 tbsp pistachio paste
500g plain flour
250g vegetable suet
Hot water to make dough
2 tbsp quince jelly

Flake the warm meat and mix with the onion marmalade and pistachio paste and set aside.

Knead the flour, suet and seasoning with hot water into a firm, smooth dough. Roll thinly into a large rectangle and spread with the quince jelly and then the lamb, before rolling up like a swiss roll. Transfer to a parchment-lined tea towel, wrap up and tie loosely at both ends to allow for lots of expansion. Steam for 1 hour until cooked. When cool enough to handle, unwrap and transfer to a clingfilm sheet, rolling tightly and securing the ends. Refrigerate to set.

To serve, thickly slice the roly poly and reheat in a hot frying pan with a little oil and butter over a medium heat until lightly golden and steaming hot throughout.

Apple parfait

This delicious autumnal dessert is more indulgent than an everyday crumble or pie. We make it even more special by plating it with thyme fudge, meringue, blackberry and chopped pistachios. Crushed biscuits work in place of the dried berries. (serves 4+)

3 egg yolks
100g sugar
1 gelatine leaf, softened
300ml apple juice
300ml double cream, whipped
Dried blackberries, crumbled

Whisk the yolks in a food mixer.

Melt the sugar and heat to 118c. Keeping the mixer running, pour the sugar carefully onto the yolks until combined. Add the gelatine while still whisking, continue until cooled and mix in the apple juice. Fold in the cream, transfer to a container and freeze until set.

To serve, scoop the parfait decoratively (here we make a sphere) and coat with the crumbled blackberries.

IAIN ON HIS...

QUICK SNACK OR MIDNIGHT FEAST?
Anything with cheese – ordinary cheddar – or chilli. I love spicy food.

WHO HAS BEEN A MENTOR?
I suppose Hywel Jones. I started my cooking life as a commis at the Mandarin Oriental Hyde Park while he was head chef and when he moved to Lola's brasserie on Upper Street [Islington] I went with him as sous chef.

BIGGEST EXTRAVAGANCE AS A CHEF?
I'm not really into truffles or caviar, but I love using ingredients when they first come into season but are still expensive. I can't wait to get some early morels at £90/kg!

INSPIRING SUFFOLK VIEW?
The sign on the A140 that says Norfolk! I live in Long Stratton so it means I'm nearly home at the end of a long day.

FAVOURITE TIME OF YEAR FOR FOOD?
Definitely autumn. British food is at its best then, without doubt. I can never wait to get the first grouse on the menu – that's the start of it for me.

BEST DISH EVER EATEN?
It was a beef cheek and lime dish that I ate about 12 years ago in Marrakech. I'd say it was the most memorable dish I've ever eaten, perhaps not the best as such. It wasn't in a fancy restaurant, just an ordinary place off the main square. The beef was incredibly tender and they left the sinew in which had gone all gooey. Delicious.

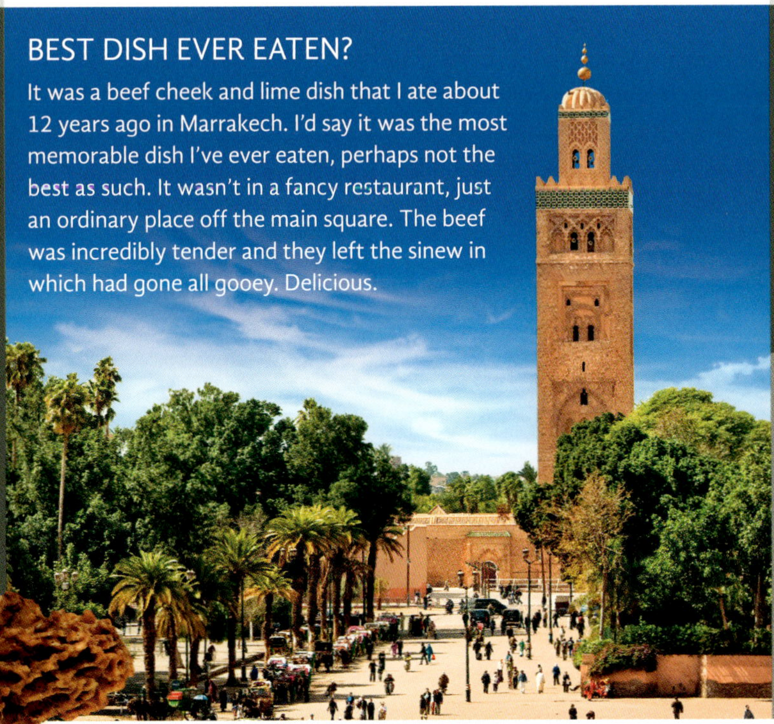

WHAT THREE QUALITIES DO YOU LIKE MOST IN PEOPLE?
Silence, distance, obedience.

'TAKE FIVE' RECIPE?
Pizza! Top the dough with a tomato and smoked chilli base, then add slices of good fennel salami, wild mushrooms and blue cheese – it's packed with flavour!

SIGNATURE DISHES

Starters
Tea- and rum-cured sea trout, sea urchin, candied lemon, fennel
Gressingham duck wonton, Asian broth, egg noodles
Roast cauliflower pannacotta, bhaji, chestnut, golden beetroot

Mains
Sea bream, ceps, herb gnocchi, parsnip
Fillet, belly and cheek of Suffolk pork, apple, mustard, wild mushrooms
Pumpkin pithivier, goats' cheese, pistachio, pickled mushrooms, celeriac

Puddings
Pear strudel, English plums, candied orange
Iced cherry parfait, meringue, pistachio, macerated cherry
Dark chocolate marquise, amaretti, hazelnuts, golden raisins

FAVOURITE COOKBOOK?
The Faviken cookbook by Magnus Nilsson. It's one of the few that I've read cover to cover. I like how he combines anecdotes of family life and other stories with the recipes; it's much more than just a cookbook.

FOOD HEROES?
Phil Howard because I got such a lot out of my time at The Square, and Angus Stovold of Lydling Farm in Surrey who has an incredible herd of Aberdeen Angus beef cattle. When I was at Pennyhill Park we bought all our beef from him.

A home, a house, a hotel

It's not every day that you can eat surrounded by stately home splendour – think high ceilings, ornate plasterwork, elegant windows, sparkling chandeliers, vast artworks – but book a table at Frederick's at The Ickworth hotel to enjoy just that. The 36-seat restaurant is a peaceful, adult-only evening retreat. Candlelit tables are set classically with white linen and simple crockery and glassware; nothing to distract from the refined, contemporary cooking that Iain Inman and his young brigade create.

The light-filled Conservatory is a family-friendly space to enjoy simpler fare such as sandwiches, soups, Dingley Dell sausages and mash, or fresh fish of the day. Come here for Sunday lunch after a walk in the spectacular grounds of the National Trust-owned House, or linger by the drawing room fire over a fresh-made afternoon tea.

The Ickworth, part of the Luxury Family Hotels collection, occupies the east wing of Ickworth House. Home to the eccentric Hervey family until the 7th Marquess of Bristol moved out in 1998, the Georgian House is famed for its Rotunda, built by the 4th Marquess to house his priceless art collection. Hotel guests are free to roam the surrounding 1,800 acres of parkland grazed by fallow deer and sheep, wander or cycle through the countryside or even take on the trim trail challenge. There's even a delightful welcome from Peaches, the hotel dog.

Frederick's, The Ickworth
Horringer, Bury St Edmunds IP29 5QE
W: ickworthhotel.co.uk
T: 01284 735350
E: info@ickworthhotel.co.uk
/TheIckworthHotel   @theickworth   /theickworthhotel

Accolades and listings: AA Two Rosettes; *Michelin*; winner, Food and Drink Tourism Attraction award, *East Anglian Daily Times* and *Eastern Daily Press* Norfolk & Suffolk Tourism Awards 2018

Food served: all week L 12-2.30 (The Conservatory); D 6-9.30 (Frederick's); afternoon tea 12-5 (Sun 2-5)

Cost: starters from £6.50; mains from £18.50; desserts from £7.50; separate lunch menu, dishes from £6.50; Sunday lunch £19.95 (two courses); afternoon tea from £21.95; wine from £23.95

Details: 36 seats (Frederick's); 52 seats (The Conservatory); separate children's menus and flexible mealtimes; private dining for up to 50; licensed for weddings; 27 bedrooms in main building, further rooms and apartments in the nearby Butler's Quarters and Lodge; free childcare and children's activities; treatment rooms; indoor pool; free admission to Ickworth House (National Trust); accessible; dogs welcome £15/night; parking

THE TABLE, WOODBRIDGE
PASCAL POMMIER

Get your skate on

Landed before his very eyes —
Pascal Pommier would be hard-pressed
to find fresher skate for his Table menu

105

"This is my dream, my dream! This is my passion as a chef." Pascal Pommier is grinning all over his face as he looks around Felixstowe Ferry and in particular at the spanking fresh seafood on offer at Springtide Fish. "It's just ten miles down the road from the restaurant, the fishermen land the fish, these guys skin them and fillet them, you can't get any better, you cannot physically get any better," Pascal enthuses. "You know it's sustainable and we get the best fish for the best price to put on our table. I think that's lovely and a good sign for the future."

He gets down on his hands and knees with fishmonger James Hunt to examine a crate of freshly landed skate, destined for diners at The Table in Woodbridge. "We've just seen it come in and tomorrow we will have it on the table for lunch. That's so wonderful," says Pascal.

Springtide Fish has been on the harbourside at Felixstowe Ferry for 50 years or more. When Dave Hicks took it over around a decade ago, it had one small counter. Since then it has grown six fold and now supplies restaurants and private customers throughout Suffolk, with any overflow going to wholesale markets.

"We buy all the local fish off the Ferry here," says James, who runs the business, including its on-site smokehouse. "We've got about a dozen boats that are licensed to fish. What they don't catch off the Suffolk coast we buy from elsewhere, mainly from British fisheries off the south coast and Scotland."

Felixstowe's fishing industry has shrunk over the years but it is business like Pascal's that helps keep the remaining fleet afloat. And the chef's obvious enthusiasm is balm to James's soul. "It means an awful lot to me. The boys here, they're not millionaires, they don't do overly great, so my passion is taking the freshest fish that I can, paying a fair price for it and then selling it on to someone that I know is going to appreciate it and is going to do it justice, someone who knows what

THE TABLE PASCAL POMMIER

they're doing," says James. "We've had a relationship with Pascal the whole time he's been here. He's got a good name for himself and that's what it's all about."

Pascal was born in Burgundy, one of France's premier food and wine regions, but has lived in Suffolk for the past 20 years. He began his training at a Michelin-starred restaurant in France, then moved to the UK, where he eventually gained his own Michelin star at the Normandie hotel in Birtle, near Bury, Greater Manchester. That was in 1995. "Obviously that was quite an achievement in those days because there were only about 30 in the whole country and not that many outside London. But it was fussy, it was quite a special occasion place. The Michelin star was great but it was not me," says Pascal. "My passion is simple food."

Pascal married Jo, whose family is from Woodbridge, and they moved to the town to open what was then The Captain's Table. After 11 successful years (and four children) Pascal took a break, leasing the building to another business. When that closed, Pascal approached his friend, restaurateur Vernon Blackmore, and the pair struck a deal, reopening as The Table.

Pascal now operates as a freelance chef, working for Vernon and for private clients. "My inspiration comes from the produce we get. Skate, Dover sole, we're blessed with the best crab in the world, the lobsters are wonderful and sweet, then we also get some lovely line-caught bass. "You don't need to do too much to it. Simply poaching, grilling, frying is just perfect. We have local vegetables and our forager Matthew Driver brings us lots of sea vegetables off the marsh. And if you've got a cut of meat, a sirloin or ribeye, some hand-cut chips, a good tossed salad, for me, that makes an amazing dish.

For a man who landed a Michelin star at the age of just 30, Pascal is modest about his achievements. Although he has some regrets about missed opportunities from that period – he says he was too shy to capitalise on his success – he is happier now. "I have my children, they are a blessing and special, and I'm very lucky to have four! I do my very best for them and push myself not only to give people pleasure through my craft but also to earn a good living so they're looked after.

"And Suffolk is wonderful, honestly. I have been to a few places in England but Suffolk's got everything for me. They say home is where your heart is and mine is definitely here."

THE TABLE PASCAL POMMIER

Skate wing, caper and lemon butter sauce, new potatoes and purple sprouting broccoli

Visiting your local port to find day boat fishermen selling their catch, maybe line-caught like ours from Felixstowe, will offer up skate in prime condition. We are very lucky to have such great produce on our doorstep. This is a wonderfully simple dish, both light and indulgent, that perfectly complements the naturally delicious skate wing. (serves 4)

Court bouillon
- 1 onion, diced
- 1 celery stick, diced
- 2 thyme sprigs
- 1 garlic clove
- 12 coriander seeds
- 2 bay leaves, preferably fresh
- 1 star anise
- 1 level tbsp salt
- 50ml white wine vinegar
- 100ml dry white wine
- 1 litre water

Simmer all the ingredients for 25 minutes before setting aside. Allow to infuse overnight or for at least 2 hours.

Minted potatoes
- 700g new or baby potatoes
- 3 sprigs of mint
- Unsalted butter

Simmer the potatoes with the mint and salt until tender, drain well, glaze with a knob or two of butter, cover and keep warm.

Sauce
- 1 small bunch of flat-leaf parsley
- 1 unwaxed lemon
- 125g unsalted butter, chilled and diced

Wash the parsley leaves, then dry and shred. Remove the peel and pith from the lemon and carefully cut out the skinless segments. Set aside.

Bring 250ml of the court bouillon to a simmer and whisk in the butter gradually into a sauce consistency. Keep warm.

To serve
- 4 good size skate wings, trimmed
- 8-10 stems of purple sprouting broccoli
- 1 heaped tbsp fine capers, rinsed

Bring the court bouillon to a boil and add the wings. Cover with a lid, bring back to a gentle boil, simmer for a few minutes and then take off the heat and leave for 15 minutes until the fish is cooked through at the thickest part.

Cook the broccoli until al dente for 4-5 minutes, size depending.

Fold the drained capers, lemon segments and parsley through the warm sauce.

Carefully drain the fish well and place on to warm plates. Season to taste. Garnish the plates with the potatoes and broccoli and serve with the butter sauce.

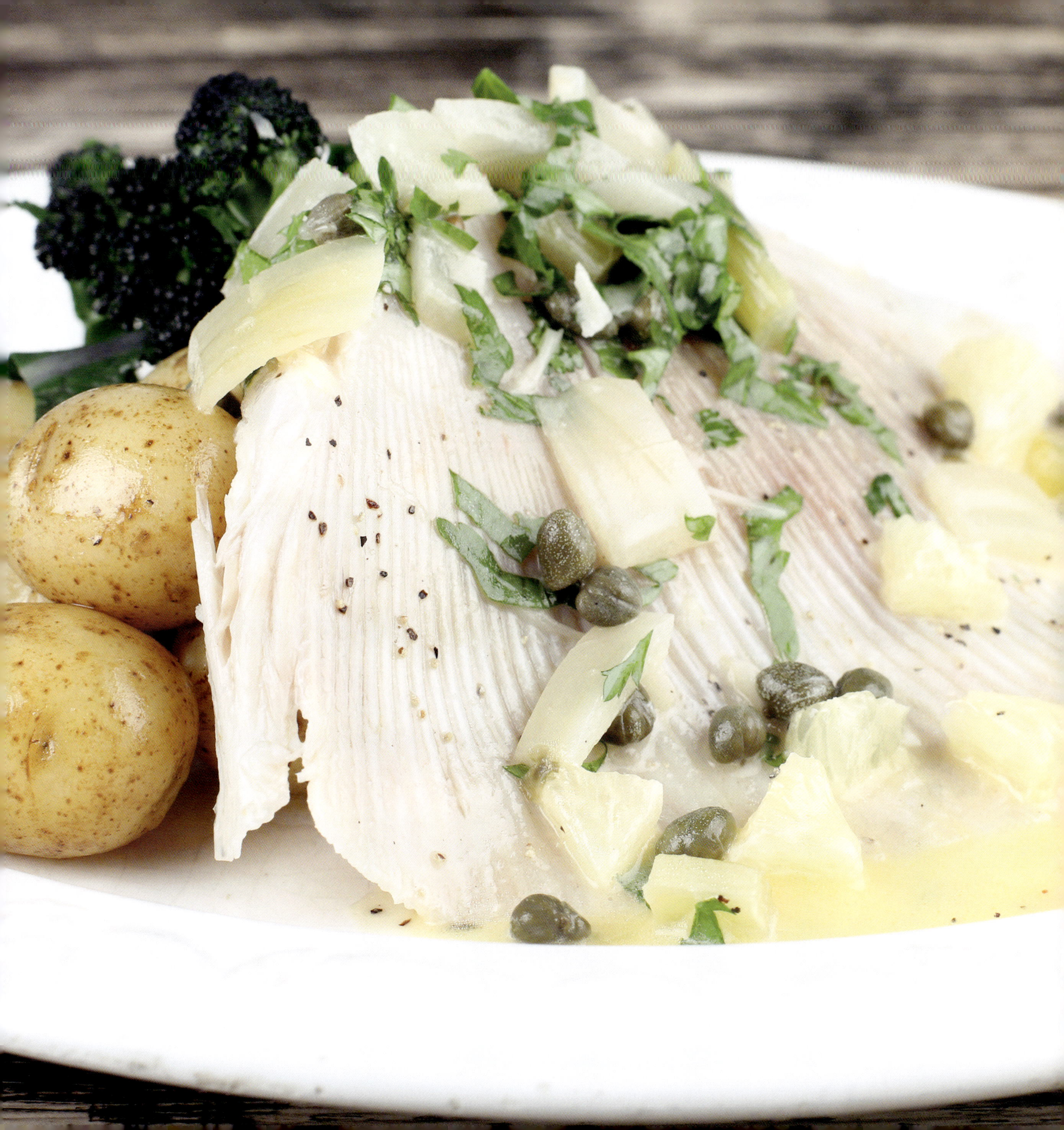

THE TABLE PASCAL POMMIER

Wild alexanders with a foraged herb dressing

A fragrant relative of carrots and cow parsley, alexanders are a tall 'weed' plant, which thrives in coastal hedgerows. They need careful identification, but the whole plant is edible, here using the lower pinkish bulbous stems where they join the roots. (serves 4)

12 alexanders bases, about 10cm long
Foraged herbs eg hedge garlic, yarrow, fennel fronds
2 tbsp unsalted butter
4 tbsp rapeseed oil
4 tsp cider vinegar

Prepare the pale pink parts of the alexanders 'bulbs', removing any leaves and green stems, pulling away loose pale outer layers and trimming off any root, before washing. Blanch in boiling water for 2 minutes and set aside.

Wash, dry and finely chop the wild herb sprigs, keeping some leaves for garnish.

Heat the butter until foaming and add the alexanders, basting for a minute. Cover with boiling water and simmer, covered, until tender. Drain and set aside.

Blend the oil and vinegar with the chopped herbs and sea salt to taste into a dressing.

Pour the dressing over the alexanders and garnish with the reserved whole leaves to serve.

Smoked duck breast, sloe jelly and beetroot

Gressingham duck is a Suffolk speciality and always on our menu. Smoked duck breasts make this a lovely colourful autumnal starter. (serves 4-6)

450g blackberries, rinsed
300g sloes, rinsed
1 whole small apple, roughly chopped
Caster sugar
1 small raw beetroot
2 smoked duck breasts

Simmer the three fruits in a stainless steel pan until all are tender, about 20 minutes. Strain through a muslin sieve overnight, squeezing through lightly to finish. Measure the juice into a heavy, large pan. For every 300ml, dissolve in 225g sugar gently and then boil hard until it reaches 105c, removing any scum. Allow to set overnight.

To serve, peel the beetroot, then grate or julienne before rinsing through a sieve and then squeezing through a tea towel to drain.

To serve, thinly slice the duck breast on to plates, scatter with the beetroot, add a teaspoon of jelly and a drizzle of olive oil.

SUFFOLK FEAST

Sticky toffee pudding

We are biased but I do think this recipe is the world's best toffee pud recipe. If you can, use Silver Spoon sugars as they support East Anglian farmers. It eats well with good vanilla ice cream. (serves 4-6)

150g dark muscovado sugar
225g dates, pitted
225g self-raising flour
175g light brown sugar
1 tsp bicarbonate of soda
4 large eggs, beaten
110g soft unsalted butter
100g light brown sugar
100g dark brown sugar
75g unsalted butter
150ml double cream

Simmer the muscovado sugar and 100ml hot water in a pan into a syrup and set aside.

Cook down the dates in 275ml hot water and set aside. Line a deep, medium roasting tray with baking parchment and pre-heat the oven to 190c.

Beat the next 5 ingredients into the date pan until batter-like. Scrape mixture into the prepared tin and bake for about 45 minutes until a skewer comes out clean.

For the butterscotch, dissolve the next 3 ingredients with a splash of water over a low heat. Remove from heat and slowly whisk in the cream. Once glossy and combined, set aside.

Remove the cooked pudding, prick lightly and pour over the syrup. Once absorbed, serve with the butterscotch.

PASCAL ON HIS...

SOMETHING THAT AMAZES YOU?
Planes. I don't know how such a big, huge heavy thing can stay up in the sky! It's frightening and amazing.

QUICK SNACK OR MIDNIGHT FEAST?
Cheese! And crackers, I'm sad to say; not bread, crackers! And chutney.

THREE QUALITIES YOU LIKE MOST?
Honesty, hard work and punctuality. And respect, I know that's four but if you respect your colleagues, respect your craft and your job, I think you can teach anyone anything. I would like to be able to teach children in a school environment how to eat, how to cook.

FOOD HERO?
Raymond Blanc. From anything simple to anything complicated, he makes it look and taste amazing. Growing, back in the 80s, his own vegetables, giving back things to the land. He's a food genius.

SIGNATURE DISHES
Starters

Vegetarian mezze with olives, sun blush tomatoes, artichoke hearts, feta, falafel, flatbread, dips

Home-cured salmon, sweet chilli & pomegranate

Serrano ham, roasted fig, balsamic salad

Mains

Char-grilled ribeye steak, horseradish crème fraîche, fries, salad

Thai red chicken curry, basmati rice, coriander chutney

Aubergine & lentil moussaka, char-grilled bread, olive salad

Puddings

Apricot brioche & butter pudding with pouring cream

Poached peach, mascarpone, meringue

Key lime pie, blueberries, chocolate sauce

FOOD NOSTALGIA?
My dad grew every single vegetable we needed and I used to love them as a little one, from Swiss chard to beetroot to chicory to unusual vegetables like salsify, that was part and parcel of my upbringing. We used to come home from school for two and a half hours break at lunchtime so every day we had lovely cooked food, from liver to boiled chicken – simple food using our garden veg.

MOST THRILLING MOMENT IN CAREER SO FAR?
My Michelin star, by far.

CHILDHOOD MEMORY?
Cooking with my mum, making a simple mayonnaise. I used to love cooking. She used to love making cakes, so, at *quatre heures*, at four o'clock, in my family there was the ritual that the coffee would come out – for us kids it was hot chocolate – and a cake or a tart. I think her apple tart was the best in the world.

FAVOURITE SUFFOLK VIEW?
Definitely here in Woodbridge, with the Pin Mill in the background, the foam on top of the river, the birds, the calm ... amazing, unparalleled, I'm very lucky to live here.

FAVOURITE COOKBOOKS?
I don't use cookery books, although I quite like Rick Stein's because I think it's very earnest, very honest food, from all around the world.

GUILTY FOOD PLEASURE?
I love puddings, toffee pudding and bread and butter pudding and crumble. English puddings, comforting puddings.

Loyalty points

Vernon Blackmore was already running The Anchor, just a few steps away, when Pascal approached him to take over at The Table. "He owns the building, I own the business, he works in the business," says Vernon. "He's an outstanding chef and I'm lucky to have him. I know that I can trust him, with major contributions from all the other chefs, to co-ordinate and get a menu together.

"The Anchor is a boozer that happens to do good food. Looking at The Table I thought I could have a lighter offer here. We do more salads, a lot of seafood, we do more vegetarian dishes.

"I've got some outstanding talent here. We all talk about menus, exchange ideas. Some of our most successful dishes have been the combination of three different dishes coming together. Everyone's very generous and there's no ego in the kitchen, which I think is very important."

Sited a short walk from Woodbridge's station, cinema and riverside, The Table's relaxed brasserie style draws in everyone from couples to families. The restaurant holds themed dining nights, including street food feasts, with an outside kitchen on the terrace adding to the fun and atmosphere in summertime.

The Table attracts a loyal clientele, loyalty being a quality, Vernon says, that Suffolk does well. "If people trust you to look after them and they like you, they will give everything for you," says Vernon. "The Suffolk countryside is beautiful, and we have the coast nearby. But it's definitely the people who keep me here."

The Table
3 Quay St, Woodbridge IP12 1BX
W: thetablewoodbridge.co.uk
T: 01394 382428
E: thetablewoodbridge@hotmail.co.uk
- /thetablewoodbridge1
- @the_table_
- the_table_

Accolades and listings: Waitrose *Good Food Guide*

Food served: L all week 10.30-3 (Sun 12-3); D Tue-Sat 6-9

Cost: starters from £5.50; mains from £11; desserts from £6; cakes and light bites from £3; wine from £19; pint £4.50

Details: 50 seats inside; 50 on terrace (seasonal); children's menu; theme nights; street food Sunday evenings in summer; bespoke menus; private room hire; accessible; pets welcome on terrace

HINTLESHAM HALL, HINT
ALAN FORD

In the mood for blue

Creamy, tangy Suffolk Blue cheese, made just a few miles from Hintlesham Hall, is a favourite of chef Alan Ford

115

HINTLESHAM HALL ALAN FORD

"My mother was from Lawshall near Bury St Edmunds, so I used to spend many a summer up here," says Alan Ford, who was born and brought up in Kent. "My nan used to take me to Felixstowe for the day, that was our big day out. We used to go to a tea house there, and to The Angel Hotel in Bury, those were her treats," he says nostalgically.

But as a little boy he never dreamed that one day he would be head chef in one of Suffolk's historic country house hotels. "I've been here for 30 years now," says Alan, looking around the plush lounge where we're chatting. "Funnily enough, this was exactly where we sat for my interview with [then owners] Ruth and David Watson. I was very nervous when I first started. It was a very challenging job."

I'll say. The Watsons had acquired Hintlesham Hall from the famous American chef, TV star and bon viveur Robert Carrier and they were involved in a major expansion. Carrier had bought the Hall in 1972 when it was badly dilapidated. He threw money at the project and turned Hintlesham into a hotel, restaurant and cookery school, but only renovated the main building.

The Watsons took it further, rescuing the surrounding outbuildings and adding more bedrooms. When Alan took over as head chef, one of his first jobs was to help design a new kitchen. He must have got it right, because three decades later he is still using the same Charvet ranges.

The Watsons moved on, but Alan, who served his apprenticeship in a series of glittering London hotels and was mentored by top chef Anton Mosimann at The Dorchester, stayed put. And although the main restaurant at Hintlesham Hall has recently been renamed Carrier's in homage to its old owner, the menus are very much Alan's. "I'm classically trained, so I use that as the basis for my food, but obviously with modern twists," he says as he puts the finishing touches to one of his elegant dishes. He's serving Dingley Dell pork fillet with a creamy mash mixed with Suffolk Blue cheese, more of the cheese mixed into a crumb scattered on top, and an Aspall cyder sauce.

Alan is not a slave to local ingredients but uses them wherever he can. Carrier's old kitchen garden has recently been brought back to life, so Alan is able to pick fresh fruit, vegetables and herbs a few steps from the kitchen door.

And he's a big fan of Suffolk Farmhouse Cheeses. "They're lovely," he says. "I put them on the cheese board and I cook with them. I do a double-baked Suffolk Gold soufflé, too, so easy to cook at home. People get flustered about soufflés but if you double-bake, you're cooking them the day before, turning them out of the mould, then heating up next day and they stay puffed up for longer.

"I think a lot of people don't recognise that Suffolk does cheeses but these have lovely clean flavours and they work well."

That's music to the ears of Jason and Katherine Salisbury, who make Suffolk Blue, Suffolk Gold and Suffolk Brie with milk from their herd of Guernseys and Jerseys at their 100-acre farm in Creeting St. Mary. Apart from farm gate sales, the Salisburys sell all their cheese through wholesalers and in this case the middle man is Will Johnston, of Hamish Johnston Fine Cheeses in Martlesham, who has backed them since they first began.

"I was so naive when we first started that I even asked Will how much he should be paying," Jason recalls. "But he gave us a fair price and he's been our longest-serving wholesaler. He's invaluable. He will give us forecasts on what we might sell, we can bounce ideas off him and he gives us feedback on our products. When he wants more cheese we up production and we make sure he has what he wants. He always gets first dibs."

Will grins. "When they started they only made ten cheeses a week and Jason told me I could only have three! Now I think on average we're taking 40 Suffolk Golds, nearly 100 Blues and 25 Bries every week and quite often we ring and say can we come and pick some more up because we've run out.

"Suffolk used to have a terrible reputation, it was renowned for producing the worst cheese in the country and there was some rhyme saying it was so bad even dogs wouldn't eat it. Now the quality's improved, the passion for East Anglian produce has grown immensely, and East Anglian cheese is probably one of our staple products."

And for a producer, there is no greater compliment than when the results of their hard work are recognised and appreciated. "The funny thing is we often don't know where the cheeses end up, because they all go out to wholesalers and the last time we see them is in the cold store," says Jason. "So it's nice when you turn up to Hintlesham and they bring it out and you think 'yeah, they've looked after that'."

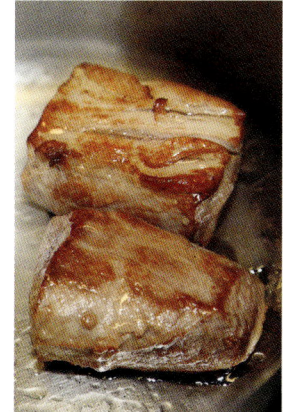

HINTLESHAM HALL ALAN FORD

Honey glazed pork tenderloin, Suffolk Blue cheese, black cabbage, Aspall cyder

I love the Salisbury farmily's Coddenham cheese, especially the blue, and it works so well alongside good Suffolk pork tenderloin (akin to fillet steak), native British apples, black cabbage (also known as cavolo nero or black kale) and of course our local Aspall cyder to give this hearty, autumnal taste of the county. It would work just as well with wild game, perhaps a sweet venison loin or breast of pheasant. We serve this with Vichy-style carrot lozenges, simmered until tender in a sweet, buttery glaze. Make the sauce, crumbs and apple garnish ahead but cook the mash and cabbage at the same time as the pork as they don't hold or reheat easily. (serves 4)

Cyder sauce
- 100ml dry cyder
- 250ml meat stock

Place the cyder in a saucepan and boil until reduced to a couple of tablespoons in volume, add the stock and reduce again until a lightly thickened gravy consistency.

Cheese crumbs
- 25g salted butter
- 3 tbsp coarse white breadcrumbs
- 100g Suffolk Blue cheese, crumbled

Heat the salted butter in a frying pan and toast the breadcrumbs until lightly coloured, cool, then fold through the blue cheese. Set aside.

Caramelised apple
- 50g caster sugar
- 2 firm apples, peeled, cored and cut into small wedges

Put the sugar into a deep frying pan with a tablespoon of water and heat on a medium-high hob. As it starts to melt, gently tip the pan to move the syrup around but do not stir. As it turns to a medium caramel colour, carefully fold in the apples to coat. Set aside somewhere warm.

Blue cheese mash
- 4 large potatoes, scrubbed
- Unsalted butter
- Large wedge of Suffolk Blue cheese
- Handful of flat leaf parsley, destalked and chopped

Pre-heat the oven to 180c and bake the potatoes until soft in the centre when skewered (alternatively simmer whole). Cool until they can be handled, cut in half and then holding in a tea towel, spoon out the centres. Put the potato flesh into a saucepan with a good knob or two of butter and seasoning to taste. Mash well before folding in the cheese and parsley, mixing together. Keep hot until required.

Pork tenderloin
- 4 x 180g portions of trimmed pork tenderloin
- 2 tbsp good honey

Pre-heat the oven to 230c. Lightly oil, season and seal the pork in a very hot pan on all sides. Roast on a tray for 6 minutes and then remove from the oven. Drain off the oil and pour over the honey, coating the meat well using tongs. Continue roasting until cooked through but still juicy, another 3-6 minutes. Remove from the oven and place the pork on a plate somewhere warm to rest for 4 minutes (tilting the plate helps the juices drain off).

Cabbage
- 4 handfuls of black cabbage, destalked, trimmed and shredded
- Unsalted butter

Place the cabbage into a deep lidded pan with a good glug of boiling water and a couple of knobs of butter plus a good grinding of seasoning. Bring to a boil, toss around with tongs and cover until wilted and al dente. Take off the heat and keep warm.

To serve
Drain the black cabbage and place on the plate. Arrange the tenderloin on top, with the mash alongside, garnishing with the caramelised apples, blue cheese crumbs and finally the cyder sauce.

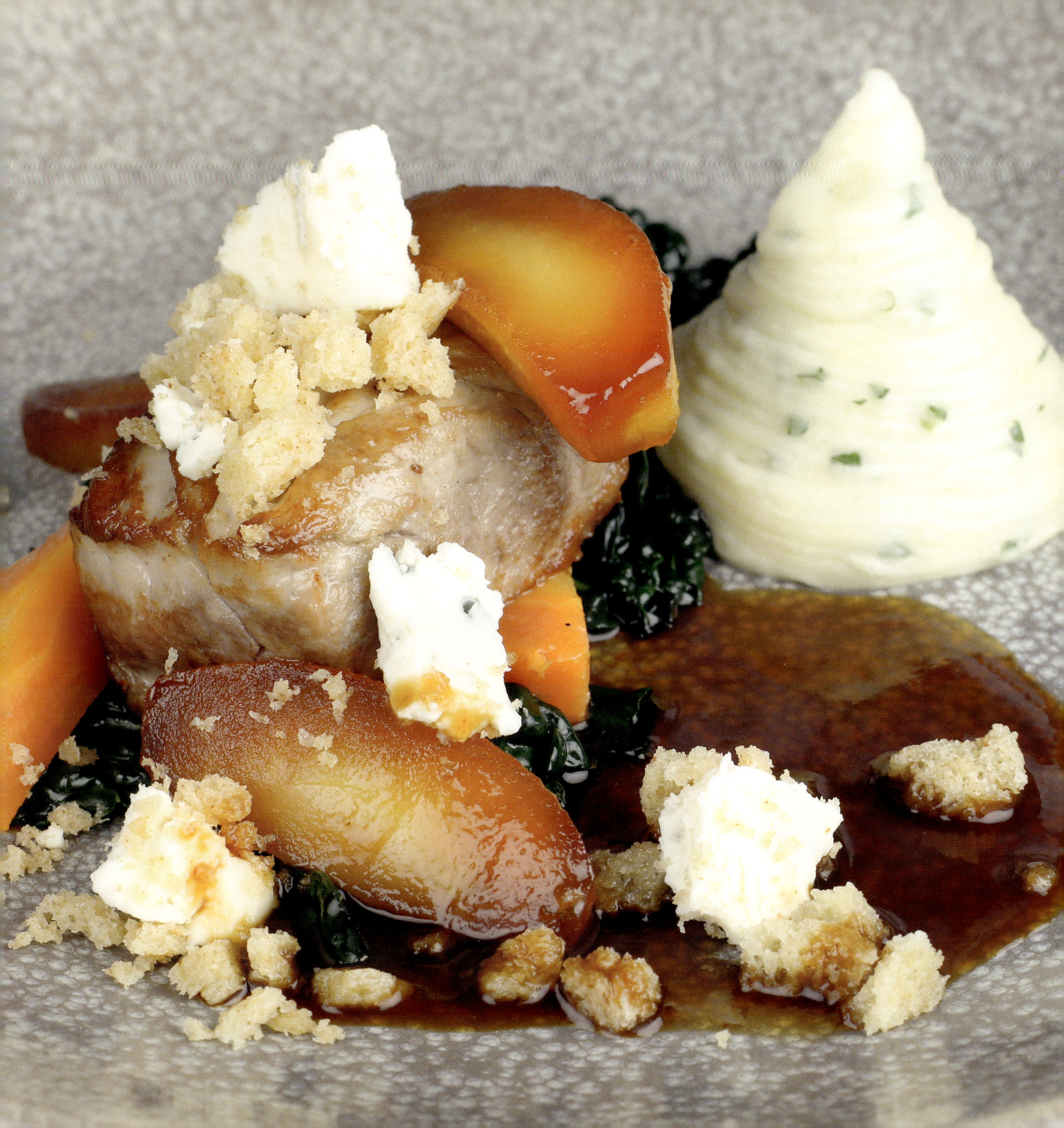

HINTLESHAM HALL ALAN FORD

Warm salad of wood pigeon

Wild game is always popular with our guests. The pigeon breasts in this savoury starter are best enjoyed cooked pink to keep the meat juicy. (serves 4)

- 2 aubergines, one cut into 12 half-cm slices, one diced
- Celeriac, 12 wafer-thin slices
- 1 garlic clove, chopped
- Pinch of thyme leaves, chopped
- 4 oven-ready pigeon crowns
- 2 tsp grain mustard
- 1 tbsp white wine vinegar
- 2 tbsp rapeseed oil
- 1 tbsp hazelnut oil
- 1 tbsp toasted hazelnuts
- Beetroot crisps
- Flat leaf parsley sprigs

Grill the oiled and seasoned aubergine and celeriac slices until softened and set aside.

Gently fry the chopped aubergine, garlic and thyme until dried out. Blend in a processor, season to taste and set aside.

Pre-heat the oven to 180c. Seal the oiled, seasoned pigeon crowns to brown on all sides. Roast for 7 minutes until pink. Rest them somewhere warm for a few minutes.

Whisk up the mustard, vinegar, oils, chopped nuts and seasoning into a dressing. Plate up the vegetable slices with the aubergine purée, top with the carved breasts, drizzle with dressing and finish with the crisps and parsley.

Herb-crusted sea bass, crab, egg tagliatelle and vegetable ribbons

The lime and parsley crust contrasts the rich seafood and the shellfish sauce. Save time if you wish by buying a good lobster bisque. Try and source wild, east coast bass, if you can. (serves 4)

- 4 nests of dried egg tagliatelle
- 250ml lobster bisque
- 2 tbsp crème fraîche
- Dash of good brandy
- 4 x 100g portions of sea bass
- Unsalted butter
- 1 small courgette, carrot and leek, cut into ribbons
- 50g young spinach leaves
- 100g white crabmeat
- Zest of 1 lime
- 2 tbsp flat leaf parsley
- 1 garlic clove, finely chopped

Cook the pasta until al dente, drain, oil and set aside. Gently simmer the bisque and whisk in the crème fraîche, brandy and seasoning to taste. Keep hot.

Pre-heat the grill to high. Fry the oiled, seasoned fish skin-side down until browned, then turn over and add a good knob of butter. Baste until just cooked through and flaking. Keep warm.

Blanch the vegetable ribbons in boiling salted water for 20 seconds, add the pasta to warm through and the spinach to wilt. Drain well and return to the pan. Fold in the crab, a splash of olive oil and seasoning to taste. Combine the zest, garlic and parsley and top the fish before warming under the grill. Serve the fish on top of the ribbons and pasta with the sauce around.

Double-baked blackberry and pear soufflé

We serve this elegant dessert with a spiced red wine syrup and a vanilla cream. (serves 6)

- 3 pears, peeled and diced
- 70g caster sugar
- 100ml water
- 150g blackberries
- 60g unsalted butter
- 70g plain flour
- 285ml whole milk
- 30g caster sugar
- Softened butter
- 1 egg yolk
- 6 egg whites
- Juice of half a lemon
- 85g caster sugar
- Icing sugar

Simmer the pears, sugar and water until soft. Add the berries and cook until no liquid remains and set aside. Melt the butter, stir in the flour and cook for 30 seconds. Add the milk gradually while whisking, then 30g of sugar before simmering for 3 minutes. Butter and sugar six ramekins. Mix two tbsp of the compote into the custard along with the egg yolk. In a clean bowl, whisk the whites, lemon juice and 85g of sugar into soft peaks. Mix half into the fruit custard before gently folding in the remainder. Fill the ramekins and clean the edges. Place the soufflés into a deep roasting tin and pour hot water halfway up. Bake at 150c for about 40 minutes (hopefully they will rise slightly!) Remove, allow to cool, turn out onto baking paper and refrigerate.

Reheat in oven set at 190c for 6 mins, dusting with icing sugar before serving alongside the remaining compote.

ALAN ON HIS...

BEST DISH EVER EATEN?
It was rock lobster with a simple lemon sauce that I ate at Rockpool, Sydney, in the early 2000s with my wife Liz and daughter Katy. An amazing dish!

FOOD NOSTALGIA?
Steamed chocolate sponge done properly in a pan of boiling water and served with chocolate custard. It was a pudding my Mum made when I was a kid.

A SPECIAL CHILDHOOD MEMORY?
Going to my Nana's in Lawshall for summer holidays, there was a croft nearby, and she promised me 5p per fish I caught. I reeled in 120 fish (probably with a few repeat catches as it was tiny), but bless her, she paid up!

INSPIRING SUFFOLK VIEW?
The coast around Dunwich in the winter is just stunning on a crisp sunny day.

IF NOT A CHEF WHAT WOULD YOU HAVE BEEN?
I wanted to be a chef from a very early age – in fact I never even considered another career. It was mainly I think because I used to experiment at home, cooking, baking cakes etc. There were not so many TV cookery shows in those days!

CHEF'S TIP?
When frying fish, if your non-stick pan is not very non-stick, place a sheet of greaseproof paper on the base of it and fry the fish as normal. Just make sure the paper does not overlap the edge of the frying pan!

'TAKE FIVE' RECIPE?
Try a quick smoked chicken pâté. Roughly blend the leg flesh of a smoked chicken, add a tablespoon each of grain mustard and mayonnaise to form a pâté texture, add chopped tarragon to taste, and season. Eat with crusty bread or toast.

SIGNATURE DISHES

Starters

Caramelised scallops, scorched cauliflower emulsion, lightly curried mussels, salted tuile

Roasted smoked quail breast, quail leg & mushroom confit, wild mushroom croquettes

Fillet of red mullet, herb crumbs, salmon & caper rillettes, cabernet sauvignon vinaigrette

Mains

Treacle-glazed pork belly, braised cheeks and roasted fillet, wild mushrooms, madeira

Loin of venison, burnt pear compote, braised endive, clove-flavoured sauce

Poached fillet of halibut, mussels, radish, fennel, lime leaf essence

Puddings

Milk chocolate custard feuilletage, toasted pear, chocolate ganache, white chocolate powder

Mango & white rum curd, grilled papaya, coconut meringue

Hintlesham Fig Mess

QUICK SNACK OR MIDNIGHT FEAST?
Ideally it's got to be blue cheese and crusty bread. Probably not at midnight though!

Say yes to the Hall

"The bride comes down our lovely 17th century staircase, the double doors into the salon are thrown open and the groom, facing a big mirror on the wall, can see his future wife in the reflection." Reservations manager Zoe Bell is describing one of the wedding options at Hintlesham Hall, adding with a grin: "You tell that to couples and they say 'We want to do that!'" The Hall has featured in the *Daily Telegraph* as one of the UK's top wedding venues, with four rooms licensed for civil ceremonies. Bride and groom can even book the entire hotel for 24-hour exclusive use.

Hintlesham Hall's elegant Georgian façade conceals an older history. Dating back to the 1400s, it is Grade 1-listed, packed with architectural features and set in 175 acres of Suffolk countryside just six miles from Ipswich. It has its own mini spa, there are shoot-and-stay breaks for guests and a championship golf course close by.

You don't need to be part of a wedding party to enjoy the restaurant of course. The dining rooms are elegant, the walls hung with vast portraits, the tall windows framed with acres of fabric, and the white-clothed tables arranged spaciously.

For all the Hall's history, it has moved with the times with rolling programmes of refurbishment, and the recent installation of a biomass boiler and electric vehicle charging points.

Hintlesham Hall
Hintlesham, Ipswich IP8 3NS
W: hintleshamhall.co.uk
T: 01473 652334
E: reservations@hintleshamhall.com
 /Hintleshamhallhotel
 @hintlesham_hall
 Hintleshamhall

Accolades and listings: AA Two Rosettes; AA Four Red Stars (accommodation); Green Tourism Silver Award; Freedom Foods accredited

Food served: all week B 7-9.30; L 12-2; D 6.30-9; all-day lounge menu 7-10; afternoon tea (booking essential) all week 2-5 (3-5 Sat & Sun)

Cost: starters from £12; mains from £25; desserts from £9; table d'hôte dinner menu £27 (two courses); set lunch from £27.50 (two courses including wine, nibbles and coffee); Sunday lunch from £22.50 (two courses); wine from £23.50; afternoon tea from £19

Details: 45 seats (Parlour); 82 seats (Salon); private dining for 16 (Justice Room); al fresco tables on terrace; 32 ensuite bedrooms including 4 suites; 6 meeting rooms seat up to 90 with full AV system; wedding licence; spa; gardens; easily accessible; pets welcome; parking

THE ANGEL HOTEL, BURY ST EDMUNDS
JAMES CARN

Angels at the table

A love of food underpins the lifelong friendship – and now business relationship – between chef James Carn and baker Will Wooster

125

THE ANGEL HOTEL JAMES CARN

It's Tuesday morning in Bardwell and the banter between James and Will begins the moment James walks through the door of Will's shop. The give and take is unfiltered, spontaneous, constant, and smacks of a deep friendship.

James Carn and Will Wooster have been mates since they no doubt caused mayhem as seven-year-old tearaways in the Honington Beavers pack, then in the playground at Ixworth Middle School. Fast forward a few years, and James quickly found his feet in the world of food, enthusiasm sparked through a work-based apprenticeship at Otley College, while Will cheffed "not very well" before moving into the family baking business, Wooster's Bakery, that he now runs.

More recently, the pair's relationship has developed another, more grown-up, dimension – that of chef and supplier. "We bake our own bread every day at the Angel," James says, referring to the molasses sourdough loaves that are baked twice a day and brought still warm and gratis to every table. Will comes back like lightning. "Yes, but I've bailed you out on more than one occasion, haven't I!" Cue more laughter before James composes himself. "Seriously, Will's sourdough is something else. His malt loaf is phenomenal – I'm thinking of putting it on as a savoury with some Baron Bigod cheese and fresh truffle – but the sourdough is incredible, especially the sprouted rye."

And while the bakery premises at Bardwell, in the lea of the Victorian windmill, drip with artisanal atmosphere (and this is where Will still has his tiny shop, run by his brother Joe), such is the demand for the Wooster loaves, focaccias, baguettes, croissants and pastries that production has moved to more practical premises near Knettishall Heath where Will can work comfortably alongside his father, and fellow baker Tom West. It's a godsend, Will says, as he tips out a living, heaving mound of sprouted rye sourdough onto the stainless steel bench, folds and turns it quickly – "it's very therapeutic doing this, but the less you touch it the better" – before returning it to the crate with a ritual two pats. He repeats the process three or four times over a period of hours. "It's a crucial stage; this is when the flavour, strength and crumb is formed."

Back in The Angel kitchen, the pace is similarly fast. Sous chef Dave Coyne is cooking a Sunday roast for the afternoon's wedding party ("but it's Thursday," he calls to whoever might be listening), Luke Cornelius (Titch to his mates) is prepping veg, Max Cameron and Toby Colletta, both demi chefs de partie, are on stoves nearby. Alan Stratton who recently returned to the team after a couple of months away from the kitchen is a relatively new recruit whose hard work has caught James' eye. "He's an incredible chef, thinks a lot, doesn't say much but when he does it's worth listening to."

It's a young, ambitious and able brigade, and this is James' first head chef role. He was ready to move on after two years at Bury St Edmunds' popular neighbourhood restaurant, Pea Porridge, and while former employers describe him as headstrong, he appears controlled, confident and to have the respect of his team. There's no question that his arrival has been a shot in the arm to the food offer at The Angel, creating a local buzz about the restaurant. There's also a neatness in that he has taken his first head chef position in the kitchen where he started his career, a very junior chef back in 2009.

As is so often the case with head chefs, pastry is not James' natural section (it's more often Alan's domain), but you only have to look at the intricacy of James' creations and taste them, to see that he's more than competent. "Pastry is something I take great pride in, and I've learnt to love it. Actually, it's probably my strongest section now," he says as he lines up the ingredients for a beautiful treacle tart. He presses sweet shortcrust pastry into a fluted mould, chills and blind bakes it as he stirs Will's crumbed sourdough into the creamy, syrupy filling, cut with zested lime and ginger. He fills the case, bakes it again briefly. It's dense and sweet, but everything else on the dish balances this: the quenelle of tangy Fen Farm buttermilk, the scattering of bee pollen from local beekeeper, Ian Hart, and the freshness of lemon verbena. A piped puddle of dulce de leche ramps up the sweetness but it is brought down a notch by the corresponding sourness of fresh and poached blueberries. "Puddings should be puddings," says James, "so sweetness is important." This one is likely to be a fixture on the menu, the fruit garnish changing with the seasons.

It's a very Instagrammable plate. James is creative, aware of how colour and shape please the eye before texture and taste are satisfied, though he insists that that flutter of micro herbs, or that scatter of pollen or onion powder are all more than cheffy touches. The dots of truffle ketchup round his dish of Denham Estate venison tartare are there "because they add taste and you get a bit of the flavour with every mouthful".

There's something nose-to-tail about his food too: the likes of Fergus Henderson and Nathan Outlaw, whose chef reputations hang on the light touch they apply to first-rate seasonal ingredients, crop up regularly as inspirations. "And of course I'll use Suffolk produce when it's the best, but I'm not religious about it – except for oysters and lobster! I'll only ever use Pinney's, and if I can't get theirs I'll put something else on, simple as that."

THE ANGEL HOTEL JAMES CARN

Wooster's sprouted rye sourdough and black treacle tart, buttermilk sorbet, blueberries, bee pollen and lemon verbena

A fantastic pudding which can be enjoyed all year round by making seasonal adjustments to the berries, replacing these blueberries with other sweet and sour fruit such as new season rhubarb or cherries.

Tart case
- 500g plain flour
- 200g unsalted butter
- 180g icing sugar
- 6 large egg yolks

To make the pastry, pulse the flour, chilled butter and sugar into fine crumbs, then mix through the egg yolks until just combined.

Wrap the pastry in clingfilm and chill for 2 hours to rest. You will only need half of the pastry to line your large, greased tart case so freeze the remainder. Pre-heat the oven to 160c. Roll the pastry to almost see-through (a few mm thick) and once the tin is lined, prick all over, line with parchment and fill with baking beans before blind-baking for 20 minutes. Remove from the oven and allow to cool.

Filling
- 310g golden syrup
- 20g black treacle
- 100g sourdough bread, in bite-sized pieces
- 50g ground almonds
- 1 large egg
- 150g double cream
- Zest of 1 lime
- 5g ginger root, grated and peeled

Pre-heat the oven to 160c. Warm the syrup and treacle until fairly liquid. Add to the other ingredients in a food processor and blend for 1 minute. Once smooth, pour into the tart case to the top and bake for 15 minutes. Remove and cool.

Sorbet
- 420g buttermilk
- 80g water
- 80g sugar

Liquidise the ingredients together and churn in an ice cream maker until set. Freeze until required.

To serve
- Fresh blueberries, bee pollen and lemon verbena to garnish

Temper the ice cream to soften before serving the dish. Slice the tart, garnish with the berries and verbena, top with the ice cream and sprinkle with pollen.

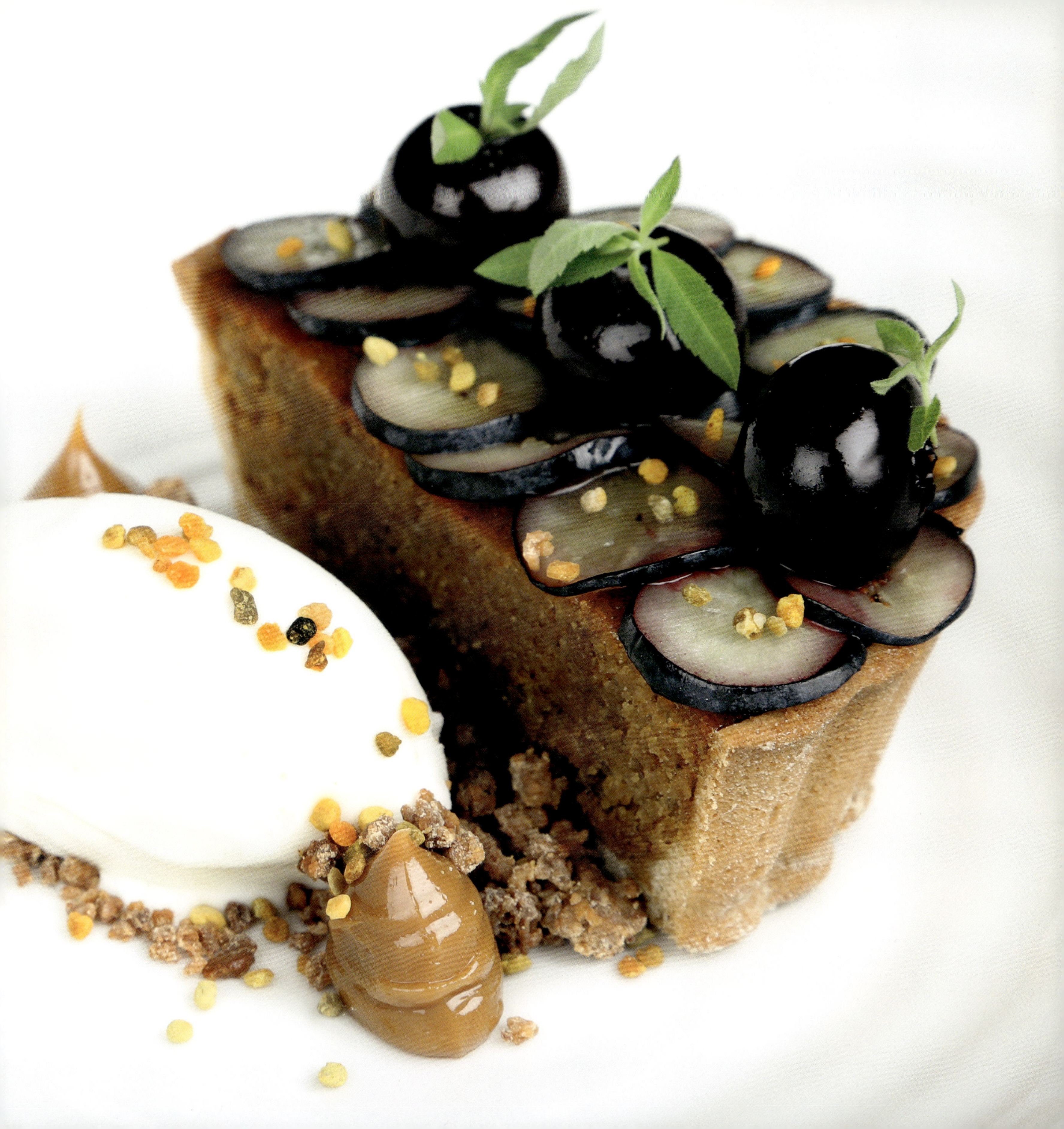

THE ANGEL HOTEL JAMES CARN

Rare-seared cutlets and ale-braised hogget breast

With more flavour than younger lamb, hogget is from a sheep in its second season. It's sweeter and less strong than mutton, but has a real savoury character. We serve this with Jerusalem artichoke purée and IPA beer-pickled red onions. (serves 4)

1kg boned hogget breast
200ml good chicken or lamb stock
50g honey
2 shallots
2 garlic cloves
500ml golden ale
2 tbsp red wine vinegar
1 rack of hogget, French-trimmed

Pre-heat the oven to 160c. Brown the seasoned breast all over and place into a deep casserole dish with the stock, shallots, garlic, honey and beer, cover and cook for 3 hours until tender. Remove and reserve the liquor. Cool and refrigerate the meat under a weighted tray until firm.

To serve, pre-heat the oven to 200c, brown the seasoned rack and then roast for about 8 minutes (for medium-rare).

Remove and rest for ten minutes somewhere warm while you reheat the breast, gently poaching it in a little liquor in a covered saucepan on the hob. Carve the rack into cutlets and serve alongside the portions of hogget breast.

Oyster tempura, seaweed salad cream and dill oil

I love Orford, and Pinney's smokehouse is probably the main reason why! All their seafood and especially their oysters are the best in the area. (serves 4 as a nibble)

2 egg yolks
1 tbsp mustard
Juice of 2 limes
200ml vegetable oil
85ml double cream
½ tsp dried dulse seaweed powder
100g plain flour
200ml sparkling water
1 small bunch of dill
100ml rapeseed oil
4 oysters, opened in the shell
Half a cucumber, finely diced

For the salad cream, whisk together the yolks, mustard and juice, slowly mix in the vegetable oil in a drizzle and whisk in the cream and seaweed powder, before refrigerating. Whisk the flour and water with a pinch of salt into a batter and refrigerate. For the herb oil, blanch the dill in boiling water for a few seconds, then submerge into iced water. Pat dry on a tea towel before blending with the rapeseed oil. To serve, dip the oyster meats in the batter and deep-fry at 180c until golden-brown. Place on a bed of cucumber in each of the half-shells, with a spoonful of salad cream and dill oil for garnish.

Venison tartare with egg yolk dressing

Tartare is one of my all-time favourite starters. Although more commonly made with beef, I think venison is just as good if not better! I serve mine with a rich egg dressing instead of just the classic raw yolk, along with pickled squash, grated black truffle, puffed crackling and a mushroom ketchup. (serves 4)

5 egg yolks
80ml rapeseed oil
2 tsp sherry vinegar
salt
150g venison loin
10g each of shallot, gherkin and capers
Tobacco to taste
Lemon juice
10g flat leaf parsley, chopped

For the egg yolk dressing, very gently poach the egg yolks in a ziplock bag in barely-bubbling water until fully set.

To make the dressing, put the yolks in a bowl and add the oil in a steady stream, whisking all the time to form an emulsion. Add the vinegar, season to taste and set aside.

For the tartare, finely chop the trimmed venison and chop the vegetables very small. Mix together, adding tobacco strands, juice and seasoning to taste before folding in the parsley.

To serve, press the chilled tartare into a ring shape and drizzle with the dressing.

JAMES ON HIS...

SPECIAL TIME OF YEAR FOR FOOD?
Summer. I love all the fresh British berries and fruits for the pastry section as well as the wide array of vegetables on offer.

BEST DISH EVER EATEN?
It would have to be the bread course at Paul Ainsworth No 6 in Padstow. The whole meal was great, but the bread was on a completely different level. Justin Sharp's snails & bone marrow dish at Pea Porridge in Bury St Edmunds is incredible, and for something sweet Heston Blumenthal's tipsy pudding is out of this world! I've been lucky enough to share all of these dishes with my wife, Sophia. Great company can make a fantastic meal even better!

WHO IS OR WAS YOUR MENTOR?
Justin Sharp at Pea Porridge, a great chef, businessman and friend.

FAVOURITE LOCAL FOODIE PLACES?
Wyken Vineyards is a lovely place to spend a morning, there's a great restaurant, a nice shop, and they produce some pretty decent wine. The farmers' market on Saturday sells some great produce, including Wooster's sourdough.

CAN'T WAIT TO EAT AT...
I would love to eat at Faviken, Magnus Nilsson's restaurant in a very remote part of Sweden. My wife's family are Swedish so I hope that we can tie it in with a family trip in the not too distant future.

FOOD NOSTALGIA?
Mussels! My first experience of them was in Normandy with my aunt and uncle when I was about 12. I can still picture the restaurant and it was probably the first moment I realised I loved food (well, eating it at least!). Mussels are still my favourite thing to eat.

PERFECT DAY OFF?
I'd spend it with my wife and our three boys in Orford having some snacks at Pump Street Bakery, and enjoying the beautiful Suffolk coastline.

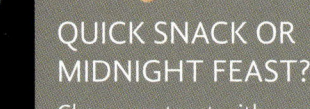

SIGNATURE DISHES

Starters

Blow-torched mackerel, rhubarb, monks beard, buttermilk, dill

Gin-cured sea trout, saffron kohlrabi, seaweed salad cream, pickled cucumber

Norfolk quail, serrano-wrapped breast, black pudding, truffle-stuffed leg, gooseberry, celeriac, tarragon

Mains

Line-caught brill, saffron mash, crab sauce, pommes soufflé, sea beet

Mangalitsa pork rib, spiced faggot, yoghurt, pomegranate, hummus

Lamb belly, crispy sweetbreads, wild garlic, fresh peas, onion

Puddings

Douglas fir sandwich, raspberry, yogurt sorbet, pistachio

Passion fruit pavlova, coconut sorbet, ginger, rum ice

Chocolate mousse, barley ice cream, dulce de leche, chocolate aero

QUICK SNACK OR MIDNIGHT FEAST?
Cheese on toast with marmite (I've eaten far more than I would care to admit!)

Devilishly stylish

The Angel Hotel always dresses for the season. Spring and summer see her clad in vivid green tangles of ivy that combine with window boxes of tumbling pink petunias to striking effect. Come autumn, she prefers more muted crimson, and a sparser covering of foliage that reveals the elegant proportions of the Georgian building. By Christmas time she sparkles joyfully with ribbons of festive lights.

At all times, The Angel retains an air of grace, as befits this landmark hotel just a stone's throw from Bury St Edmunds' historic Abbey Gardens and ancient ruins, and its stunning cathedral.

Owned by the Gough family for over 50 years, the hotel is part of a trio of properties that includes the Salthouse Harbour Hotel in Ipswich and Southwold Pier. Like its sister hotel, The Angel is packed with art from Robert and Claire Gough's private collection, an eclectic array of conventional portraiture, landscapes and photography, as well as *objets*, contemporary sculpture and unique furniture. Sink into one of the deep sofas by the open fire in the lounge for afternoon tea, and you'll have plenty to look at.

The Green Room with its spectacular chandelier and striking patchwork chairs is the place for private dining or business meetings, and the Wingspan cocktail bar in the medieval underground vaults is a quirky spot for evening drinks.

The Angel Hotel
Angel Hill, Bury St Edmunds IP33 1LT
W: theangel.co.uk
T: 01284 714000
E: reservations@theangel.co.uk
 /TheAngelHotelBury
 @AngelHotelBury
 /angel_hotel_bury

Accolades and listings: Waitrose *Good Food Guide*; AA Two Rosettes; AA Four Stars (accommodation); *Michelin*; winner, *EADT* Food & Drink Awards, Chef of the Year 2017 (David Coyne) & 2016 (James Carn), Young Chef of the Year 2016 (Max Cameron) & finalist Luke Cornelius

Food served: B Mon-Fri 7-10; L all week 12-2:30; D Mon-Sat 6-9:30; Sun L 12-9

Cost: starters from £7; mains from £15; desserts from £8; express menu available at certain times from £11.95 (one course); Sunday lunch from £22.50; wine from £19

Details: 85 seats in main restaurant; children's menu; 77 bedrooms; Wingspan cocktail bar available for private hire for up to 40; Green Room with full AV system available for private hire, seats up to 16; accessible; parking

THE UNRULY PIG, BROMESWELL
DAVE WALL

A bittersweet love

Dave Wall teases out the complex flavours of single-estate Pump Street chocolate, an ingredient he adores

135

The Unruly Pig kitchen is busy. Chefs weave around each other, familiar with the space and intent on tasks. Senior sous Karl Green is breaking down hare on one bench, chef de partie Emile Tilston is purposefully rolling gnocchi over a wooden paddle to score the traditional ridges in the dough – they'll go with lamb and the puttanesca punch of anchovies, garlic, olives, capers and tomatoes, and sweet peperonata. Elsewhere, octopus tentacles, ready for a swift grilling, spill over the side of a metal bowl, and firm stalks of rhubarb, flushed with the promise that winter's grip is finally relaxing, wait to become a compote that will meet a white chocolate pannacotta infused with cardamom, lemongrass and basil. This is a place with a generous slug of warm-hearted Italian influences on the menu – 'Britalian' food as owner Brendan Padfield calls it.

Karl looks up from his hare to light charcoal in the wood-fired oven that is at the heart of this workspace; Inka adds her voice as she roars up to temperature.

Dave, meanwhile, is focused coolly on chocolate. He builds a stylish pudding, one that he developed with Karl. "It's great to have a talented chap like Karl to work alongside and bounce ideas off, particularly over a large glass of red!" he says. The dish celebrates chocolate in all its sweet, rich, bitter, smooth, fruity, snappy tastes and textures. Triangular tuiles sandwich a mousse, there are cubes of brownie, and flavours of blood orange (campari-soaked slices, fresh segments, and a burnt orange purée) that counter the richness. "I adore blood oranges," says Dave, "there's a fantastic bittersweet flavour to the purée that cuts right through the chocolate. The campari was Karl's idea and it really works." Rough-cut chunks of honeycomb add crunch to a dish that is a masterclass in balance.

The chocolate is a Madagascan 72% from Pump Street. Using it is a no-brainer for Dave, and not just because the beans are turned into glossy couverture just a few miles from The Unruly Pig. "I love the Pump Street ethos, the way the team has worked hard to make the business a success," says Dave as we head to meet owner, Chris Brennan, and customer manager Sally Jones. "We'd be mad not to use their product. As a chef, it's magical to find ingredients that inspire." At Pump Street's chocolate headquarters at Bentwaters, Chris explains the process from the arrival of hessian sacks of cocoa beans from single-estate growers (the beans are meticulously sorted, then carefully roasted, conched, tempered, poured, and beautifully packaged) up to their dispatch to customers as local as The Unruly Pig, and as far afield as Hong Kong and the USA.

THE UNRULY PIG DAVE WALL

Chris travels regularly to visit farmers around the world's cacao-growing belt. "That connection is essential because the quality of our chocolate is all down to how farms are run," he explains as we taste squares of chocolate from romantic-sounding places where the *terroir* and climate lend subtleties of flavour. There are hints of rum and raisin in the Jamaican 75%, but more citrussy notes in the Madagascan used in the recipe today. "Tasting this gets me thinking straight away about dishes," says Dave. "I always start with the core ingredient, then ideas flow. I love the Ecuador 85% which we use in a marquise – you really keep the power of the chocolate with that one."

We pay a pilgrimage to Orford and the Pump Street Bakery, the tiny shop and café where the buns are sticky, the loaves are crusty and the hot chocolate is thickly rich. It is the spiritual home of the multi-award-winning business created by Chris and his daughter Jo as a way of satisfying their desire for really good bread. "When we opened The Unruly Pig in 2015 and I began scouting for suppliers, my first port of call was Orford," says Dave. "We've used Pump Street right from the start, first the sourdough, and the brioche buns for burgers, and baguettes for sandwiches, then the chocolate. And Pinney's down on the quay there are a joy to work with." He uses Pinney's oysters in a velouté [see recipe], their smoked duck for a duck liver parfait garnish, and smoked mackerel in a sandwich. "We use their day boat fish too – skate roasted with butter, lemon and capers is just delicious."

Previous chef positions in the Gordon Ramsay Group may have instilled in Dave the importance of systems – "it was intense at the Boxwood Café and Claridges, they were operational machines" – but it was Michelin-trained Suffolk chef, Carl Shillingford, who inspired him as a commis at The Anchor Inn, Nayland, back in 2007. "I want my chefs to be cooks, to understand food and ingredients and how French classic cooking is at the cornerstone of any good kitchen – even in a place like this with our 'Britalian' food. The Anchor was an incredible place to learn. It was owned by farmers, and we used all their meat, whole animals, never bought any in. We made our own bread and ketchup, we went foraging for mushrooms. At the time, I thought 'why would anyone want to do this?'. I didn't realise how good it was. Now I understand."

SUFFOLK FEAST

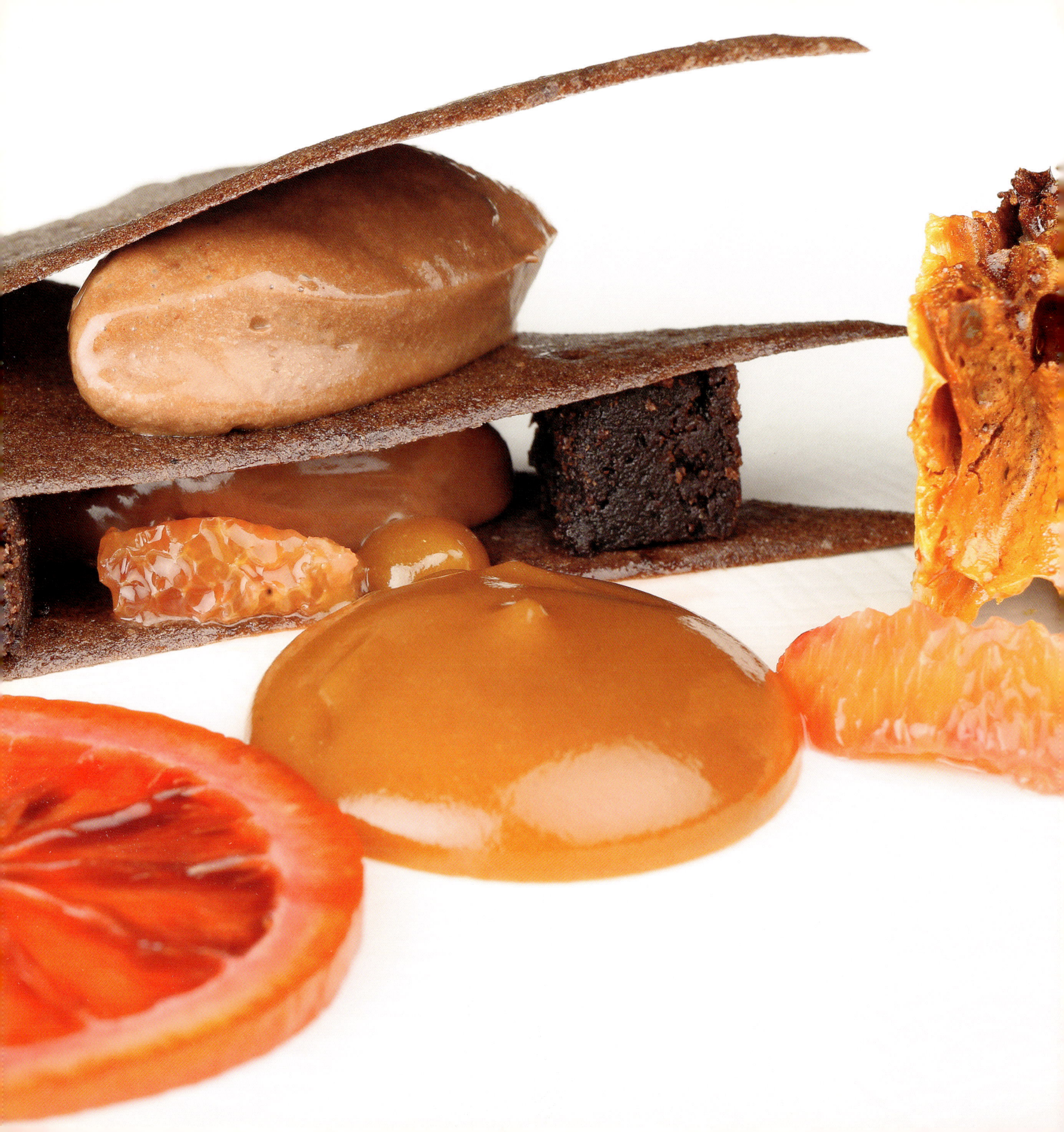

THE UNRULY PIG DAVE WALL

Dark chocolate, campari, blood orange and honeycomb

This is one of my and sous chef Karl's favourite creations. The blood orange and dark chocolate (we generally use Pump Street's 72% Madagascan) work so well with the bittersweet campari in the purée and the honeycomb crunch.

Space precludes the inclusion of my brownie and honeycomb recipes. Make your own or buy the best quality you can find. The orange purée and confit can be made the day before. (serves 4)

Orange purée
- **2 seedless blood oranges, unpeeled**
- **200g sugar**
- **200ml water**
- **25ml sherry vinegar**
- **80ml campari**

Score the oranges 6 times from top to bottom ½ cm deep. Place in cold water and simmer for 5 minutes. Drain and repeat 4 more times. Refill again with cold water and simmer for 30 minutes until very soft. Drain and mash with a wooden spoon into a pulp.

Make a caramel by melting the sugar in the water over a very low heat without stirring (cautiously shaking the pan occasionally if needed). When it turns a dark mahogany colour, remove from the heat, carefully add the orange pulp and combine. Stir in the vinegar and campari and simmer well for about 10 minutes, reducing it by a third. Liquidise for 5 minutes until silky smooth and then set aside.

Orange confit
- **1 blood orange, very thinly sliced**
- **100g caster sugar**
- **80ml campari**
- **80ml water**

Pre-heat the oven to 100c (fan off). Lay the oranges out on a shallow-lipped baking tray. Melt the other ingredients together and pour over the oranges. Cover with parchment and bake for approx. 1 hour until the slices are soft.

Chocolate mousse
- **4 egg yolks, whisked to pale**
- **90g caster sugar**
- **90ml water**
- **200g dark chocolate (the best you can find), melted**
- **400g whipping cream, whipped to soft peaks**

Put the whisked yolks in a saucepan. In a separate pan, heat the sugar and water to 121c on a cooking thermometer. Carefully pour the syrup over the yolks and whisk on a high speed until the mix is cool and has doubled in size. Fold a third of the yolk mix into the chocolate, then another third, and then the remainder, keeping it airy. Repeat with the whipped cream. Refrigerate to set.

Tuile biscuits
- **15g cocoa**
- **85g icing sugar**
- **90g plain flour**
- **100g unsalted butter, softened**
- **2 egg whites, lightly whisked**

Sift the first three ingredients together, then combine with the butter and egg whites, beating well. Place a triangular outline stencil (you can cut one out of a clear plastic lid) on a silicone baking mat on a roasting tray and spread the mix over the stencil to create triangles as thin as you can. Remove the stencil. Bake the tuiles for 5 minutes, then allow to cool a little, before lifting carefully onto a cooling rack. Repeat to create 12 tuiles in total. When cold, store airtight.

To serve
- **Chocolate brownie, cut into 12 1cm cubes**
- **1 blood orange in pithless segments**
- **Honeycomb, broken into shards**

To plate up, place spoonfuls of the mousse and the brownie pieces between the tuile biscuits (see picture). Arrange the confit orange slices, some fresh segments, shards of honeycomb and the purée attractively on the plate.

THE UNRULY PIG DAVE WALL

Chorizo, brie and spicy 'nduja arancini

Arancini are the most fantastic of Italian appetisers, crisp oozy fritters of leftover risotto. 'Nduja is a soft, very spicy, pâté-like Italian sausage. Buy it either whole or in a jar. A little yoghurt works well as a cooling dip. (serves 4 as nibbles)

1 onion, finely diced
100g butter
375g chorizo, skinned and diced
50g 'nduja
300g risotto rice (I prefer carnaroli)
100ml white wine
400ml good chicken stock, hot
100g brie, diced small
Beaten egg and seasoned flour
2 handfuls of panko crumbs

Soften the onions in the butter before adding the chorizo and 'nduja. Fry gently for a few minutes, then stir in the rice. Turn up the heat and stir-fry for a minute or two before pouring in the wine. Once absorbed, add all the stock a ladle at a time over a low-medium heat, stirring until absorbed.

When the rice is cooked, pour it onto a roasting tray and cool for 10 minutes. Fold in the cheese and roll into ping pong-sized balls. Chill until set.

Dust the balls in flour, then egg, before coating in the crumbs. Deep-fry until crisp and golden before draining and transferring to kitchen paper. Season to taste and serve.

Oyster velouté

We love oysters at The Pig and this velouté is always a crowd-pleaser, especially if you aren't keen on the texture of oysters. It goes well with smoked eel alongside a little pickled apple and celery. (serves 4)

1 medium leek, washed and finely sliced
100g butter
Leaves from 10 sprigs of thyme
250ml good fish or chicken stock
400ml whipping cream
4 oysters, meats and sieved juices
Juice of half a lemon

Gently soften the leek with the butter and a pinch of salt. Add the thyme and stock, before boiling hard to reduce by half. Add the cream and gently simmer for 10 minutes until reduced by a quarter.

Cool for about 10 minutes, then process with the oyster meats and juices. Finish by blending in the lemon juice and seasoning to taste.

Buck rarebit

Cheese on toast and poached egg, but with attitude! Our rarebit packs a punch, seasoned with plenty of mustard, worcestershire sauce and tabasco. The addition of a poached duck egg adds immensely. (serves 4)

50g butter
50g flour
450ml milk, hot
200g very mature hard cheese, grated
50g good blue cheese, crumbled
1 heaped tbsp English mustard
Worcestershire and tabasco sauces
4 thick slices of sourdough toast
4 poached duck eggs
2 spring onions, finely shredded

Beat the melted butter and flour over a medium heat into a roux. Gradually whisk in the milk, creating a thick, silky white sauce. Simmer gently for 10 minutes.

Whisk in three-quarters of both cheeses until melted, and stir in the mustard, plus generous amounts of both sauces and seasoning to taste. Allow to cool.

Pre-heat the grill. Spread the sauce thickly on the warm toast and sprinkle on the remaining cheeses. Grill until golden and bubbling, adding the eggs on top and sprinkling on the spring onions before serving.

DAVE ON HIS...

MOST THRILLING MOMENT IN YOUR CAREER TO DATE?

Cooking in the Roux Scholarship competition. The first year I was in it (2013) was the 30th anniversary and it was all televised. I'll never forget as I filleted my bass the legendary Albert Roux popping up from nowhere and ogling my knife skills from inches away, with the camera zoning in seemingly desperate for me to gash the fish and see a reaction from Albert! Luckily I nailed it!

HOW DID YOU CELEBRATE YOUR LAST BIRTHDAY?

Brendan who owns The Unruly Pig, sent me and my wife to his favourite restaurant, The River Café. It was fantastic!

FAVOURITE TIME OF YEAR FOR FOOD?

I love the shoulder season between winter and spring, when it's still cold enough to slow-cook but there are lots of exciting ingredients around: blood oranges, asparagus, morels, wild garlic.

GUILTY FOOD PLEASURE?

I don't feel too guilty about it but I love 'nduja, the Italian sausage akin to a paste of chilli and fatty pork.

WHAT GETS YOU UP IN THE MORNING?

I never ever tire of cooking, and the buzz of a busy restaurant is an inimitable magic.

PERFECT DAY OFF?

Southwold with my wife, Michelle, and our kids. We love the seaside and Southwold is so traditional still, it's great.

MENTOR?

My first head chef, Carl Shillingford. He'd worked at the highest level throughout his career, took me on as a commis and gave me the most fantastic education in all the cornerstone foundations of cookery, doing things the right way. A great chef and brilliant teacher.

WHAT IS YOUR BIGGEST EXTRAVAGANCE AS A CHEF?

Butter. Its price has seen exorbitant rises in the last year but I love cooking with it and still lash it in everything (wincing at the hit on margin every time!).

SIGNATURE DISHES

Starters

Chicken, raviolo, onion, wild garlic

Short rib, oyster, kohlrabi, apple

Octopus, 'nduja tortellini, burrata

Mains

Quail, potato terrine, cauliflower, black pudding

Cod, risotto, clams, brown crab, blood orange, chilli

Hare, parsley root, chocolate, blackberry

Puddings

Salted caramel tart, milk purée, honeycomb

Pannacotta, white chocolate, rhubarb, basil

Pump Street chocolate marquise, pistachio ice cream

QUICK SNACK OR MIDNIGHT FEAST?

I graze all day and I'm more than partial to a little late-night tuck, particularly cheese! I have been known to finish off a Vacherin Mont D'Or in one go. Cheese with a bottle of Brunello and I am in heaven...

WHAT'S ON YOUR KITCHEN PLAYLIST?

We tend to like it loud and pumping! Lots of house and techno.

SUFFOLK FEAST

Good pig

The Unruly Pig may look like a pub, albeit a tidied-up one, but the banners celebrating recent awards hint that it's in a different league from your average watering hole.

Bought in 2015 by Brendan Padfield who left a high-powered legal career to become a restaurateur, this partly 16th century roadside spot outside Woodbridge has attracted national attention in a short space of time. Quirky, art-filled interiors instantly set the place apart; the pieces are Brendan's and he periodically changes things around to keep regular guests on their toes. Likewise, the seamless melding of pub (you can come for a pint and bar snacks) and comfortable destination restaurant with a notable wine list, curated largely by Brendan, is cleverly achieved.

The skills of the front-of-house team were recognised in the respected Estrella Damm UK Top 50 Gastropubs Awards 2018 where the Unruly Pig won Front of House Team of the Year, a follow-up to winning the Best Pub in Suffolk award in the Great British Pub Awards 2016.

"We've set out our stall," says Brendan. "Right from the start, we wanted to create an accessible food offer but with high-end cooking." It must be pragmatic too, he adds, by which he means that crowd-pleasers such as the Unruly burger will never be off the menu.

The Unruly Pig
Orford Road, Bromeswell, Woodbridge IP12 2PU
W: theunrulypig.co.uk
T: 01394 460310
E: brendan@theunrulypig.co.uk
/unrulypig   @unrulypig   /unrulypig

Accolades and listings: Waitrose *Good Food Guide*; *Michelin*; *Harden's*; *Good Pub Guide*; AA *Pub Guide*; winner, Best Restaurant, *Eat Suffolk* Food & Drink Awards 2018; winner, Front of House Team of the Year, Estrella Damm UK Top 50 Gastropub Awards 2018; winner, Best Suffolk Pub, Great British Pub Awards 2016 & 2017; winner, Best Gastropub 2017, *Luxury Lifestyle* magazine

Food served: Mon-Fri L 12-2.30 (Sat 12-3); D 6-9 (Sat 5-9); Sun and BH L 12-8

Cost: starters from £6.95; mains from £10.95; puddings from £7.50; set menu (Mon-Thu L and D, Fri L and 6-7pm, Sat L) £16 (two courses), £19 (three courses); wine from £15; pint from £4.25

Details: 90 seats inside; outside decking area 40 seats; five course taster menu £49 with optional £29 wine flight; 'Bespoke Roast' Sunday lunch by arrangement; separate vegetarian and free-from menus; children's menu; upstairs private dining room seats up to 22; garden with mini football goal; accessible; dogs welcome; parking

THE BOARDING HOUSE DINING ROOMS, HALESWORTH
TYLER TORRANCE

144

Local manifesto

Tyler Torrance is persuasive as he argues the case for supporting local food producers such as Blythburgh Free Range Pork

THE BOARDING HOUSE DINING ROOMS TYLER TORRANCE

Too many people take their local suppliers for granted, according to Halesworth chef Tyler Torrance. "Right now we are at the cusp of great change in the UK and we either support the artisanal producers or we lose them," Tyler says. "If you don't use your local fishmonger, they're not going to be there. If you don't go to your local butcher, they're not going to be there. And that would be an absolute shame."

Tyler, owner of The Boarding House Dining Rooms in Halesworth, is putting his money where his mouth is. "I'm building a business based on local products, local food, local people and I'm hoping the rest of the community will get out and support them as well. And by showcasing them, I'm hoping it shines a little light on what we do here. I think it's a very, very simple symbiotic relationship."

Outgoing, charismatic and usually talking a mile a minute, Canadian-born Tyler expresses a boundless passion for Suffolk produce. "It is second to nothing in the world. I've cooked internationally and worked with the best, and the produce that I've got here in Suffolk has blown me away. Pork, lamb, beef, fish, some of the best cheesemakers in England with Fen Farm Dairy, and Hodmedods [English-grown pulses] just up the way." His menu proves the point: this is a place to come for Emmerdale Farm sirloin, locally reared guinea fowl, cod fished from the North Sea, and a cheeseboard fragrant with the likes of Suffolk Gold and Baron Bigod.

Today, however, is all about Blythburgh Free Range Pork, the business that belongs to pig farmer Jimmy Butler who runs it with his sons, Stuart and Alastair. The family's pigs – there are some 24,000 at any one time – are born and live outside on the light sandy land of the Suffolk coast where they are allowed to grow slowly, rootle, dig and play until 26 weeks of age. After slaughter, the meat is stamped boldly with the brand, and delivered to butchers around the UK.

One such butcher is Richard Thickitt, who arrives at Tyler's kitchen from his shop in Bramfield, carrying an enormous side of Blythburgh pork. Tyler salivates at the sight of it, his mind working nineteen to the dozen to come up with recipe ideas; he loves cheaper cuts as much as premium ones and has little patience with chefs who rack up unnecessary food miles. What's important for Tyler is the ability to showcase what's on the doorstep in the best possible way.

It's a view that chimes with Alastair, who is delighted to see the whole animal used in creative, delicious ways on Tyler's menu. He gets frustrated by chefs who buy only the prime cuts. "Chefs have to be flexible and not just ask for 20 bellies a week. They may have to have a shoulder or a leg too. There are of course chefs like Tyler, who say 'in order to use a premium product like Blythburgh pork I need to use the whole pig'."

We watch as Tyler creates a dish using pork collar alongside the loin and a black pudding bonbon. "The collar is slow-cooked, the fat melts in and bastes the meat. The pork loin, immensely moist, with lovely, locally produced pancetta lightly wrapped around it; it's beautiful. There's nothing better if you know where to look, if you know what to do; if you take just that little bit of care and love, you're going to find the beauty in the produce." The pork is served with roasted root vegetables, cavolo nero and the braising juices. The flavours are robust but the finished dish is far from rustic. Although Tyler uses cuts unloved by many chefs, in his hands they are transformed into something elegant.

Richard approves. With the Thickitt family being Tyler's landlord as well as his butcher, there's a close relationship, and Richard is convinced that Tyler's business could help revitalise the old market town: "There's a lot of people in and around Halesworth and at the moment I don't think people are using the town as much as they perhaps could. Places like this [The Boarding House], they're going to bring people into the town and hopefully everything else should be able to feed off it."

For Tyler, who headed up kitchens at The Crown in Southwold and then The Brudenell Hotel in Aldeburgh before embarking on his first solo venture, the network of local suppliers that he has nurtured over the years is crucial. "What I love about Suffolk is the community. I know the people that my daughters go to school with. I know who's growing my vegetables. I know Charlie who comes with my little leaves. I'm so grateful to our staff for their help and support. The connection to the land, to the community, being part of that is where you make your life. And being mindful of what is in front of you and finding happiness in that is probably one of my biggest influences in cooking."

SUFFOLK FEAST

THE BOARDING HOUSE DINING ROOMS TYLER TORRANCE

Blythburgh pork selection

From snout to tail, the noble pig offers a tasty array of superb cuts. This recipe celebrates just a few. Nothing gives me more pleasure than showcasing Suffolk's outstanding free range pork and for me the Butlers' Blythburgh meat is simply the best. The robust flavour of the slow-cooked collar contrasts with the lighter pork loin and the spicy, crisp black pudding fritters. As pictured, I serve this with burnt onion purée, roasted roots, wilted cavolo nero and a pork jus made from the roasting juices of the pancetta-wrapped loin and some of the braising liquor from the collar (save the remainder as a fantastic base for another dish).

Ideally, roast the loin to serve after it has rested, rather than reheating. Remember to remove the bonbons and the collar from the fridge 45 minutes before they are required to bring to room temperature before finishing. (serves 4)

Pork collar
- 1 pork collar joint
- 2 medium onions, diced
- 2 carrots, diced
- 1 head of garlic
- 5 sprigs of thyme
- 5 star anise
- 1.5 litres light chicken stock, simmering
- 1 tbsp Chinese five-spice

Pre-heat the oven to 160c. Place the collar of pork in a covered hobproof dish with all the ingredients except the five-spice and reserving a little of the stock. Ensure the collar is fully submerged. Bring to a simmer and transfer to the oven to braise for about 3 hours until the meat is tender and flaking. Remove the collar from the liquor. Once cool enough to handle, flake off the meat, including some of the soft fat for succulence. Fold in the reserved stock, the five-spice and seasoning to taste. Press into a mould and cool before refrigerating to set. When cold, cut the terrine into portions.

Black pudding bonbons
- 1 good quality black pudding ring
- Seasoned flour
- Beaten egg
- Panko bread crumbs

Remove the casing from the black pudding and mould the mixture into bite-size balls. Prepare separate bowls of the flour, egg and crumbs and dip the balls into each in turn, shaking off any excess at each stage, and pressing the crumbs on firmly. Transfer to a tray and refrigerate.

Pork loin
- 500g thinly sliced pancetta
- 1kg eye of pork loin

Lay the pancetta onto a rectangle of cling film sheets to give enough coverage to fully wrap the loin. Season, then wrap the pork in the pancetta, rolling firmly and using more cling film if necessary to seal it tightly. Refrigerate until fully chilled.

Pre-heat the oven to 180c. Heat an oiled frying pan over a high hob, unwrap the pork and brown on all sides carefully. Bake in the oven to finish roasting. This will not take long. Keep monitoring after 20 minutes, returning for another 5-10 minutes and checking again, until it is cooked as you like it (I tend to keep it a little pink inside). Remove the loin to somewhere hot to rest under loose foil for 15-20 minutes. This keeps it perfectly juicy.

To serve
- Oil and butter

You will need to pan-fry the collar portions, deep fry the bonbons and carve the loin simultaneously.

Heat your deep fryer to 180c. Pan-fry the collar portions in a little hot oil and foaming butter until golden-brown on both sides and heated through. Deep-fry the bonbons until golden, drain and then transfer to kitchen paper and season. Thickly carve the loin. Arrange all three piggy delights attractively onto warmed plates.

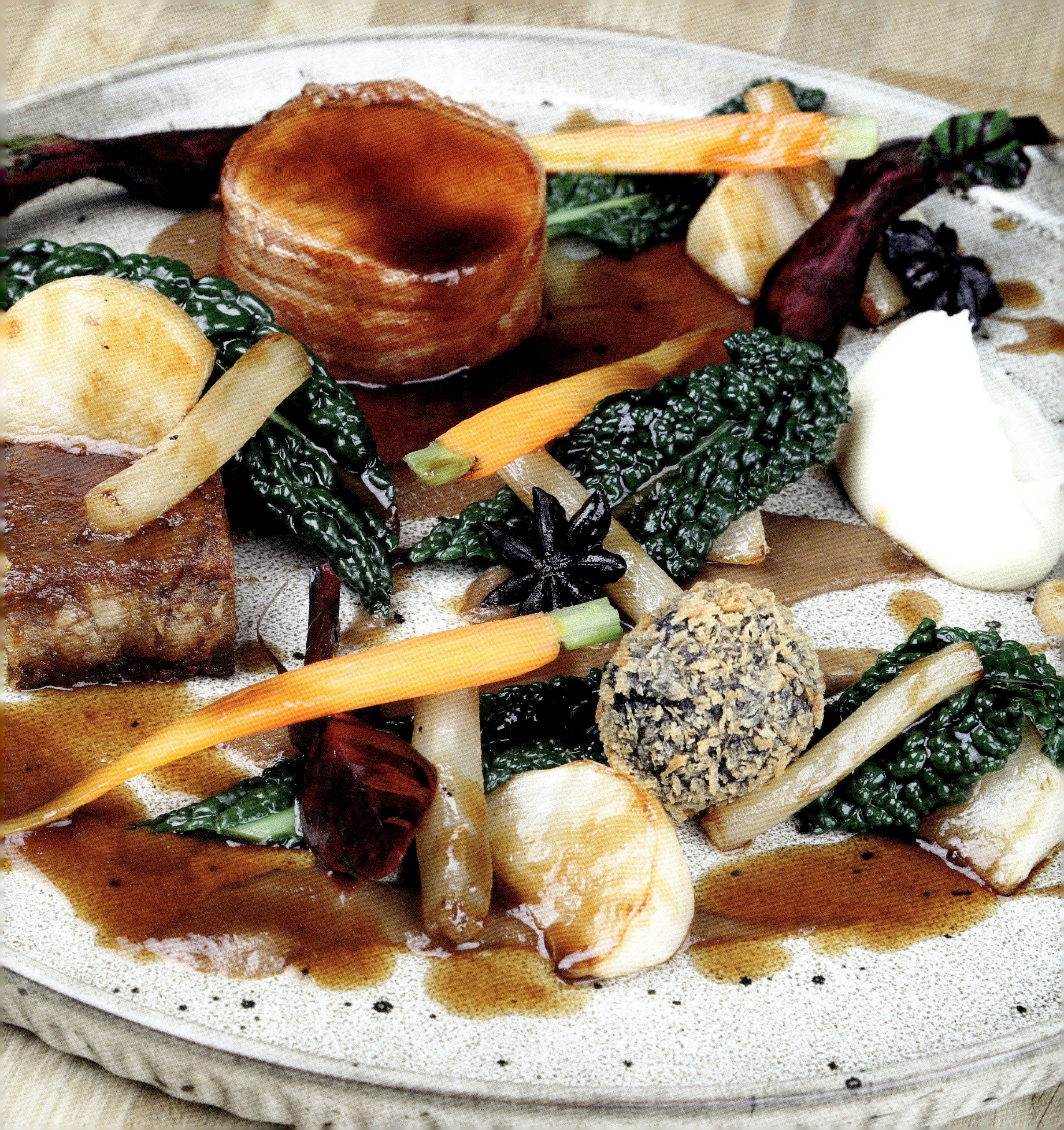

THE BOARDING HOUSE DINING ROOMS TYLER TORRANCE

Smoked haddock crumble, foraged samphire and tiger prawns

The sauce in this versatile dish is based on a classic nage, a reduction of white wine, water, and aromatics – here I use fennel, lemongrass and turmeric – finished with a little cream. It's a light, fragrant sauce that works perfectly with all seafood. Use any sea greens instead of samphire, and local crab or lobster instead of the prawns if you wish. (serves 4)

2 large handfuls of samphire
1 large handful of raw tiger prawns
100g plain flour
50g unsalted butter
25g caster sugar
1 tbsp thyme leaves
100g panko bread crumbs
750ml approx. of hot nage
4 good portions of smoked haddock

Pre-heat the oven to 180c. Blanch the samphire and prawns until just cooked in boiling water. Drain and keep warm.

Make a crumble by processing the flour, butter and sugar together with generous pepper and a little salt into a fine crumb. Fold through the thyme and panko crumbs before setting aside. Cut the fish into chunks and poach in the gently simmering nage until flaking. Place the haddock in a gratin dish, cover with a good layer of the crumble and bake for a few minutes till golden. Serve on hot plates garnished with the prawns and samphire.

Venison scrumpets

This is my very, very favourite recipe for game and works best with a shoulder of delicious venison. Its deep, rich flavour is brought out with slow braising. The crunchy fritters are a great way to convert newcomers to wild game, especially with our red onion and mustard seed relish and dressed watercress. (serves 4)

1 whole shoulder of roe deer
2 onions and 2 carrots, diced
1 head of garlic, halved
5 sprigs of thyme
5 star anise
1 tbsp quatre épices spice blend
1500ml good game stock
Flour, eggs and panko breadcrumbs

Pre-heat the oven to 160c. Braise the venison in a heavy, lidded casserole with the vegetables, garlic, herbs, spices, sea salt and simmering stock (keep a little aside for the next stage) for about 3 hours until tender and flaking.

Remove the shoulder from the braising liquor and flake the meat from the bone into a bowl. Combine with a little stock and seasoning to taste, and press into a terrine mould. Cool and refrigerate.

Once chilled, cut into fingers. Dip alternately into separate bowls of seasoned flour, beaten egg and crumbs. Deep fry in hot oil until golden, before draining and transferring to kitchen paper. Serve sprinkled with a little salt.

Lemon curd

Every chef has a few go-to recipes and here is one of my favourites. A perfect palate cleanser, and part of many of my favourite desserts, here our lemon curd joins textures of meringue, crisp pastry, and flavours of raspberry. It's simply delicious! Using agar agar helps it to set lighter than the classic preserve. (serves 4+)

300g sugar
300g squeezed lemon juice
5g agar agar
300g eggs, beaten
300g butter

Melt the sugar and juice in a pan and bring to a simmer. Whisk in the agar agar and boil for 2 minutes. Add the egg, whisk again and bring back to a simmer, whilst stirring. Take off the heat and whisk in the butter until melted and incorporated.

Process in a blender for several minutes and sieve into a container. Once cooled, beat thoroughly in a food mixer. Sieve again before chilling.

TYLER ON HIS...

HOW DID YOU CELEBRATE YOUR LAST BIRTHDAY?
A few friends, a nice meal, a little bit of whisky and a damn good cigar.

FAVOURITE TIME OF THE YEAR FOR FOOD?
I love autumn but each season has its strengths, its showcase, its moment. I enjoy seasonality. The first glimmer of rhubarb in January, the perfect summer strawberry, foraging for berries with the girls in autumn.

GUILTY FOOD PLEASURE?
Noodles, noodles all the way. Any type: fried, noodles in broth, sometimes even at midnight, the quick ones that you're never supposed to eat! As long as they're spicy.

PERFECT DAY OFF?
A quiet day at home, me, Pauline and the girls. A lazy breakfast, nice cup of coffee, just a nice home day. Building a business it's very easy to work seven days a week, so yeah, the opportunity to have a day at home with my girls, to have one-on-one time with them.

LAST THING TO GIVE YOU A BELLY LAUGH?
My kids make me laugh on a daily basis. It's like being surrounded by squirrels.

HOW FAR FROM YOUR BIRTHPLACE DO YOU LIVE NOW?
I couldn't tell you, it's the other side of the world. Let's look at Google maps. It's 3,644 miles.

CHEF'S TIP?
Sharpen your damn knife! If you're working with a dull knife you're wrecking your food.

FAVOURITE BIT OF KITCHEN EQUIPMENT?
Refer to previous question! My knives are all called Lucille, you've got to treat them like a lady. I love knives and fire.

RESTAURANT BUCKET LIST?
I've always wanted to visit Hong Kong. But I would probably take a simple meal in Bora Bora. I like the idea of a coconut on a white sand beach. Nothing complicated, just my family, peaceful, calm … is it a meal? No, it's an experience. Everything is perfect when you've got the right people around you.

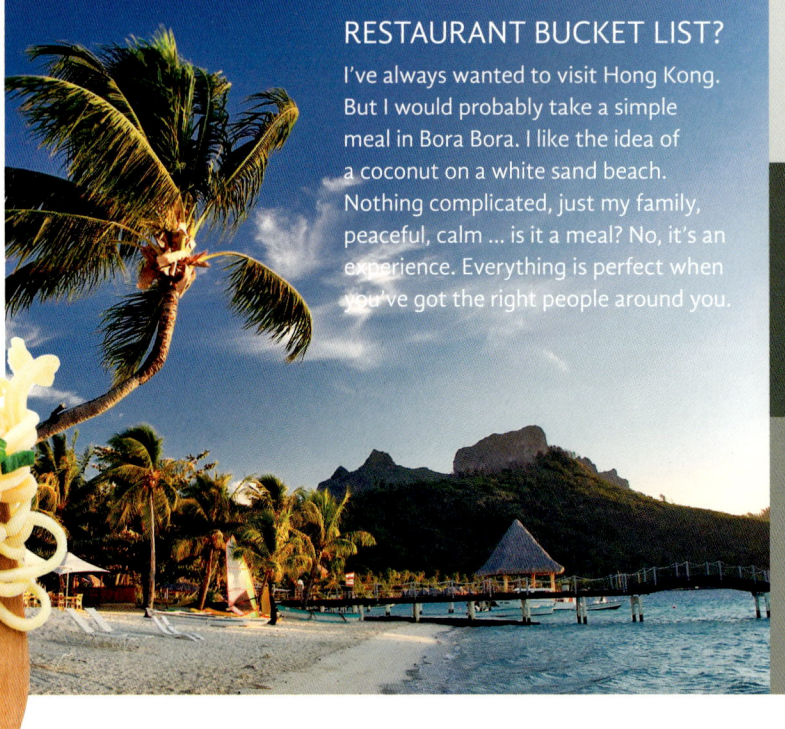

SIGNATURE DISHES

Starters
Whipped goats' cheese, roasted beetroot, fine beans, beetroot & horseradish salsa

Local wood pigeon, Anya potato, broccoli, bacon

Tiger prawn & Suffolk cod gratin, lemongrass cream, lime

Mains
Emmerdale Farm sirloin and ox cheek, beetroot & potato presse, kale, turnip, braising jus

Sea trout fillet, brown shrimp, purple sprouting broccoli, cucumber pickle, wasabi

Local guinea fowl, butternut squash, cavolo nero, hazelnut, butternut squash jam

Puddings
Blackberry bavarois, meringue, candied beetroot, blackberry sorbet

Apricot & saffron tarte tatin, sweet potato & crème fraîche ice cream

Chocolate & peanut butter delice, bacon & caramel ice cream

KITCHEN PLAYLIST?
I always tend to play punk rock, everything from The Ramones to modern punk, classic punk, pop punk. If it's loud and raunchy I'm usually quite happy.

SPECIAL CHILDHOOD MEMORY?
[long pause] Meh. I think I was hatched.

A grand design

The Boarding House is an imposing building, its elegant proportions and large windows commanding a prime position on Halesworth's Market Place. Its history is a bit of a mystery but it's thought it was built in the 17th century as a commercial building, with shops on the ground floor and meeting rooms above.

It was turned into a residential property in Georgian times, but when Tyler and his wife Pauline took over, it had been a tea room with a vintage shop upstairs. They fell in love with the place, took over the lease, gave it a lick of paint and opened two weeks later, in July 2016.

They have gone on to renovate the dining rooms and have planning permission to turn the upstairs, bit by bit, into seven bedrooms as part of a five-year plan. "We didn't want just any business, we wanted something that felt right to us," says Pauline. Tyler adds: "It's a bigger project than I ever thought we'd do for our first restaurant. But we've gone from strength to strength, growing the only way you can in Suffolk, through word of mouth."

The couple run supper clubs, they display local artists' work, and are keen for The Boarding House to be a relaxed place for socialising. "Our idea of a restaurant is for everyone to have good food and for it to be accessible to everyone. People can come for anything from coffee and a cake to a three-course meal, a bespoke menu or just for a cocktail. We want to keep it local, keep it fun."

The Boarding House Dining Rooms
10 Market Place, Halesworth IP19 8BA
W: boardinghousehalesworth.com
T: 01986 948306
E: tyler@boardinghousehalesworth.com
- /boardinghousehalesworth
- @BHHalesworth
- /boardinghousediningrooms

Food served: Wed-Sat B 10-12; L 12-3 (12-2 Sun, plus all-day B); D 6-9.30. Please check website for updates

Cost: starters from £6; mains from £13; desserts from £6; set lunch £16 (two courses), £21 (three courses); brunch from £3.50; Sunday lunch (pre-booked) £16; wine from £19.50; pint from £4.70

Details: 45 seats in restaurant, 30 in garden; children's menu; monthly supper club; special event dining; art exhibitions; accessible; pets welcome; public parking

Alan's apples

With Boxford Farm on his doorstep, Alan Paton buys the freshest fruit grown just a shout from his busy kitchen

LAKES RESTAURANT, STOKE BY NAYLAND HOTEL, GOLF & SPA
ALAN PATON

STOKE BY NAYLAND HOTEL, GOLF & SPA ALAN PATON

There's something powerfully promising about the turn of the year in an orchard. The trees at Boxford Farm – rows of apples, cherries, plums – are yet to be clothed in their prettiest springtime garb of feathery blossom, pink-white petals and fresh green leaves, but with the tight-shut buds waiting to open, the hints of that season are there.

Farm manager Robert England enjoys this anticipation; he just needs the dormancy to continue for a little longer, and for spring to coax the trees from their slumber with gradual, rather than too-sudden, warmth. He crunches into a Royal Gala, as bright and crisp-flavoured as if it had been picked yesterday, throws one to his boss Robert Rendall, and another to Alan Paton. The trio talk fruit, flavour, farm practice and future plans.

We head back to The Stoke by Nayland Hotel, and the kitchen which Alan has run as executive head chef for the past nine years. It is moments from Boxford Farm, and with both hotel and farm owned by the same family – Robert Rendall, who runs the farming enterprise, is the grandson of founders Bill and Devora Peake – there's an easy, deep connection between chef and producer.

Apples (40 varieties are grown and stored at the farm, including several heritage types grown here by the Peake family since 1938), berries, rhubarb, asparagus, Morello cherries and plums all find their way from orchard to prep board to be used fresh in season, or preserved, pickled, chutney'd or jammed. "For a chef it's incredible to have this on the doorstep," says Alan. "I'm lucky, and we'd be mad not to take full advantage of it on our menu."

So he does just that. Asparagus is celebrated during its too-brief season steamed and served with an apple consommé and Café de Paris butter, or wrapped with smoked bacon and served with parmesan 'cream egg'; slivers of strawberries might be set around a white chocolate cup filled with icing sugar-coated berries, strawberry sorbet and a korma yoghurt ice that cuts smartly through the fruit-chocolate combination. Raspberries create pretty-as-you-like pictures with an airy mousse and crisp puffed tapioca sprinkled with sharp powdered raspberry, and rhubarb, cherries and berries will be used fresh or in sauces, ketchups and marinades for savoury dishes.

But today is about Boxford Farm apples, and in particular Alan's take on apple crumble. He talks as he preps the dish, sharing colourful stories of years in kitchens. There was an inevitability in his métier, coming as he does from a family of chefs and hoteliers, and his career has taken him from his native Scotland to hotels in London, Jersey, Dublin and Suffolk via stints on Cunard liners and time on a South African game reserve. Alan's anecdotes flow in between instructions to his two sous chefs, but he focuses as he plates up. He spoons appley, brandy-fragrant caramel over a peeled, halved and scooped-out Royal Gala that has been dried in a low oven, placing the apple on a pile of spiced oats ("lots of crunch, and I am Scottish after all!"), and filling the centre with an Aspall cyder crème anglaise, cubes of fresh apple, curls of green apple-infused chocolate. He puts the apple lid on, adds a little more custard, apple cubes and a scattering of the chocolate, and the pretty plate is done.

Pastry is not Alan's natural habitat, however. He'd far rather leave sweet intricacies to his fiancée, Layla, who works with him on menu development as well as being a talented ("I'm a little OCD") pastry chef – and be given a joint of pork. "There's nothing you can't do with pork. It's the most versatile meat. I love it." It'll appear perhaps as a charcuterie platter on the Lounge menu, as smoked belly in a hearty white bean soup with chorizo and lardo, or as pork butt braised slowly with Aspall cyder. A 'surf n turf' dish has been popular, meaty pan-fried cod cheeks served alongside the caramelised ones of a pig, truffle cream, beluga lentils, pancetta and onions, and his homemade black pudding, rich with Persian spices. The pudding is made to a recipe that Alan will divulge to nobody. "It's written down in a folder... but only I know where that folder is," he says conspiratorially.

When the demands of a full-service hotel allow, Alan jumps at the chance to mentor young chefs like apprentice Ashleigh Shephard who was one of 12 finalists in the nationwide 2016 FutureChef competition. He supports other industry charities, and is an active member of the Craft Guild of Chefs and Master Chefs of Great Britain. But for all that, Alan's focus remains the hotel and his (in an ideal world) 20-strong brigade. He is hungry to push the menu at the main Lakes Restaurant still further from the 'melon and parma ham' offer that greeted him nine years ago. "We will always sell huge amounts of steak, and chicken liver parfait will never come off the menu, but there's potential to offer something different too," he says. "I'd like the Lakes to become a destination restaurant, I'd like to develop a range of chutneys and pickles to sell in Pippin [the hotel's gift, produce and leisurewear shop], and I'm working with Layla to create some fantastic new breads such as a sourdough loaf with fermented apple." Ideas? Drive? There's plenty of both in this kitchen.

SUFFOLK FEAST

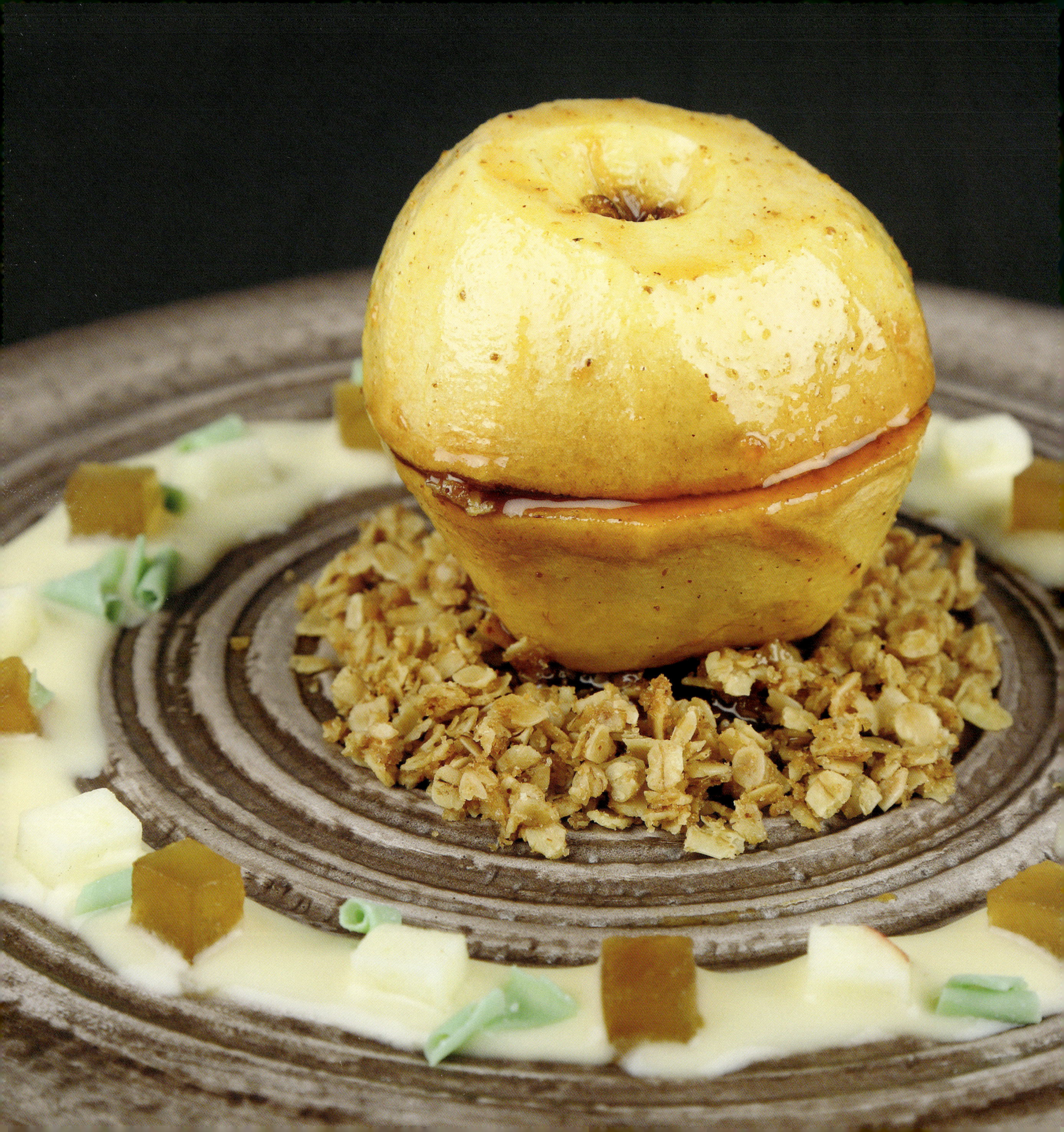

STOKE BY NAYLAND HOTEL, GOLF & SPA ALAN PATON

Apple crumble and custard

The third generation of the family behind the Stoke by Nayland Hotel, Golf & Spa runs Peake Fruit, a business the family created from their farming estate. We of course use the farm for our fabulous apples, strawberries, raspberries, blueberries, morello cherries, rhubarb and asparagus, clocking up some seriously low food miles! We have access to many great apple varieties, and picked from so close to the kitchen, that's fantastic for a chef! In this take on apple crumble, we finish the dish with curls of apple-infused chocolate. (serves 4)

Baked apples

- **4 Royal Gala apples or Braeburn apples**
- **Ground cinnamon**

Pre-heat the oven to 100c. Peel the apple, cut in half horizontally and remove the core with melon baller. Rub the insides with ground cinnamon. Place in a shallow roasting tin and bake for 1 hour to dry. Remove and set aside.

Apple syrup

- **700ml apple juice**
- **4 tbsp good brandy**

Boil the apple juice, reduce by half and add the brandy before setting aside.

Cyder anglaise

- **4 egg yolks**
- **50g caster sugar**
- **120ml double cream**
- **120ml dry cyder**
- **1 tsp vanilla paste**

Whisk the yolks and sugar until pale and creamy. Heat the cream, cyder and vanilla until near boiling then cool to 80c. Slowly whisk the cream mixture into the yolks until all incorporated. Return mixture to the pan and cook over a medium heat until sufficiently thick to coat the back of a spoon. Remove from the heat and stir for 3 minutes to cool. Refrigerate until required.

Oat crumble

- **½ teaspoon of mixed spice**
- **Small pinch ground cinnamon**
- **Small pinch allspice**
- **150g rolled oats**
- **70g rapeseed oil**
- **70g light brown sugar**
- **Pinch of salt**

Pre-heat the oven to 160c. Cook the spices over a medium heat in a dry pan for 1 minute. Allow to cool. Mix well with the remaining ingredients and lay out on a shallow roasting tin, lined with parchment. Bake for about 10 minutes until light-golden. Set aside.

Apple cubes

- **1 Braeburn apple, peeled and cored**
- **100ml apple juice**

Cut the apple into small cubes and stir into the apple juice before refrigerating.

To finish

- **125g unsalted butter, softened**

Poach the apple halves in the apple syrup over a low-medium heat, gently stirring in the butter and basting the fruit. Once cooked through, remove from the heat and keep the apples and sauce hot.

Dress warmed plates with the oats and the anglaise. Top with the bottom halves of the apples, pour some anglaise in the well, top with more oats and the apple cubes, and put the top halves in place. Finish the plate with more apple cubes and the syrup.

STOKE BY NAYLAND HOTEL, GOLF & SPA ALAN PATON

Celeriac and apple

This dish was created firstly out of my love for celeriac and secondly as a great option for diners that do not perhaps eat meat, dairy or gluten. We add to the interest with juniper salt and candied walnuts. (serves 6)

    1 medium sized celeriac, peeled
    1 small bay leaf
    Light vegetable stock
    2 Royal Gala apples, cored
    50ml apple juice
    50g caster sugar
    ½ tsp ground ginger
    1 Cox apple, peeled and cored

Cut 6 discs, 5cm wide and 2cm deep from the celeriac (keeping the off-cuts) and lay out in a snug, deep roasting tray. Add the bay leaf and a shallow layer of stock before covering with parchment and foil. Bake for about 20 minutes until tender.

Roughly chop the remainder of the celeriac and simmer with stock and a pinch of salt until tender. Drain, reserving the liquor and process the flesh to a smooth, thick purée (adding the liquor if needed). Season to taste, sieve and set aside.

Cut one Royal Gala apple into segments and the other into small dice. Heat the juice, sugar and ginger together until melted. Remove from the heat and stir in the segments. Allow to cool then add the dice. Chop up the Cox apple and cook with a little water until soft before sieving into a purée. Spoon the celeriac purée onto hot plates, top with the discs and apple shapes, before spooning the apple purée around.

Spiced pigs' cheeks, black pudding and spinach

A hearty starter that combines some of my favourite piggy delights. It is pictured here with citrus purée, spiced pomegranate yoghurt, crisp onion, apple, spiced pancetta and kale sprigs. (serves 4)

    4 pigs' cheeks, trimmed
    80g butter
    1 carrot, shallot and celery stick, cut into ½cm dice
    1 cinnamon stick
    ½ tbsp tomato purée
    1 tsp ras el hanout
    400ml pork stock
    100g washed baby spinach
    200ml double cream
    Black pudding in ½cm discs

Seal the cheeks in foaming butter until golden. Remove and add the vegetables and cinnamon and stir-fry until dark gold. Stir in the purée and ras el hanout, then cook for 2 minutes. Return the cheeks along with the stock to the pan. Simmer gently for about 2 hours until tender. Remove from the heat, cool and refrigerate together till ready to serve. Remove the cheeks from the stock. Boil the stock to reduce by half. Sieve. Wilt the spinach in a little water. Drain, cool and liquidise with the cream and seasoning to taste. Keep warm.

Reheat the cheeks gently in the liquor. Reduce the liquor to a sauce. Grill or fry the black pudding until crisp. Spoon the spinach onto hot plates before adding the black pudding and pigs' cheeks.

Strawberries and cream

First created for a special dinner with Hardeep Singh Kohli, the broadcaster, this dessert uses spices, chocolate and strawberries, an unusual but great combination. We accompany the dish with a strawberry sorbet and korma ice cream. You will need to buy or make 4 white chocolate cups (shape them by pouring melted chocolate over a small, upturned, clingfilmed bowl and refrigerating). (serves 4)

500g strawberries, hulled
50g icing sugar
3 spiced chai teabags
1 tbsp caster sugar
32 large strawberries, hulled
250ml double cream in soft peaks
4 white chocolate cups
Ice cream and sorbet to serve
Dried strawberries and baby mint

Cook the strawberries with the icing sugar to a purée, sieve and chill. Simmer the teabags with 100ml hot water for a few minutes, squeeze out and discard the bags. Add the sugar to the tea and boil until reduced to a syrup. Cool and chill. Slice 4 strawberries thinly lengthways and cut the remainder into halves and quarters. Add 4 tbsp of the purée into the cream and beat until stiff. Build small circles of the sliced strawberries on cold plates and fill the centre with purée. Place a chocolate cup on top and add strawberry pieces as a bed for a neat scoop of sorbet and ice cream. Decorate the plate with more purée, cream, dried strawberries and mint.

ALAN ON HIS...

LAST BELLY LAUGH?
I love driving and some of the less dangerous antics you see on the road every day can raise an incredulous laugh. Watching Billy Connolly does it for me too.

FAVOURITE LOCAL PLACES TO EAT OUT?
I love my local, The Hare and Hounds run by Chantal and Will Raymond – great food and drink – and I recently ate at The Angel, Bury St Edmunds which was fantastic. I also love Chris Lee's cooking at The Bildeston Crown. We don't go there enough!

PERFECT DAY OFF?
I would go to the west of Ireland for breakfast, then to the French Laundry in the Napa Valley for lunch, Vienna for afternoon tea, then to Massimo Bottura's restaurant Osteria Francescana in Modena for dinner, finishing in Japan with sushi and sake. I would be with Layla, and it would be a perfect day off together.

'TAKE FIVE' RECIPE?
Coat some monkfish pieces in panko, fry off some smoked bacon, butter some fantastic bread, deep fry the monkfish, chop some gem lettuce, fill the sandwich and finish with some sriracha sauce. Perfect!

WHAT GETS YOU UP IN THE MORNING?
Paying the bills and school runs.

HOW FAR FROM YOUR BIRTHPLACE DO YOU NOW LIVE?
410 miles. I was born in Paisley, Scotland.

WHAT IS YOUR NICKNAME?
When I worked at the Turnberry Hotel one of the sous chefs nicknamed me Satan. I never ever did find out why...

IF NOT A CHEF WHAT WOULD YOU HAVE BEEN?
Ah, that's easy – either an air traffic controller, an undercover customs and excise detective, or James Bond.

SIGNATURE DISHES

Starters

Goats' cheese with beetroot and bran, baked onion purée, Aspall cyder, cheese & onion 'crisps'

Treacle-cured pollock, lemon, ginger, pumpkin seed, pomegranate

Norfolk quail, charred spring onion, red mojo sauce, caramelised pineapple, pine nuts

Mains

Pork belly, fillet, osso buco of shin, glazed cheek, sauerkraut, apples, beetroot, pork quaver, lardo

Seared monkfish, bacon hummus, heritage potato, romanesco, blackberry, beetroot, Moroccan red onion relish

Spinach gnocchi, king oyster mushroom, truffled egg yolk, wild mushroom broth, piccolo parsnips, pickled girolles, black garlic

Puddings

Bread & butter pudding, blue cheese & white chocolate ice cream, raisin compote

Boxford Farm raspberry gluten-free sponge, raspberry gin tea, rosemary sugar, lime jam, whipped raspberry cream

Warm dark chocolate mousse, parfait, mint yogurt, cocoa crunch, chocolate cookie crumble

WHAT IS YOUR BIGGEST EXTRAVAGANCE AS A CHEF?
Butter! And pastry chef ingredient requests. Our new development chef has an unending list of requirements!

Pretty as a picture

If ever 'rolling' were to be the apt descriptor for a location, it's here. Everything in this gorgeous corner of Constable Country rolls and undulates, from the gently wooded golf-course landscape with its slopes and gullies that dip into streams, ponds and lakes, to the gliding service of food from kitchen to restaurant table. It all rolls smoothly.

Maybe that's partly because this is a business in which the family owners remain hands-on; four of founder Devora and Bill Peake's five children are directors in the business with the third generation represented by Robert Rendall who runs Peake Fruit and Boxford Farm. It was the Peake's vision, and risk-taking, that led to their original 120 acre fruit farm from the 1940s being expanded into the collection of businesses it is today: fruit growing, storage and processing (this is the family behind the Copella brand of farm-pressed juice, now owned by Tropicana UK), and the hotel, golf club, spa and conference centre.

Robert's grandparents would no doubt be glad to see that their vision is being pushed forward even now, with plans in the pipeline to expand the spa and build another nine holes for the golfers to enjoy. For the time being, though, the Lakes Restaurant remains a spacious room in which to enjoy Alan's menu of contemporary food mixed with old favourites. Tables are bare, set without pomp and ceremony, and the vast windows make the most of the stunning views.

Stoke by Nayland Hotel, Golf & Spa
Keepers Lane, Leavenheath, Colchester C06 4PZ
W: stokebynayland.com
T: 01206 262836
E: sales@stokebynayland.com
/SbNHotel   @StokebyNaylandH
/stoke-by-nayland-hotel-golf-spa

Accolades and listings: AA Two Rosettes; winner, Young Restaurant Team of the Year 2014; AA Four Stars; winner, Best Hotel and Best Business Tourism Venue, Essex Tourism & Hospitality Awards 2015; silver award, Best Business Tourism Venue, VisitEngland Awards 2016; Sustainable Tourism, Visit Suffolk Greenest County Awards 2016

Food served: all week B 7-10 (7.30-10.30 Sat, Sun); Mon-Sat L 12-2, Sun 12.30-4 (buffet); D 6.30-10

Cost: starters from £7.25; mains from £14.75; desserts from £5.95; afternoon tea £17.95; Mon-Sat (buffet) L £9.95 (main course); Sun L £12.50 (one course) - £19.50 (three courses); wine from £18.95; pint from £3.50

Details: 120 seats (Lakes Restaurant); 80 seat (Gallery Restaurant for buffet lunch); all-day lounge menu; al fresco tables; banqueting for up to 450; private dining; 80 bedrooms; 5 self-catering Country Lodges; spa and gym; two championship golf courses; accessible; parking

Herd instinct

Oli Burnside only had to look at the Kenton Hall cattle to know that English Longhorn beef would be perfect for his pub menu

THE PLOUGH & SAIL, SNAPE
OLI BURNSIDE

THE FOOD HUB

Everyone must ask the same question of twin brothers Oli and Alex Burnside: who is older? Alex patiently replies that Oli is 13 minutes older, and yes he does try to pull rank sometimes. But they appear to work together seamlessly at the Plough & Sail at Snape, Oli leading his team of six chefs, and concentrating on producing thoroughly good food, and Alex, with his front of house experience, making sure everything runs like clockwork. Both brothers are quietly spoken, exuding competence and capability, and together they have created a pub with a deserved reputation.

Oli is content that most of the menu uses ingredients from nearby suppliers, and that it is necessarily seasonal. He enjoys being flexible and creative with his cooking, drawing on his experience to push the boundaries of traditional style, but his guiding philosophy is very simple: "I cook what I like, the sort of food I want to eat. I alter and adjust recipes as I go along to use what's available and to get the best taste and combinations of flavours. Pastries of course have to follow strict recipes, but the starters and main courses can be much less rigid and more adventurous." One of his accompaniments today is gnocchi made with the wild garlic that grows abundantly in the area, but he chooses to make them in less conventional sausage shapes before pan-frying them and plating them as neatly angled columns. The asparagus is a regional speciality too of course, the county's fields in spring bristling with fresh green spears.

As Oli carefully arranges the components of his main dish – English Longhorn beef fillet and bonbons – he enthuses about the meat. "Just look at the structure," he says, pointing out the delicate veins of fat. "I see that, and I just know it will be tender and taste delicious. The little bonbons are simply balls of pulled beef, crumbed and pan-fried to give another dimension.

"I first came across Kenton Hall beef here at Snape Farmers' Market, and I recognised instantly how good it is. Sunday lunches are always very popular here – people come from miles around – and traditional roast beef is a favourite. I get well-aged forerib or a prime sirloin from Kenton Hall, because the meat is the main event after all, and you have to get it right. You only have to see the cows on the farm and in the fields, and the way they are treated to understand why it's in such huge demand."

Down at the farm, Lucy McVeigh is a somewhat unlikely stock-person. Young and slight she certainly doesn't conform to the stereotype, but watch her with her pedigree herd of English Longhorn cattle, and it's obvious she is a natural. Talking nineteen to the dozen about the finer points of raising beef, Lucy's knowledge is impressive and

THE PLOUGH & SAIL OLI BURNSIDE

riveting. She casually jumps into a pen with a group of three-year olds. Most store cattle have an on-hoof weight of about 700kg, which is a lot of cow to get pushed by; add in the dramatic horns and it's even more important to know how to handle the livestock and pre-empt any skittishness. In their custom-built cartwheel pen — designed by Lucy's engineer father, David — the cattle rustle about in deep straw, each section holding different groups divided according to age or gender.

Lucy points out individual cows. "They all have names," she says, patting Esme on the back, "because it's the way we know which animal we're talking about. We could use their numbers but they're about sixteen digits long!" Esme's horns are spectacularly long, sticking way out at each side of her head. "They look impressive," says Lucy, "but they make it hard to get her in or out of confined spaces." In another pen, the family favourite, Fleur ("we've had so many marvellous calves from her") is eleven years old and is kept now more or less as a pet.

Separately, the vast, muscular bull, Tetford Top Gun, stomps around in the straw, keeping a wary eye on the unusual goings-on. Known around the farm as Charlie, this five-year-old beast has sired more than 20 calves, passing on the pedigree of the breed. "We're certified and have got protected status now," Lucy says, justifiably proud, "which means that only genuine pedigree English Longhorn cattle can claim the name, and no-one can try to pass off inferior beef. We raise our beef for over 30 months, and feed them properly — muesli and molasses for breakfast and home-grown grain — then from spring they graze in the fields."

Away from the pens a walk-in fridge holds several carcasses, each weighing about 360kg. Lucy explains how foreribs are the constant best-sellers, followed by sirloins, then fillets, shin and other cuts, all with the same full flavour and tenderness. It's these attributes, coupled with impeccable husbandry, which convinced the Burnsides to buy from Kenton Hall. Their customers just know they're getting some of the tastiest beef in Suffolk.

THE PLOUGH & SAIL OLI BURNSIDE

Fillet of Longhorn beef, crispy bonbon, asparagus and wild garlic gnocchi

This is an elegant dinner party main course, a real showcase for well-bred, well-fed local beef and worth the extra effort to do justice to its rich, luxurious flavour. Fresh wild garlic from the woods, local asparagus and good horseradish sauce give the dish a zingy finish. Squash purée makes a colourful addition. (serves 6)

Shin bonbons
- 800g sliced, boneless shin of beef
- 750ml good red wine
- 2 tbsp horseradish sauce
- 100g plain flour
- 4 eggs
- 100g panko breadcrumbs

The day before, season and sear the shin of beef until browned well on both sides. Decant to a deep roasting tin, cover with the red wine and slowly braise in a 150c oven for 4 hours. Remove the shin with a fish slice and allow to cool. Cool and refrigerate the red wine liquor overnight.

Flake the beef and mix with the horseradish and seasoning to taste. Roll the beef into 18 balls, approximately walnut sized. Allow to set in the fridge. Set up separate bowls of the flour, whisked egg and breadcrumbs.

Roll the bonbons a few at a time in each bowl in turn, allowing any excess flour and then egg to fall off before pressing well into the crumbs. Place them, not touching, on a clingfilmed tray and refrigerate.

Red wine sauce
- 2kg beef bones
- 250g redcurrant jelly

Roast the beef bones for 40 minutes at 180c. Transfer the bones to a stockpot, cover with boiling water and simmer for 10 hours, skimming off any impurities. Cool, sieve and chill overnight. The next morning, remove any surface fat, add the reserved red wine liquor and redcurrant jelly, bring to the boil and reduce to a sauce consistency. Cool and sieve through muslin before setting aside.

Gnocchi
- 100g wild garlic leaves, washed
- Rapeseed oil
- 5 large Maris Piper potatoes (we need 500g once cooked)
- 170g plain flour
- 1 egg
- Plain flour to dust

Blanch the wild garlic in boiling water for 10 seconds and plunge into iced water. Drain and dry before liquidising with a drizzle of oil into a purée. Bake the potatoes for 40 minutes or until tender. Cut in half and scrape the insides before pushing through a potato ricer or fine sieve. Mix the flour and egg into the potato, followed by the wild garlic purée. Knead on a dusted board into a dough, adding more flour if too sticky. Roll into six 4cm-wide logs and clingfilm tightly.

Bring a large pan of water to a rolling boil and drop the wrapped gnocchi in one at a time. Cook for 10 minutes until expanded and firm, place into iced water and set aside.

To serve
- 3 x 250g portions of beef fillet, oven-ready
- Butter
- 2 bunches asparagus, trimmed
- Squash purée, warmed

To serve, you need to cook the beef, blanch the asparagus, brown the gnocchi, deep fry the bonbons and simmer the sauce simultaneously.

Pre-heat the oven to 180c. Season and seal the fillet portions on all sides until golden-brown before roasting for 4-6 minutes for medium rare (cook longer if preferred). Rest somewhere warm. Unwrap the gnocchi and pan-fry in melted butter until golden brown on all sides. Deep fry the bonbons at 200c for 4 minutes. Blanch the asparagus in boiling water for 2 minutes and drain. Bring the sauce to a simmer.

Plate up the thickly carved fillet with the bonbons, asparagus, and squash purée, if using. Drizzle with the sauce before serving.

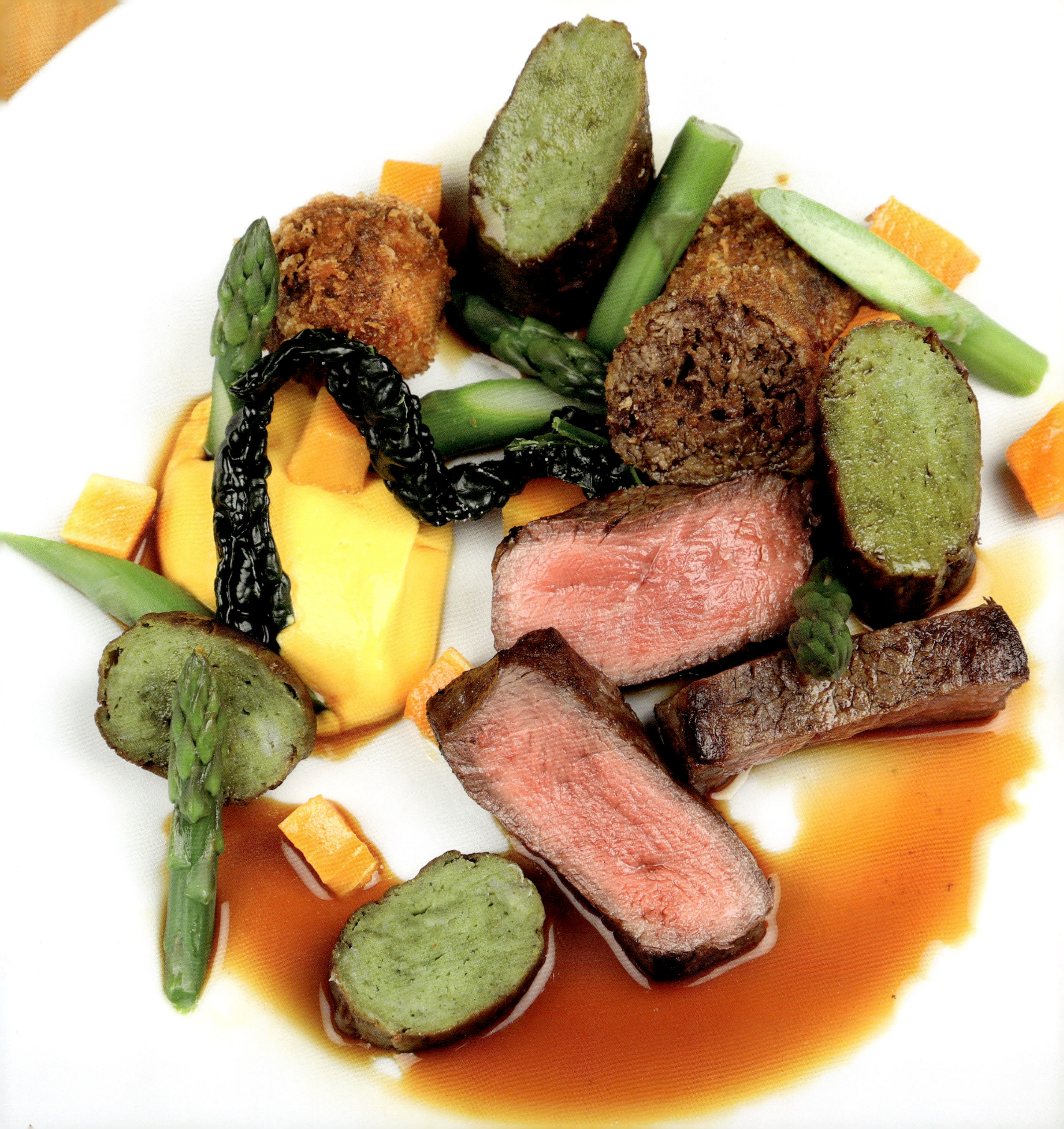

THE PLOUGH & SAIL OLI BURNSIDE

Pan-fried skate wing with prawn and cucumber butter

A light but flavoursome fishy main course, we serve this with sauté new potatoes and wilted baby spinach. (serves 6)

6 medium-sized skate wings
Plain flour
Rapeseed oil
150g unsalted butter
1 small cucumber, deseeded and finely diced
24 raw tiger prawns, shelled
1 handful flat leaf parsley, chopped
6 lemon wedges, to garnish

Preheat the oven to 180c. Shallow-fry the seasoned and floured wings fat-side down in a shallow layer of hot oil and 50g of melted butter until golden. Turn over onto a baking tray and and oven bake for 15 minutes or until flaking.

Meanwhile, melt the remaining butter in the same pan, then fold in the cucumber and prawns. Simmer, bubbling, for one minute until the prawns are cooked. Stir in the parsley and serve alongside the skate wings with the lemon wedges for squeezing.

Sticky chicken wings and blue cheese dip

This simple, tangy starter has zesty creaminess and rich, glazed meat. (serves 6)

60ml dark soy sauce
50ml orange juice
60g clear honey
60g dark brown sugar
2 tsp five-spice powder
2 tbsp sesame oil
2 tbsp tomato ketchup
24 large chicken wings
5 spring onions, finely chopped
75g blue cheese, crumbled
Seeds of 1 pomegranate
100ml crème fraîche
50ml sour cream
Rocket leaves, to garnish

Combine the first 7 ingredients in a large bowl. Add the wings, stir to coat, cover and refrigerate for 24 hours.

Pre-heat the oven to 180c. Season the wings, tip onto a baking tray and cook for an hour, until tender. Remove the wings from the tray to somewhere warm, reduce the sauce to a sticky glaze if needed and adjust the seasoning.

Combine the remaining ingredients, season to taste. Serve the wings and the dip, garnished with the rocket, with the jug of warm glaze.

Vanilla cheesecake and berry compote

I use thick Suffolk cream from Marybelle Dairy for this simply delicious dessert, and serve it with tangy local berries such as strawberries, raspberries and blackberries to cut through the richness. (serves 6+)

75g butter
150g digestive biscuits
415g double cream
2 vanilla pods, split and seeds scraped
5 gelatine leaves, softened
1kg cream cheese
165g caster sugar
3 punnets of berries, hulled
50g caster sugar

Mix the butter and finely crushed biscuits together before pressing into a parchment-lined and buttered 23cm-wide loose-bottomed tin. Chill the base for 1 hour.

Scald 2 tbsp of the cream with the vanilla pod and seeds, take off the heat and whisk in the drained gelatine until dissolved. In a large bowl, mix the cream cheese and 165g of sugar. Beat in the gelatine, vanilla and cream mixture. Separately whisk the remaining cream to soft peaks and fold into the cream cheese. Smooth the mixture over the base. Chill for 12 hours.

Take a quarter of the chopped berries and slowly heat with the 50g of sugar until the fruit starts to break down. Fold through the remaining berries and refrigerate. Serve with the wedges of cheesecake.

OLI ON HIS...

'TAKE FIVE' RECIPE?

Cook some diced pancetta in a small pan. Discard the woody bits of the asparagus, blanch the spears and refresh. Cut some tomatoes into bite-size chunks and warm gently, then pan-fry the scallops. Mix everything together and sprinkle with a reduction made from rapeseed oil and balsamic vinegar. Spoon everything onto a pile of small salad leaves. Apart from the scallops, all these ingredients are local, and this makes a quick and very tasty meal – just don't overcook the scallops!

PERFECT DAY OFF?

With my wife, daughter and son at the beach at Southwold which is just up the road so we don't spend hours in the car. We play games on the sand, have a walk and then early tea somewhere. Nothing fancy, just plain simple fun. Days like that are special. My brother Alex and I are best friends too and our families spend time together whenever we can.

FAVOURITE TIME OF YEAR FOR FOOD?

Spring and early summer when there's lots of wild garlic and new asparagus and other new season vegetables. I love the freshness and sweetness of small new potatoes, beets and carrots just out of the ground. Everything – meat too – seems to have such an intense flavour. I get inspired and I like coming up with new spring recipes using all these ingredients. Another advantage of living in the country is that it's all right here around us.

WHO IS YOUR MENTOR?

Robert Mabey from The Regatta Restaurant in Aldeburgh. He taught me a lot and is still very supportive.

BIGGEST EXTRAVAGANCE AS A CHEF?

Butter. You can't beat the taste of good butter. If you have just-baked bread with a thick layer of lovely yellow butter on it it's one of the simplest and most enjoyable flavour combinations. A bit of butter added to most things gives an extra richness which I love, even if my waistline doesn't!

QUICK SNACK OR MIDNIGHT FEAST?

Peanut butter on toast. We always have some in the kitchen and when I've been cooking all sorts of different things all day it's a bit of a treat to have a simple filling snack.

INSPIRING SUFFOLK VIEW?

The incredible view from Snape Concert Hall over the marshes and reed beds. It's also the view from where I got married.

SIGNATURE DISHES

Starters

Spiced pear salad, Binham Blue, chicory, madeira dressing, sugared walnuts

Mediterranean fish soup, rouille, gruyère, crostini

Pressed ham hock, confit shallots, pea purée, melba toast

Mains

Breast of Gressingham duck, carrot, beetroot, potato fondants, carrot purée, jus

Slow-roast pork belly, cabbage slaw, peanuts, pomegranates, maple & lime leaf dressing

Herb-crusted fillet of cod, shellfish bisque, samphire, herb-crushed new potatoes

Puddings

Lemon cream, white chocolate & raspberry fudge, raspberry sorbet

Strawberry & almond frangipane tart, clotted cream

Dark chocolate mousse, pomegranates, sugared hazelnuts

CHEF'S TIP?

Add lemon to new potatoes when cooking in water. Squeeze the juice into the water, then put the lemon itself into the pan. As the potatoes cook, the lemon keeps them beautifully white. It also adds a citrus note which I really like. Just add butter to serve.

SUFFOLK FEAST

Come dine with us

Thirty-five-year-old twins Oli and Alex Burnside bought the Plough & Sail pub at Snape in 2012, combining their respective experience in hospitality (Oli as Ruth Watson's sous chef at the Crown & Castle, Orford; Alex in the management team at Aldeburgh's Regatta Restaurant) to create their first venture together.

A rambling roadside building at the front of the Snape Maltings venue, the pub needed attention to haul it out of a slightly run-down state into its incarnation as a 'country dining pub'. The Burnsides have created a light, inviting dining space, an adjacent bar area with a homely feel, and a cosy snug with sofas and armchairs arranged around a log fire that crackles all day during winter. A mezzanine level and plenty of outside tables mean that numbers even on the busiest of Sundays can be accommodated.

The pub has been the perfect place for Oli to showcase his non-formulaic cooking style, and Alex to run the business with his trademark easy efficiency. They've no doubt been helped by the pub's location at Snape Maltings with its crowd-pulling shops, cultural activities and monthly farmers' market, not to mention the abundance of local food producers. "We joined the Suffolk Young Producers group, and a lot of them supply us now – the likes of Suffolk Meadow ice cream and The Cake Shop Bakery in Woodbridge."

The brothers took on the more informal Golden Key pub, just 30 seconds' drive away from the Plough & Sail, in 2017. The two properties employ five full-time chefs, plus Oli, and 20 others in front-of-house and management roles.

The Plough & Sail
Snape Maltings, Snape IP17 1SR
W: theploughandsailsnape.com
T: 01728 688413
E: alexburnside@hotmail.com
   /ThePloughAndSail
   @PloughandSail
   /ploughandsailsnape

Accolades and listings: Waitrose *Good Food Guide*; *Harden's*; *Good Pub Guide*

Food served: all week L 12-2.30; D 6-late

Cost: starters from £4; mains from £12; puddings from £5.50; wine from £14.50; pint average £3.80

Details: 80 seats in main restaurant; private dining space for up to 30; al fresco tables; separate light bites and Sunday lunch menu; walks from pub through reed beds; cultural events, markets, festivals and shopping at Snape Maltings; accessible; dogs welcome; parking

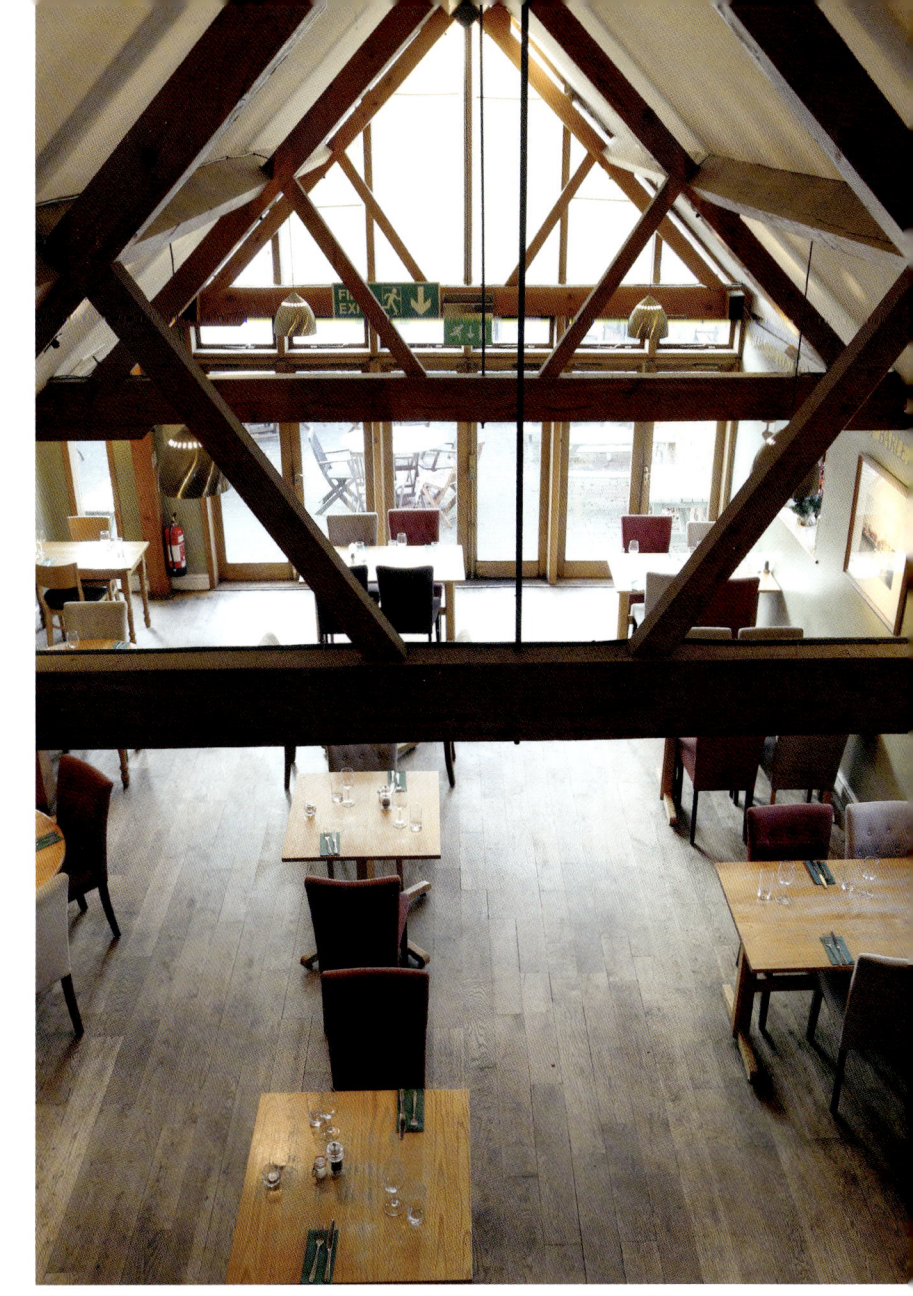

THE WEEPING WILLOW, BARROW
NICK CLAXTON-WEBB

Whatever the feather

Game birds feature in all their guises on Nick Claxton-Webb's menu at this contemporary village pub, but today is all about locally shot pheasant

175

Is it a pub? Is it a restaurant? Owner Peter Romaniuk shrugs, then laughs. "It is whatever guests want it to be," he decides. "Actually, what I really want to create is Suffolk's first modern pub." By that, Peter means somewhere for good food at sensible prices, and a menu that offers everything from homemade scotch eggs at the bar, or sausage and mash from the Magnificent Seven line-up of pub classics to a full à la carte menu perhaps enjoyed at the 'chef's table' seats which have a prime view of the kitchen. He means it to be a place that is attractive, lively, a bit different, where bar staff are as happy to pour a glass of Champagne as a pint of real ale.

Nick Claxton-Webb heads up — with calm authority — a seven-strong brigade including his senior sous chef Hannah Jenness who came with him from his previous job. He gets Peter's idea. Open the menu and you can indeed have a fish finger sandwich, or a plate of cheesy chips, or a homemade sausage roll with a pint. "We've created an egalitarian menu," he says. "Burgers, moules-frites, ham egg and chips, goulash all sell well." It goes without saying, however, that the burger is made from local Aberdeen Angus beef and comes inside a brioche bun with sides of cured red onion, roasted artichokes and slow-roast tomatoes, and that the ham (lightly smoked) is from locally reared pigs. The cheesy chips? They're hand cut, hot and crisp outside, floury and soft inside, and come with parmesan shavings, a heady whiff of truffle oil and homemade béarnaise for dipping. The vast sausage roll is a handsome beast of snack, Blythburgh pork encased in crisp, buttery pastry and served with mustard mayonnaise.

But today, Nick is focused on one of the à la carte dishes. He loves cooking game and — like those sausage rolls — this pheasant dish flies out. "It's the holy trinity isn't it: pheasant, mushrooms and cream. People love it. We did 40 birds last Friday evening alone." He tucks three substantial cock bird crowns into a pan, sealing them in generous amounts of hot butter and oil; they spit and sizzle and smell good, the fat keeping the lean meat moist. He oven-roasts them for just a few minutes, and allows the meat to rest before slicing the breasts off easily. The legs — they've been marinated in juniper, oranges and herbs for several hours — are confit'd to tenderness separately in duck fat; that meat is then shredded and mixed through generous amounts of cream, porcini and oyster mushrooms, a slosh of white wine, and a handful of chestnut gnocchi. Nick tastes, tastes, tastes as he goes, but rather than season the fricassée in the conventional way, he uses capers and anchovies, finishing everything with a squeeze of lemon juice. "It's more natural, less harsh," he explains. Plated up with charred leeks or steamed greens, it is a strapping dish that fits the time of year.

SUFFOLK FEAST

THE WEEPING WILLOW NICK CLAXTON-WEBB

"I've bought my game from Malcolm for years," says Nick as we head to Hopleys Farm in Horringer, a village just west of Bury St Edmunds, where Malcolm Payne runs a small shoot. "Malcolm's daughter used to work at The Ickworth hotel when I was head chef there, and we used his pheasant and partridge then too." We arrive to be greeted by Darcy, Rosie and Mollie and the bouncing vim and vigour that is second nature to cocker spaniels. Malcolm calls them to heel, and we head off on foot along farmland paths, the trio of dogs hunting, searching, rooting in the undergrowth after delicious scents, but also showing their best side – on Malcolm's command – for a few pictures. "I'm a property developer by day; the game is very much a hobby," he says. "We put down about 2,000 birds, and keep bags to around 80. It really is just for friends and family and I like it that way." Birds not taken home by his guests are prepped at the nearby game farm before being delivered to Nick and a few other local chef customers.

Pheasant takes centre stage on the day of our visit, but Nick switches comfortably to other feathered game during the colder months.

Partridge (also from Malcolm) is popular pot-roasted and served with petit salé (cured pork belly), charred leeks, wilted greens and bacon tuiles, while hay-smoked quail is often on the menu with Jerusalem artichokes and king oyster mushrooms, and mallard duck with vanilla-lime mash, salt-baked beets, roast cauliflower and collard greens. Furred game might appear as a rare-roasted saddle of Denham Estate venison with pickled red cabbage and potato gratin with smoked Lincolnshire poacher cheese, or cannelloni stuffed with confit rabbit, leek and sage.

But for all his love of game, you're probably most likely to find Nick loitering around the pastry section. "I've got a very sweet tooth," he admits. "I can't walk past a cake or tart without having a quick taste." It's not surprising, then, that the puddings ('to round you off' as it says on the menu), include such heart-stoppers as pumpkin pie with dulce de leche, cinder toffee and cinnamon ice cream, or warm plum and frangipane tart, or that most crowd-pleasing and utterly egalitarian of British desserts, sticky toffee pudding.

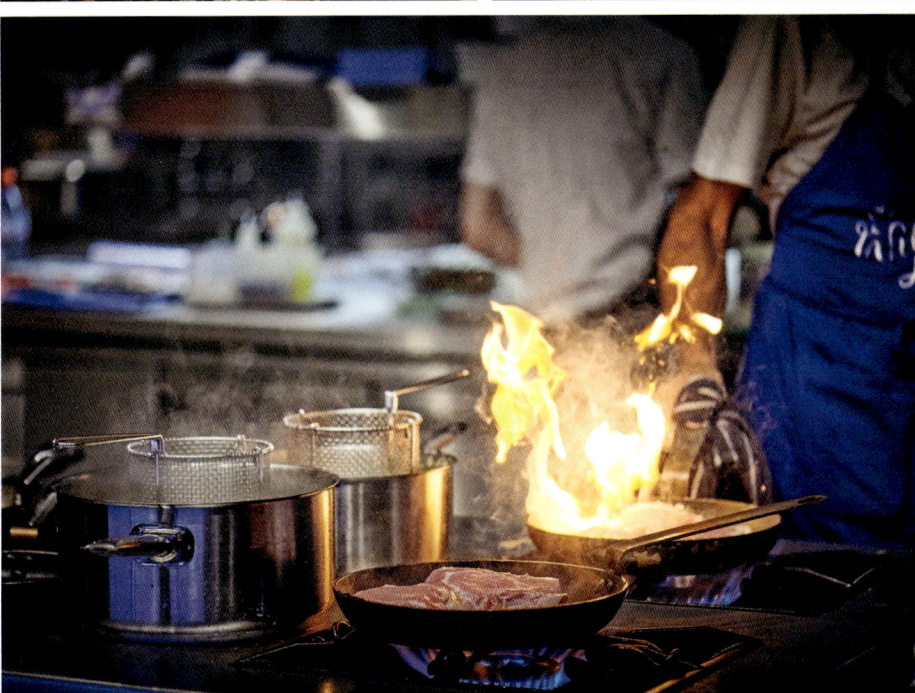

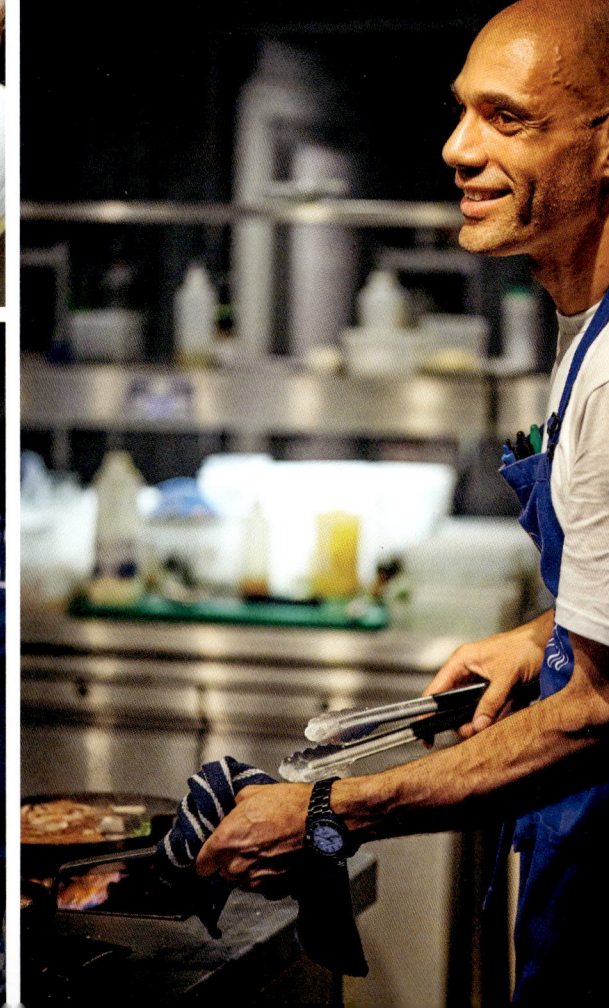

THE WEEPING WILLOW NICK CLAXTON-WEBB

Roasted pheasant, chestnut gnocchi and truffle-scented wild mushroom fricassée

An Italian inspired earthy, autumnal main course, which would also work well with other feathered wild game or even guinea fowl. Source a good selection of fungi for this dish to bring a variety of shades and textures. Serve with wilted greens or sea vegetables. (serves 4)

Pheasant legs
- 2 young cock pheasants
- 50g rock salt
- 2 or 3 sprigs of thyme
- 2 or 3 cloves of crushed garlic
- 2 or 3 juniper berries
- 2 or 3 peelings of orange zest
- 500g duck or goose fat

Separate the pheasants into crowns (both breasts attached to the rib cage) and legs. Combine the next 5 ingredients into a cure and rub well into the legs before refrigerating for 2 hours. Wash off the marinade and dry with a clean cloth. Carefully simmer the duck fat and use to cook the legs gently for 1 to 2 hours until soft and tender. Allow the legs to cool in the fat, then remove and shred off the meat before refrigerating.

Gnocchi
- 1kg unpeeled starchy potatoes
- 250g tipo 00 pasta flour
- 70g chestnut flour
- 2 small eggs, lightly beaten

Simmer the whole potatoes for 45-60 minutes until soft. Peel the potatoes and pass through a ricer. Combine the flours and add two-thirds to the potato with the egg and a good pinch of salt.

If necessary, add more flour to produce a soft but not sticky dough. Divide into four pieces and roll each out into a cylinder on a floured board. Cut into 1.5cm pieces and squeeze into pillow shapes. Place untouching on a lightly floured tray.

Prepare a large bowl of iced water. Bring a stockpot of salted water to the boil, scatter in the gnocchi carefully and keeping on a high heat, cook until they float. Remove with a slotted spoon and drop into the iced water. Once cooled, remove, drain and set aside.

Fricassée
- 100g dried wild mushrooms
- 200g fresh wild mushrooms, bite-sized
- 1 large white onion, diced
- Good pinch of baby lilliput capers
- Few sprigs of thyme, leaves chopped
- 2 cloves of garlic
- 30g unsalted butter
- 50ml white wine
- 300ml chicken stock
- 300ml double cream

Pour boiling water onto the dried mushrooms, cover and allow to swell for 20 minutes. Drain and replace the boiling water, cover again and leave until softened. Drain and tear into bite-sized pieces. Gently soften the onions, capers, thyme and garlic in the butter. Add the fresh and rehydrated mushrooms and cook until tender. Add the wine and stock, boiling hard to reduce by two thirds. Add the cream and reduce by one third. Set aside.

To serve
- Pheasant breasts
- 2 crushed garlic cloves
- Sprig of thyme
- Rapeseed oil
- Unsalted butter
- Drizzle of white truffle oil
- Lemon half

Pre-heat the oven to 180c. Oil a hot, heavy, ovenproof pan and seal off the breasts until browned on both sides, add the garlic and thyme sprig before roasting for 4 minutes, turn over and cook for 4 more minutes. Remove from the pan and allow to rest for 10 minutes somewhere warm. Carve off the breasts and keep warm.

Fry the gnocchi in a hot pan of foaming oil and butter until golden, allowing 7 per person. Add the gnocchi and the leg meat to the fricassée and warm until heated through. Stir through truffle oil and a squeeze of lemon.

Spoon into hot soup plates and top with the carved breasts.

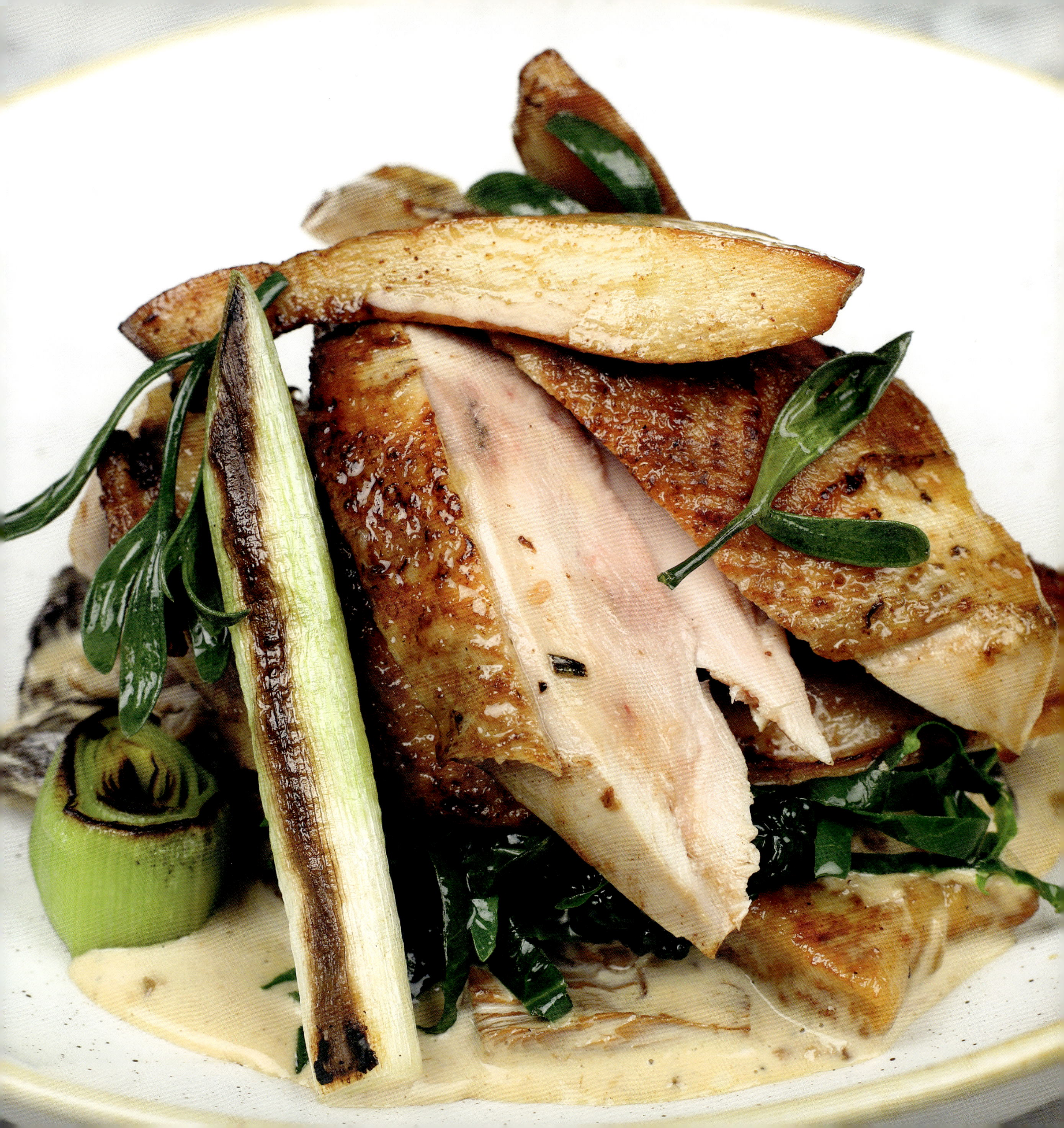

THE WEEPING WILLOW NICK CLAXTON-WEBB

Rare-roasted venison steaks with heritage baby beets

Beetroot and venison is a well-suited combination. We serve this with sweet orange and thyme-braised carrots, tangy pickled red cabbage and a savoury, fragrant granola crumb. (serves 4)

- 4 venison haunch steaks
- 1 splash of olive oil
- 2 sprigs of thyme
- 3 peelings of orange
- 6 juniper berries, crushed
- 4 handfuls of mixed beets, trimmed
- Olive oil and balsamic vinegar
- Butter
- 1 sprig of rosemary and thyme

Marinate the venison steaks in the next 4 ingredients, cover and leave for an hour.

Pre-heat the oven to 180c. Sprinkle the beets with a splash of oil and balsamic plus a pinch of sea salt in a snug tin and bake for approx. 20 minutes until softened. Allow to cool slightly and gently rub the skins off. Set aside.

Pre-heat the oven to 200c. Wipe off the venison steaks (reserving the marinade) and quickly sear in a hot, oiled pan until browned all over. Add two knobs of butter and the herbs, orange and juniper from the marinade. Place the pan in the oven for 2 minutes then remove, turn the steaks and baste well. Transfer to a warmed plate and rest for 10 minutes somewhere hot. Arrange the beetroots onto warmed plates and top with the carved venison.

Heritage tomato, semi-dried olive and artichoke linguine

This is a nice vegan dish but it could be finished with feta, roasted hake or chicken if you wish. (serves 4)

- 400g heritage tomatoes, halved
- Olive oil
- Caster sugar
- Leaves from 4 sprigs of thyme
- 100g whole olives
- 320g quality dried linguine
- 100g roasted artichokes, chopped
- 2 tbsp salsa verde

Line two baking trays with silicon paper. Halve the tomatoes width ways and remove the eye of the stalks. Lay the tomatoes cut side up on one of the trays and sprinkle with olive oil, a good pinch of salt, sugar and half the thyme. Tear the olives roughly and place on the second tray, sprinkling the same way as the tomatoes. Put both trays in the oven on its lowest setting and allow to dry out for approx. 6-8 hours until shrivelled. Set aside, reserving the syrupy juices.

Cook the linguine in plenty of salted boiling water. Drain and stir with a third each of the tomatoes, artichokes and olives in a deep sauté pan over a high heat. Once heated, fold in the salsa verde and mix carefully, using tongs. Divide between hot pasta bowls and top with the remaining vegetables. Garnish with the olive oil and the retained tomato juices.

SUFFOLK FEAST

White chocolate and vanilla pannacotta

A flexible friend of a dessert, this eats well with all manner of fresh fruits and something frozen for contrast. Here it's pictured with spiced, grenadine-poached rhubarb and our stem ginger ice cream. (serves 4)

250ml milk
250ml double cream
40g grated white chocolate
25g caster sugar
1 split and scraped vanilla pod and seeds
3 gelatine leaves, softened

Simmer the first 5 ingredients together, stirring for a minute or two. Set aside for 20 minutes to steep. Whisk in the gelatine until melted. Sieve the mixture and pour into 4 small clingfilm-lined moulds, then cool and refrigerate for a few hours to set. Turn the pannacotta out onto chilled plates.

NICK ON HIS...

FOODIE NOSTALGIA?
Cassoulet! I'm a real Francophile; I lived in France for 10 years and I just love the language and the whole approach to food and life. It's very regional, with each region proud of its particular food. We had a fantastic holiday a few years ago in Carcassonne in the south of France where the food is all about confit meat, salamis, and cassoulet which I love for its richness and depth of flavour.

FAVOURITE SUFFOLK VIEW?
From Dunwich beach looking out to sea. We've had some great cottage holidays around there. We've got a big extended family so every so often we'll rent a big place and get as many of us together as we can.

SIGNATURE DISHES

Starters

Roast beetroot pesto linguine, blue cheese, sea vegetables, pine nuts

Oak smoked salmon, honey-soused cabbage, yuzu, pickles, toasted ciabatta

Roasted tomato and artichoke salad, rocket pesto, feta, watercress

Mains

Rare-roasted rump of Suffolk lamb, fondant potato, pickled red cabbage, piccolo parsnips

Pan-roasted hake, olive oil crushed new potatoes, mussel and smoked anchovy velouté

Butter and thyme-roasted chicken, caesar salad, soft poached egg

Puddings

Bourbon crème brûlée, berry compote, butter shortbread

Hot chocolate fondant, peanut butter ice cream, cherry gel

Sticky toffee pudding, vanilla ice cream, butterscotch sauce

HOW DID YOU SPEND YOUR LAST BIRTHDAY?
Punting in Cambridge with my family! It was great fun. I have a summer birthday so it's generally a BBQ every year, but I don't like BBQs!

CAN'T WAIT TO EAT AT...?
Moor Hall [Aughton, Lancashire]. It's all about the produce, very real as you'd expect from Mark [Birchall, chef patron and former executive chef for Simon Rogan's restaurant, L'Enclume, Cartmel]. They have their own meat-aging rooms, and make their own cheese. I'd love to do a stage there.

'TAKE FIVE' RECIPE?
Croque Madame. It's a cheese and ham toastie with béchamel and fried egg. The kids love it but it's not for me. I don't eat cheese.

GUILTY FOOD PLEASURE?
The trimmings from a cake or tart or shortbread or biscuits... anything like that. I have a very sweet tooth. I can't walk past a tray of sticky toffee pudding without tidying up the edges!

QUICK SNACK OR MIDNIGHT FEAST?
Scotch eggs and sausage rolls from our bar menu. I've eaten an awful lot of them recently!

FAVOURITE TIME OF YEAR FOR FOOD?
Autumn-winter. I love game, mushrooms and being able to make pies and goulash with loads of creamy mash.

WHAT THREE QUALITIES DO YOU ADMIRE IN PEOPLE?
Loyalty, hard work, honesty about what you're doing and why, about being true to yourself.

Colour me beautiful

The bright red front door is a hint that what lies beyond The Weeping Willow's conventional cappuccino-coloured exterior is not run-of-the-mill.

Peter Romaniuk and his wife, Paula Pryke OBE, bought the freehold in August 2015, and poured creativity, energy and enthusiasm into a nine-month renovation, opening their (almost) local pub after a three-year closure in September 2017.

It is not surprising, given Peter's reputation as an architect, that the interior is striking. Wherever you sit, there's an interesting aspect, whether of the garden, flowerbeds and terrace dining area, the kitchen, or the rest of the pub with its mix of preserved original detail and bright modern spaces. There are no gloomy corners. The light-filled main dining room, with two glass walls and airily high ceiling, looks over the meadow and the eponymous willow. "The tree and the potential of the outside space were what sold the place to me," says Peter. "Well, that and the fact that I like beer!"

Paula's exceptional career as an internationally renowned florist, meanwhile, means that every table, sill and shelf is brightened with something of colourful interest, whether a dramatic seasonal arrangement on the bar, simple table posies, or centrepieces in the unabashedly pink semi-private Raspberry Room. Her creative eye means that upholstery is bold too, the pub furnished with royal blue sofas, stools upholstered in jewel colours, and high-backed armchairs and dining chairs covered in elaborate textiles. Artwork on the walls is striking: a series of plates painted with dogs of various breeds draws the eye, while huge abstract contemporary paintings fill other spaces.

The Weeping Willow
Bury Road, Barrow, Bury St Edmunds IP29 5AB
W: theweepingwillow.co.uk
T: 01284 771881
E: hello@theweepingwillow.co.uk
- /theweepingwillowpub
- @WWBarrow
- /theweepingwillowpub

Food served: Mon-Sat L 12-2.30; D 6-9; Sun L 12-5.30

Cost: starters from £5.90; mains from £12.90; desserts from £6.50; separate snack and bar menu; wine from £20; beer from £3.40

Details: 62 seats in main restaurant (plus 8 Chef's Table seats); 34 seats in bar area; semi-private Raspberry Room (seats 12); 32 seats on terrace; large garden; play area; accessible; dogs welcome; parking

THE ANGEL INN, STOKE BY NAYLAND
DAN RUSSEL

Stalking point

Muntjac is a sustainable, healthy, delicious meat. Dan Russell discovers more on a morning out with Lavenham Butchers' Greg Strolenberg

185

Dan Russell has changed out of his chef's whites and he's tiptoeing through a wood behind Greg Strolenberg of Lavenham Butchers, trying not to step on dry twigs. They're not out for a country stroll, they're stalking deer. Greg is carrying a high-powered rifle and he is hoping to spot a muntjac.

The wood is a Site of Special Scientific Interest (SSSI) and Greg and his business partner Gareth Doherty, both licensed stalkers, have been asked to manage the deer population for the landowner, because the animals are capable of stripping the woodland through their non-stop browsing. Left to breed unchecked, Greg says, they can do untold damage to their habitats, literally eating themselves out of house and home.

Dan and Greg move slowly though the wood, stopping every few hundred yards as Greg scans the undergrowth for the camouflaged, cautious deer. And although the pair leave empty-handed from this outing, Greg says it hasn't been a wasted afternoon. "Taking Dan out so he can see first-hand what's involved in getting the meat, that's really satisfying," he says.

It's that connection that fires Dan with enthusiasm. He loves the robust cooking of autumn and winter: one of his key dishes at The Angel Inn is a muntjac loin cooked as a wellington, the fine-grained meat covered with a layer of finely chopped mushrooms, and wrapped in flaky, buttery pastry, before being cooked to a perfect rosy pink. "I enjoy it when the game season starts: the colder evenings, lighting the fire in the restaurant, setting the ambience and making the food that matches it, the big earthy flavours, the mushrooms, the venison.

"And Suffolk produce is phenomenal. It's some of the best I've used in my career. I've been lucky to work in some luxury places and I believe the Suffolk suppliers that we use compete with the best out there, especially Lavenham Butchers. I just can't rave enough about them at the moment! They hunt the meat, they butcher it, they sell it, and I really buy into that field-to-fork idea."

Greg makes a point of getting out from behind his butcher's counter to visit chefs – he was previously a chef himself – as frequently as he can. "I tell them what I've got that's good, and hopefully help them think of things they can put on the menu that are different, maybe slow-roasted shoulder of venison rather than just your beef and pork which you can get anywhere."

THE ANGEL INN DAN RUSSELL

He adds: "The joy of game is that you're not limited as you are with other meats. It works with everything from chocolate and chillies to berries and fruits or wines, and there's always something in season to shoot." Muntjac is one of the six species of deer resident in the UK. Brought over from China in the early 20th century to populate Woburn Park in Bedfordshire, they escaped and quickly established themselves in the forests of eastern, central and southern England.

It's not all about hearty dishes at The Angel, however. Dan's menu is carefully devised to appeal both to customers who want traditional pub food, and those looking for something more adventurous. His desserts are takes on old favourites and textures – a crème brûlée spiced up with ginger and sharpened with a plum compote, a chocolate tart given crunch and contrast with honeycomb and cinnamon ice cream.

Dan's college tutor, Alan Whatley, was also the chair of the Association of Pastry Chefs, so he was taught by an expert. "That was a great experience. He spent three years training me in the pâtisserie section, and landed me my first job at The Ritz Hotel, which was amazing. It was very, very hard work but I loved every minute of it."

With his father also a Ritz-trained chef, Dan clearly has cooking is in his blood. He spent five years working in the French Alps as well as in gastro-pubs from Yorkshire to Surrey, but in the past year he has put down roots in Suffolk as head chef at The Angel. "I'm really enjoying it," says Dan, back in the pub and taking a rare half-hour out to chat in the bar. "Suffolk is gorgeous. I catch myself, especially round here in Dedham Vale, driving round with my mouth wide open at some of the views."

His ambition is to win a second AA Rosette for the restaurant and his modern British food is already getting good reviews. "I like simple food. I know that sounds crazy, because when you look at it, it's not necessarily simple, but I'm not one of those chefs that puts nine, ten, twelve different elements on a plate. I like very simple, very clean flavours."

As many as possible of his ingredients are locally sourced. "When we launch our next menu we're thinking about putting a number next to every dish and that will be how many metres away that core ingredient has come from the pub." Now that's what makes a local, local.

THE ANGEL INN DAN RUSSELL

Muntjac wellington, buttered heritage vegetables, butternut squash and red wine sauce

We have five main varieties of deer in East Anglia and muntjac, the smallest, gives us the sweetest, tenderest venison. Try sourcing it from your local butcher's or a friendly gamekeeper. As it is available all year round, we change the garnish according to the seasons, for example wild mushrooms in autumn, or lovely tender greens in spring. (serves 4)

Stuffing
- 50g butter
- 250g button mushrooms, finely chopped
- 1 garlic clove, finely chopped
- Good pinch of thyme leaves

Melt the butter in a hot pan, before adding the mushrooms, garlic, thyme leaves and seasoning. Cook over a medium heat until softening and drying out. Cool, then place the mushrooms in a clean cloth and squeeze tightly to remove excess liquid. Unwrap into a container and set aside.

Pancakes
- 2 large eggs, beaten
- 50g plain flour
- 50ml full fat milk
- Small handful of flat leaf parsley

Mix the eggs, flour and milk with the chopped parsley leaves into a batter. Using a hot, oiled pan, make 3 or 4 large thin pancakes and set aside.

Wellington
- 1 large, whole muntjac loin
- 4 slices good parma ham
- 500g puff pastry, rolled to half cm thickness
- Eggwash

Season the loin and brown on all sides in a hot oiled pan. Cool.

Make a large layer of clingfilm of overlapping strips with sufficient width for the length of the venison loin. Lay the pancakes on top in a row, top with the ham and spread with the mushroom mix. Place the loin on top horizontally near the leading edge and using the clingfilm, roll everything together away from you, wrapping it up firmly into a tight cylinder (ensuring that clingfilm stays outside the roll). Use more clinglfilm to help keep it together and then knot the ends of the clingfilm and refrigerate the parcel for at least 6 hours.

Next cut the pastry into a rectangle, sized to fit the unwrapped muntjac parcel. Roll up tightly and neatly in the pastry, sealing the edges with eggwash and tucking in the ends underneath. Cut air vents in the top and score decoratively. Chill back in the fridge to firm up for at least an hour.

Buttered vegetables
- 12 baby carrots
- 12 baby leeks
- 6 baby courgettes

Cook the vegetables al dente in boiling, salted water and then drain and plunge into iced water. Drain and set aside.

Squash purée
- 1 butternut squash, peeled and deseeded
- Rapeseed oil
- Unsalted butter

Dice the squash. Oil and season before roasting at 180c for about 25 minutes until browned and tender. Process while hot to a purée and push through a sieve for smoothness. Beat in butter and adjust the seasoning. Keep warm.

To serve
- 500ml good dark meat stock
- 500ml drinkable rich red wine
- Thyme sprigs
- Unsalted butter

Bake the wellington at 180c for around 25 minutes. Allow to rest while you reduce the stock and wine together till a thick jus. Pan-fry the vegetables in butter, thyme sprigs and seasoning to reheat.

Slice the wellington thickly and place on hot plates with the vegetables and purée. Finish with the jus.

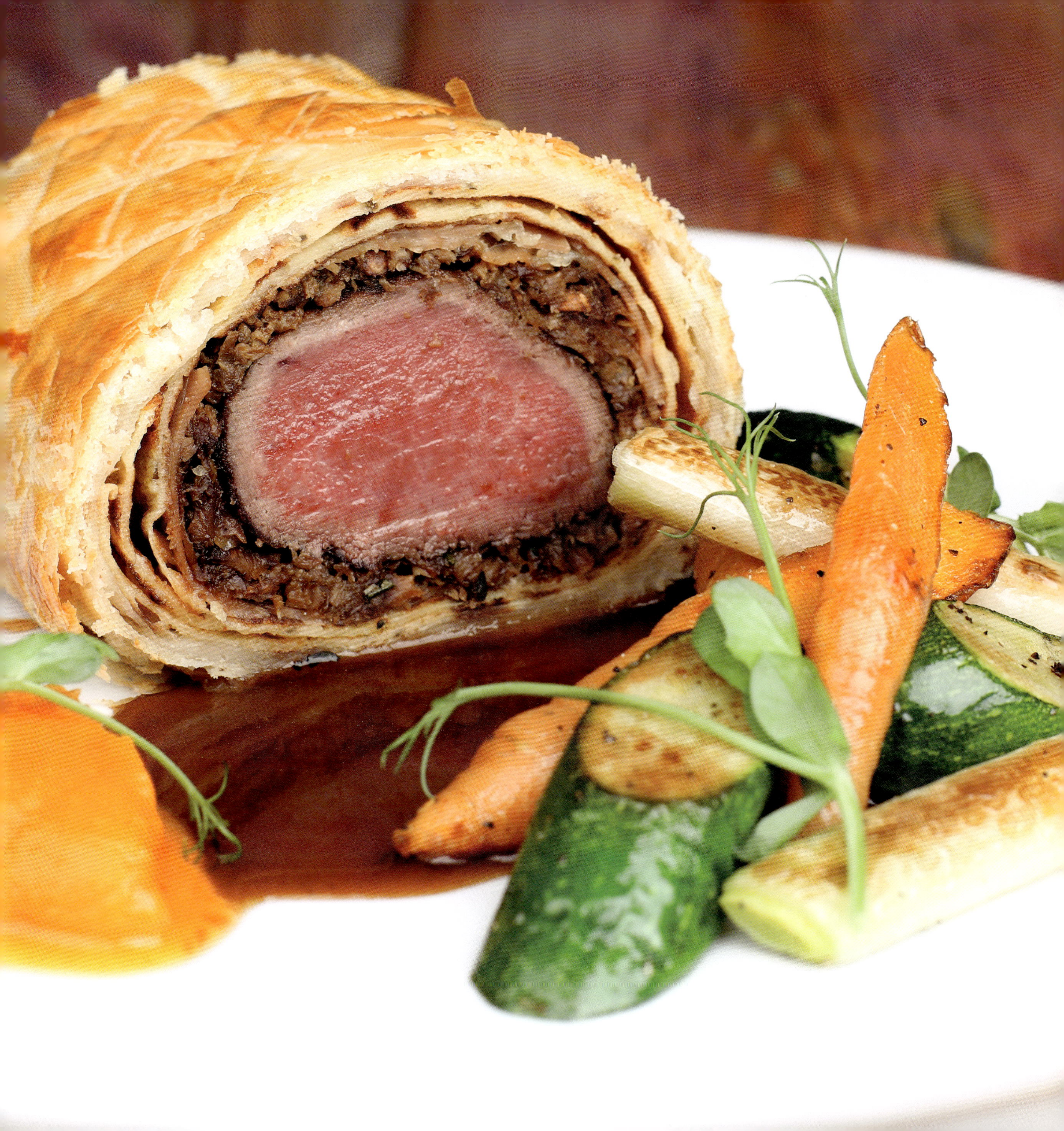

THE ANGEL INN DAN RUSSELL

Chocolate fondant puddings

An elegant dinner party dessert that always wows and satisfies. We add to its appeal with marshmallow, honeycomb and interesting ice creams. (serves 4)

180g good, dark chocolate
180g unsalted butter
80g caster sugar
3 large egg yolks
2 whole eggs
50g plain flour
Butter and cocoa powder

Pre-heat the oven to 190c. Melt the chocolate and butter over a pan of simmering water. Separately whisk the sugar, yolks and whole eggs together. Stir gradually into the chocolate mixture off the heat. Sieve in the flour and mix well.

Butter 4 dariole moulds and coat with cocoa powder. Knock out excess and then fill three-quarters full with the mixture.

Bake for 12 minutes. Remove from the oven and rest for two minutes before carefully turning the fondants out onto plates.

Beetroot-cured salmon, pickled beets and burnt orange

A great, colourful alternative to classic smoked salmon, garnished with micro herbs. Enjoy alongside an iced artisan gin and good tonic. (serves 6)

2 large red beetroot, peeled and quartered
2 lemons, zested
6 tbsp coarse salt
2 tbsp demerara sugar
60ml good gin
800g wild salmon fillet, skin-on and deboned
3 mixed beetroots
250ml white wine vinegar
200g caster sugar
2 star anise
1 cinnamon stick
1 large orange

Process the red beetroot and zest into a smooth paste and then mix with the salt, sugar and gin. Lay the salmon skinside down on to a piece of parchment and cover evenly with the mixture. Lay on more parchment and tightly wrap several times in clingfilm before refrigerating in a dish for 48 hours.

Slice the mixed beets thinly and place in 3 separate bowls. Make a syrup of the vinegar, sugar and spices, before pouring over equally. Allow to macerate for 6 hours or overnight. Peel and segment the orange (no pith!), then char lightly with a blowtorch. Plate the thinly sliced salmon with the beetroot and charred oranges.

Ginger crème brûlée

A simply luscious dessert to prepare in advance and divine served with some crumbly shortbread and a spiced plum compote. (serves 4)

1 vanilla pod (or 2 tsp extract)
450ml double cream
100g mascarpone
10cm piece of root ginger
6 egg yolks
60g light brown sugar, plus more for dusting

Preheat the oven to 120c and prepare 4 ramekins in a snug, deep roasting tin.

Scrape the seeds from the split vanilla pod and place both parts (or the extract) with the cream and mascarpone in a pan. Bring to a simmer and set aside. Leave to infuse for a few minutes and then remove the pod. Stir in the peeled, grated ginger. Whisk the egg yolks and sugar until light and fluffy.

Gradually stir in the ginger cream. Decant into the ramekins. Pour boiling water into the tin halfway up the sides of the ramekins. Bake until the brûlées are set, for approx. 20 minutes. Remove, cool and refrigerate for 3 hours.

Dust the tops with more sugar and glaze with a blowtorch or under a grill to get a crisp, caramelised finish.

Dedham Vale

DAN ON HIS...

INSPIRING SUFFOLK VIEW?
Probably the one you get as you look towards the Dedham Vale here in Stoke by Nayland.

BEST DISH YOU'VE EVER EATEN?
Two things come to mind: the first time I ever had fondue when I was in the Alps. I know it's just a pot of molten cheese but wow, what an experience! Up in the mountains with the snow and that setting, it was great. The second one, I was very lucky to go the The Square in London when Philip Howard was there. I had sea bass and I remember it was the first time I was ever blown away by a fish dish in a restaurant, it was just absolutely phenomenal.

FOOD HERO?
I can name 100 chefs who I think are phenomenal but at the moment, Massimo Bottura, Gordon Ramsay and probably someone like Philip Howard, whose food is very clean, very simple. Hopefully he'll never hear me say that because I'm sure it's not as simple as it looks! But I just like the way they put the food together, nothing overly fancy, just good honest cooking.

GUILTY FOOD PLEASURE?
I've got a sweet tooth, I always have had, so probably something like a bag of Haribos.

LAST BELLY LAUGH?
When I proposed to my girlfriend. I got down on my knees and she said 'what the **** are you doing?' and it made me laugh a lot. She will kill me for telling you that.

PERFECT DAY OFF?
Just relaxing. I like going out and eating in different restaurants in the area. I like going to the cinema as well.

WHICH HABIT WOULD YOU STRUGGLE TO KICK?
Coffee. I drink coffee probably more than I drink water. I've kicked all my other bad habits. Coffee just keeps me going.

IF NOT A CHEF...
I used to enjoy drama at school. I might have gone down that route but I think honestly, since I was 14 when I did work experience in a kitchen, I've wanted to be a chef. My dad was a chef as well so I always had it in my blood.

SOMETHING THAT AMAZES YOU?
Space. Space is fascinating, the far reaches of wherever it goes. I can't quite get my head around it sometimes. I like reading up on astronomy, I'm a bit of a geek really.

SIGNATURE DISHES

Starters

Ham hock ballotine, breaded hen's egg, white bean purée

Whipped goats' cheese, pickled baby vegetables, sweetcorn textures

Creamed wild mushrooms on brioche, poached duck eggs, wild rocket

Mains

Fillet of beef, horseradish mash, tenderstem, parsnip chips, jus

Pan-roasted hake, warm tomato coulis, roasted baby veg, chorizo, buttered new potatoes

Roasted butternut squash risotto, blue cheese, sage, rocket

Puddings

Chocolate tart, honeycomb, cinnamon ice cream

Apple & blackcurrant crumble, custard

Sticky toffee pudding, toffee sauce, vanilla ice cream

WHAT THREE QUALITIES DO YOU LIKE MOST IN PEOPLE?
Someone who can make me laugh. Someone friendly. And I like people that are honest.

QUICK SNACK?
A chocolate bar, just to boost those energy levels up. It's naughty, I know, but that's me!

Well looked after

It's not every pub that has a 30-metre deep well at the entrance to the dining room, but as The Angel's manager Becky King quickly points out, it does have a brick parapet and a grate. This 16th century coaching inn takes good care of its guests.

"We try and make it a home from home. When people go out, I think they need to be wowed and spoiled, and that's what we try to do here," says Becky. With its ancient beams and modern service culture, The Angel is a cosy and comfortable place.

For wine lovers, in addition to the regular list, there is a selection of high-end bottles - mainly French - bought at the cellar door. "We have several special bottles at affordable prices because they've been bought direct," says Becky. "A bottle that might normally cost £120, we will sell for maybe £50-60."

And unlike many pubs with restaurants, The Angel has retained a snug bar, so people looking for a quiet pint will feel welcome here. Plenty of locals come through the doors, but Stoke by Nayland's location on the edge of Dedham Vale means the pub also attracts holidaymakers, walkers and cyclists touring Constable Country. Customers range from people in their mid-20s to those in their mid-80s, some coming from as far afield as the USA, Australia and Holland.

The Angel Inn
Polstead Street, Stoke by Nayland CO6 4SA
W: angelinnsuffolk.co.uk
T: 01206 263245
E: info@angelinnsuffolk
 /AngelInnsuffolk
 @AngelInnSuffolk
 /angelinnsuffolk

Accolades and listings: Waitrose *Good Food Guide*; AA One Rosette; AA Five Stars (Inn)

Food served: Mon-Fri B 8-10; L 12-2.30; D 6-9.30; Sat-Sun B 8.30-10; L 12-3 (12-4 Sun); D 6-9.30 (6-9 Sun); Mon-Sat afternoon tea (pre-booked) 2.30-5.30

Cost: starters from £5.25; mains from £12.95; desserts from £5.95; set lunch £15.95 (two courses), £18.95 (three courses); set Sunday lunch menu £18.95 (two courses), £21.95 (three courses); afternoon tea (pre-booked) £12.95; wine from £16.95; pint from £3.60

Details: 30 seats in restaurant, 50 in bar, 39 in courtyard; private dining for 12-28; children's menu; 6 en suite bedrooms; room service; conference space for 15-25; airport/station transport available on request; secure cycle storage; parking

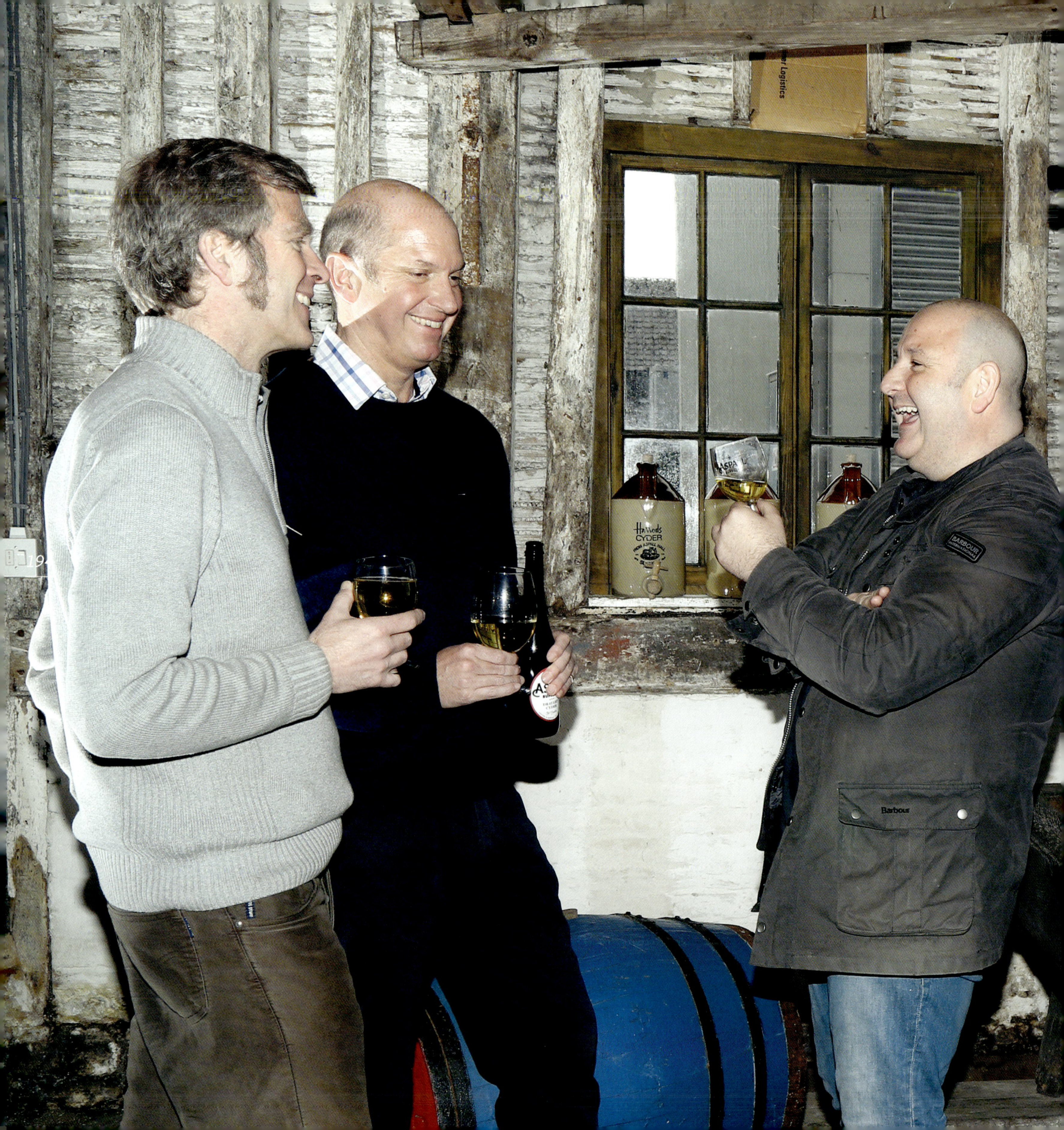
Harrods
CYDER
Barbour

THE KITCHEN@THORPENESS
CAMERON MARSHALL

An apple cyder a day

The lively flavour of Aspall Premier Cru cyder gives perky, sweet-sour notes to Cameron Marshall's crowd-pleasing dishes

Cameron Marshall is in his element as he tours the Aspall production unit with Barry and Henry Chevallier Guild; he has long been a fan of the amber drink, which since the 18th century has been made from apples grown, pressed, fermented and bottled on this site, tucked deep in the Suffolk countryside near Debenham.

The sleek of Aspall's modern-day operation stands cheek-by-jowl with the collection of original wooden presses that have been carefully preserved as a reminder of the deep-rooted Suffolk heritage of the brand. The elegant moated home of the Chevallier Guilds is surrounded by orchards first planted by Aspall founder Clement Chevallier when he moved into Aspall Hall in 1728. The story goes that he was out planting apple trees within days of moving in, much to the incredulity of locals who couldn't understand the sense in replacing fine arable land with orchards. They no doubt reaped the benefit of Clement's activity when it came to mid-January wassailing, however, when a bowl of hot cyder, fortified with brandy or sherry, would have been shared as a toast to the slumbering trees, and in anticipation of a healthy crop of apples. None of Clement's original plantings survive of course, but many of the current trees are a gnarly century old, standing alongside vigorous new plantings that will provide fruit for cyders to come.

Cameron will rarely say no to a glass of Aspall, but today is about getting creative with it at his informal, family friendly café-restaurant, The Kitchen@Thorpeness. "I love the flavour, I love the taste of Aspall. It goes well with desserts, starters, dressings, and we use the vinegar as a staple in the kitchen too." Cooking a cured pork ribeye, he de-glazes the pan with Aspall Premier Cru and flambés it to give a sweet-sour flavour and delicious sauce. He uses the same method but to different effect for Gressingham duck livers that he serves with fresh pomegranate, sautéed smoked bacon and a cyder dressing [see recipe]. "The dressing for the duck is Dijon mustard, a bit of maple syrup, some of the cyder and just a touch of extra virgin olive oil. I use a hand whisk so it is almost splitty," says Cameron enthusiastically. "And for the buttered apples around the pudding [apple and muscovado sugar parfait – see recipe], I de-glaze the pan with cyder which adds sweetness. I didn't add any sugar to that dish, apart from what's in the actual parfait."

SUFFOLK FEAST

THE KITCHEN@THORPENESS CAMERON MARSHALL

The Kitchen menu is rich with local produce: salads from Thorpeness Leaves, Thorpeness asparagus (Cameron swears you can taste the sea air in the spears), meat from a local butcher. Ingredients are combined to create a menu of comfort food, the sort you'd come back for time and again. Morning hunger will be satisfied by a stack of pancakes served the American way with streaky bacon and maple syrup, or poached eggs with hollandaise sauce, a dish that channels flavours from closer to home with generously cut Suffolk ham. Come at lunch for a trio of local sausages with horseradish mash and onion gravy, or at weekends and school holidays for a flavour-packed pizza.

Henry Chevallier Guild and his brother Barry, eighth-generation cyder-makers, recently sold Aspall to the American brewing giant, Molson Coors, but the pair remain brand ambassadors and as keen as ever for the cyder to be used creatively. "It's such a multi-faceted product," Henry says. "It's always great to see chefs coming up with different uses. It goes well with food in a pint or wine glass, but when chefs use it as an ingredient you can see it actually has more in common with wine than beer – it's really a fruit wine. It's very adaptable, very flexible."

Like all good chefs, Cameron thinks on his feet, apparently plucking ideas out of the air and turning them at high-speed into something deliciously, deceptively simple. But he's had a lot of practice. "I started cooking when I was seven or eight. Mum was a terrible cook. She'd go out on a Saturday and say 'now, don't do any cooking' and the first thing I did as she walked out the door was make bread or cakes. It was a learning curve. I did throw away an awful lot, and there was always mess; she hated all the mess. But that was my first cooking experience." Before long, Cameron was taking orders from friends and neighbours for birthday cakes – not bad for a ten-year-old.

He went on to catering college at 16 before taking a variety of positions as a chef and hotel and restaurant manager. It was good practice for when he and his wife Claire bought the Dedham Boathouse in 2002. They opened it as a café and in the first season made enough money to completely renovate the property and transform it into the popular restaurant it is today. The opportunity to open The Kitchen@Thorpeness came, he says, out of the blue in 2014, but Cameron saw huge potential and now lives mid-way between the two businesses, shuttling between them, rarely getting a day off.

He doesn't mind though, and he's happy to be ensconced in Suffolk. "I was born on the Wirral, I'm a Wirral lad and I still often go back to see my parents. But East Anglia is home now, it's been home for a long time, and I really, really love it here."

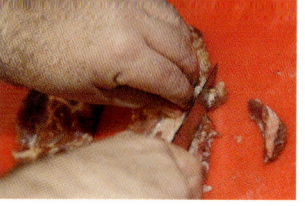

THE KITCHEN@THORPENESS CAMERON MARSHALL

Cured pork ribeye, sweetheart cabbage, roast parsnips and a cyder and mushroom cream sauce

Ribeye of pork is a hearty cut for hearty appetites, making for a tasty, autumn dish with sweet, moist meat and a deep flavour. Swap the 'tame' mushrooms for any edible, wild fungi you have foraged. Other roots work as well as the parsnips too, perhaps celeriac or beets. I am a distinct fan of Aspall and their cyders, but you could use a dry white wine or vermouth instead. An apple and shallot compote would be a delicious addition at the table. (serves 4)

Curing
- 1 litre water
- 1 heaped tbsp salt
- 3 heaped tbsp brown sugar
- Juice of a large orange
- Half small bunch of thyme
- 4 200g portions of pork ribeye steak

Heat a few tbsp of the water in a pan large enough to fit the pork. Melt the salt and sugar in the water, add the juice and thyme, and then the rest of the cold water. Submerge the pork and leave for at least 8 hours in the refrigerator.

Sauce
- 1 small onion, finely diced
- Rapeseed oil and butter for frying
- 100g chestnut mushrooms, sliced
- 100ml dry cyder
- 100ml double cream
- 1 rounded tsp Dijon-style mustard

Soften the onion in a little oil and a few knobs of foaming butter in a hot, deep sauté pan over a low-medium heat before stirring in the mushrooms. Turn up the heat and stir-fry for about 5 minutes until tender. Deglaze the pan with the cyder over a high heat, scraping the pan as you stir. When well-reduced, mix in the mustard and double cream and season to taste. Leave to simmer for 2-3 minutes and then set aside somewhere warm.

Cabbage
- 1 sweetheart cabbage, leaves only
- Rapeseed oil and butter for frying

Finely shred the cabbage. Toss in a little oil and a few knobs of foaming butter in a deep sauté pan over a high heat. Stir-fry until tender, seasoning to taste and continue until crisping at the edges. Remove and keep warm.

Parsnips
- 3 large parsnips, peeled and cored
- Rapeseed oil

Pre-heat the oven to 190c. Put a shallow layer of rapeseed oil into a deep roasting tin and heat. Slice the parsnips thickly and parboil in salted, boiling water for 5 minutes and then drain well. Carefully toss in the oiled tray to coat the parsnips all over, season generously and then roast until golden-brown. Set aside somewhere warm.

To serve
- Rapessed oil and butter

Pre-heat the oven to 190c. Drain the pork and dry on a clean cloth. Season well with pepper. Pan fry the ribeyes in a hot, deep ovenproof sauté pan over a high heat in a little oil and a few knobs of foaming butter. Turn over when crisp on one side and repeat on the other. Transfer to the oven to roast for another 5-8 minutes until just cooked through (we like to serve it a little pink). Rest the meat somewhere warm.

Ensure the cabbage and parsnips are hot and place on warmed plates with the carved pork, before generously saucing with the mushroom cream.

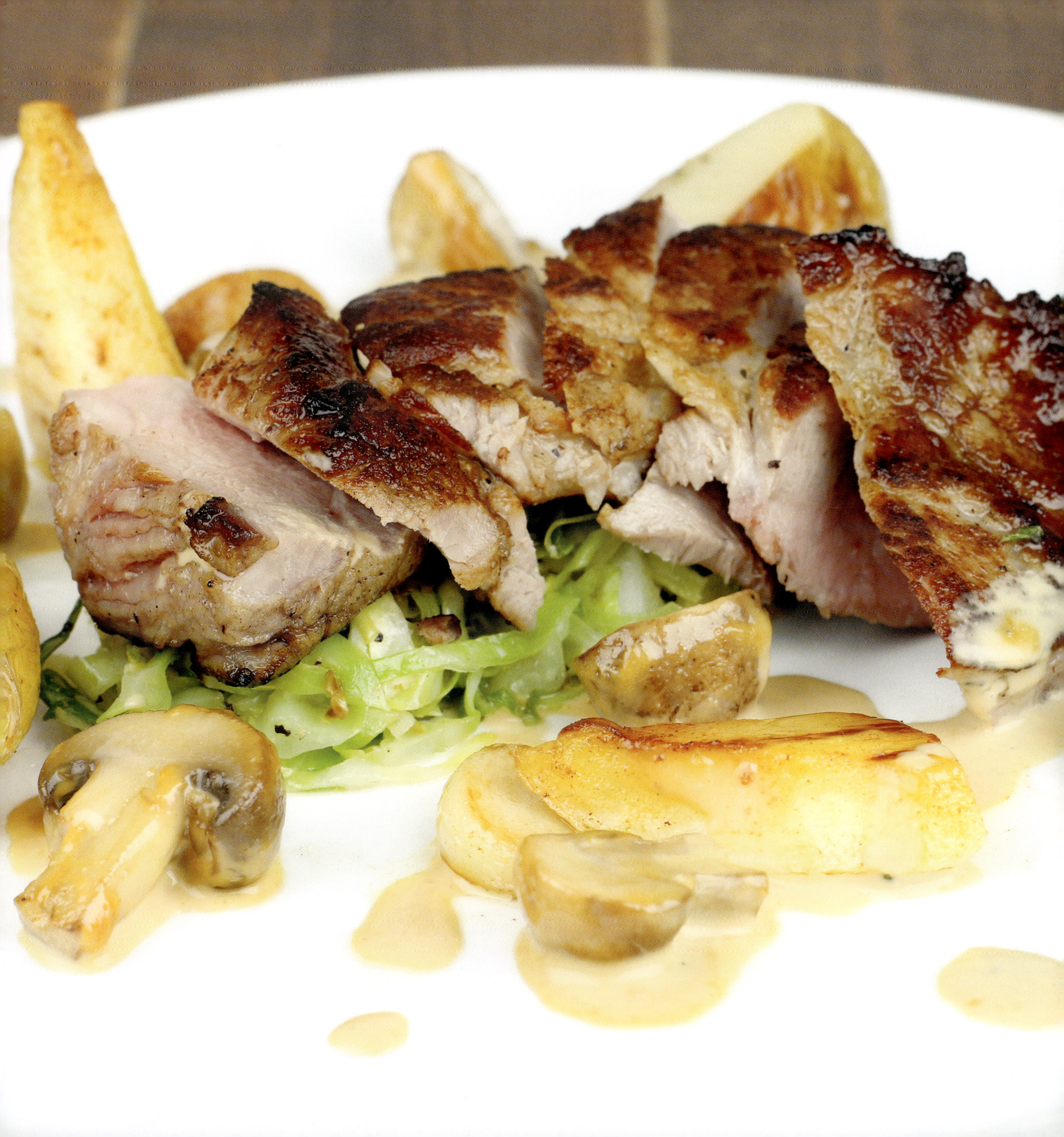

THE KITCHEN@THORPENESS CAMERON MARSHALL

Tossed salad of crispy duck livers, smoked bacon and a cyder dressing

Poultry offal like that of all the farmed meats is distinctly underrated, full of nutrients and great in a warm salad. We are advised to serve it thoroughly cooked through but I do like it pink for juicy flavour. (serves 4)

1 tsp Dijon-style mustard
100ml dry cyder
2 tbsp cyder vinegar
Runny honey to taste
50ml light olive oil
100g streaky smoked bacon, diced
Rapeseed oil
Unsalted butter
250g duck livers, trimmed
2 handfuls of mixed salad leaves
Seeds from half a pomegranate

Whisk the mustard, cyder, vinegar and honey together and mix in the oil slowly. Season to taste and set aside.

Stir-fry the bacon over a high heat with a little oil and a few knobs of foaming butter in a hot, deep sauté pan until browned. Add the livers and continue frying until caramelised all over (for well done, cook for a few more minutes until firm). Add half the dressing to the pan to warm through. Tip the contents of the pan into a large bowl and mix with the salad leaves and pomegranate seeds. Serve on warmed plates and drizzle the remaining dressing around.

Pan-fried smoked mackerel, with a horseradish and potato salad

Smoked fish is a particular favourite and horseradish is a natural complement to the smoked seafood flavour. Some sweet-sour beetroot would be great on the side too. (serves 4)

250g smoked mackerel fillets
500g new potatoes, cold boiled
4 tbsp good mayonnaise
2 tsp of grated horseradish
1 bunch of dill, chopped
Juice of 1 lemon
100ml olive oil
cracked black pepper

Remove the mackerel skin and set aside. Dice the cooked potatoes, fold in the mayonnaise, horseradish, half the dill, half the lemon juice and cracked pepper and salt to taste.

Separately, whisk the remaining juice with the oil and more pepper and salt to taste.

Fry the mackerel in a dry medium-hot pan until crisp on both sides. Plate up the potato salad, topped with the mackerel and drizzle over the dressing, finishing with the remaining dill for decoration.

Apple and muscovado sugar parfait, walnuts and butterscotch

A light but indulgent dessert at the end of a heavy meal, this is basically posh ice cream for grown-ups. (serves 4+)

3 Bramley apples, peeled
Unsalted butter for frying
275g light muscovado sugar
50ml water
5 egg yolks
250ml double cream
150g walnuts
100g unsalted butter
150ml double cream

Core and dice the apples and sauté in foaming butter on a high heat until golden-brown but still crisp (before they start to stew). Set aside. Carefully boil 125g of sugar and the water for 3-4 minutes and set aside. Beat the yolks until fluffy, then slowly pour in the syrup, whisking continuously till the mixture cools. Whip the 250ml cream to soft peaks in a large bowl, fold in the yolk mixture and three-quarters of the apple. Decant into a clingfilm-lined loaf tin and freeze for 3-4 hours.

For the crumble, pre-heat the oven to 190c, mix the walnuts with 50g of the sugar and bake on a shallow tray for 10-15 minutes. Allow to cool. For the butterscotch sauce, heat the last 2 ingredients plus 100g of the sugar gently. Simmer till golden-brown. Turn out the parfait onto cold plates, decorate with the apples and crumbled nuts plus a good drizzle of butterscotch.

CAMERON ON HIS...

FAVOURITE TIME OF THE YEAR FOR FOOD?
April and May for the first asparagus which they grow round here in Thorpeness. But I also love all the beetroots and squashes, the colours and flavours of autumn.

THREE QUALITIES YOU LIKE MOST IN PEOPLE?
Honesty, loyalty, and a good sense of humour are really important.

WHICH OF YOUR VICES WOULD YOU FIND HARDEST TO GIVE UP?
I don't smoke, I've never smoked, but I do like a drink – a cider or a beer. I don't drink much but I'd miss it.

'TAKE FIVE' RECIPE?
Asparagus, plain and simple: put a knob of butter in a pan, add the asparagus then transfer the pan to the grill and just warm through. Add some fresh grated parmesan and black pepper and a touch of oil – delicious! Or another one would be the beets: boil the beets in a mix of white wine vinegar, warm water, mustard seeds and fresh herbs, let them steep and go cold and then drain and chop them into cubes, reserving the liquid. Mix the beets through feta cheese and some salad leaves. You don't even need any dressing, just a napping of that sauce and that's it, fantastic!

INSPIRING SUFFOLK VIEW?
The road into Thorpeness when I'm driving to work very early in the morning. I've got the water tower one way and the power station the other, Red Poll cows on one side, the pebble beach with the seashell sculpture on the other, then as you come into Thorpeness you've got the Meare. It is really special.

LAST BELLY LAUGH?
Peter Kay's Car Share sketches. I just love him, he's hilarious.

SOMETHING ABOUT YOU THAT NOBODY KNOWS?
I wanted to be a hairdresser! I still have a knack, I can do a braid! Or an actor. I used to go to an after school thing at the Glenda Jackson Theatre in Birkenhead but then cheffing took over. That was the real calling.

SIGNATURE DISHES

Starters

Shaved cauliflower, broccoli & orange salad, pomegranate, sunflower seeds

Home-smoked salmon, pickles, crispy capers, celeriac remoulade

Crumbled feta, roast tomatoes, beetroot & pine nut salad

Mains

Shakshuka with toasted flatbread

Macaroni cheese, Suffolk ham, leek, parmesan shavings

Cured breast of chicken, smoked bacon, avocado, toasted cashews, pesto dressing

Puddings

Lemon tart, sweet vanilla cream

Coffee & walnut gateau, toffee fudge ice cream

The Kitchen's own giant florentine

GUILTY FOOD PLEASURE?
Ice cream and fruit cake! I love Christmas cake.

KITCHEN PLAY LIST?
I've got two different ones. At the Boathouse in Dedham it's a lot of 90s drum and bass. At The Kitchen the boys like old school rock 'n' roll.

Food and fantasy

Thorpeness is a curious place. Built by the Ogilvie family in the early 20th century as an upmarket holiday village, it is perhaps best known for its Peter Pan-themed boating lake, the Meare, and the water tower that has been converted into the iconic House in the Clouds holiday let.

The village, with its quirky mock-Tudor houses, is held in great affection by its devotees, some of whom have lived or holidayed there for generations. So there was consternation when the old Estate Office, midway between the Meare and the beach, was demolished to make way for a new building in 2013, with apartments above and a restaurant and vintage shop below.

Cameron and Claire Marshall, who were already running the successful Boathouse at Dedham, stepped in to open the restaurant, and local opinion swiftly changed. The Kitchen is open seven days a week and its relaxed dining means it's busy even midweek in winter. In summer, it's packed. "I could tell it was going to be another Dedham and I just knew it would be crazily busy in the summer," says Cameron. "It is a lovely room, the outlook is perfect. It really is a fantastic spot."

He describes the food as "restaurant-style, but to-go" and in addition to the regular menu he does a roaring trade in pizzas, either eat-in or takeaway. "Technically, the only takeaways are the pizzas," Cameron grins. "But sometimes people will say 'can I have the chicken and I'll bring the plate back tomorrow?' And that's fine."

The Kitchen@Thorpeness
Remembrance Road, Thorpeness IP16 4NW
W: thekitchenthorpeness.co.uk
T: 01728 453266
E: enquiries@thekitchenthorpeness.co.uk
- /TheKitchenThorpeness
- @thekitchenthorpeness
- /thekitchenthorpeness

Food served: all week B 9-11.30; L 12-3; Sunday brunch 9-3; D 5-8 Fri-Sat, July-Aug

Cost: starters from £4.95; mains from £7.50; desserts from £1; breakfast from £3; Sunday brunch from £3; wine from £15; pint from £4

Details: 40 seats in restaurant, 80 on terrace; private hire; event nights; dairy- and gluten-free cakes and savouries; children's menu; pizza menu including takeaways; double apartment available for rent; disabled access; dog-friendly; public parking

THE SAIL LOFT, SOUTHWOLD
JONATHAN NICHOLSON

The egg men

William Kendall's organic eggs travel a scant few miles to become the golden-yolked mainstays of Jonathan Nicholson's relaxed seaside menu

205

THE SAIL LOFT JONATHAN NICHOLSON

Jonathan Nicholson is smiling from ear-to-ear as he moves about the kitchen. He moves like a dancer, with the assurance of an accomplished chef who is comfortable and competent in his domain. This isn't surprising because Jonathan has been cooking for decades, having worked in large London restaurants and been chef proprietor of The Bell at Sax' before taking on The Sail Loft too in 2016 and dividing his time between the two properties. As he works, he explains how The Sail Loft has an easy informality to it and how, because of his expert co-chefs, it can cope with the stream of walk-ins and the demands of being open all day, every day, for good, freshly cooked food.

One of the joys, he says, of being in charge is that he is free to change menus on a whim, and to use local ingredients which are at their best on any particular day – this can even include plants foraged from the beach opposite.

On a shelf sits a tray of eggs from Maple Farm, the stars of The Sail Loft show today. "These beauties are really delicious and the yolks really yellow," says Jonathan with another big grin, "and they taste so fresh and rich, quite unlike anything you get in the average supermarket. You can use eggs to make so many things too; they're so versatile – mayonnaise, hollandaise, meringues, puddings or just on top of a croque madame or eggs benedict. And all those dishes taste better if you use proper eggs."

He darts from flaming cooker to worktop at speed, whisking, stirring, chopping the assembled ingredients. Seemingly in a trice the first of his dishes appears: a smoked haddock scotch egg with his own piccalilli. The plate is finished with pea shoots and a splash of vivid lemon zest oil. As he cuts the crunchy sphere in half the brightness of the yolk zings against the creamy soft casing and is, of course, the perfect consistency. "You see," he proclaims, "there's nothing like a genuine free-range egg when you're making it the centrepiece of a dish! Look at that colour! And I know exactly where these eggs come from and where the hens live – outside, running around like they should."

Three more plates of food are completed to Jonathan's satisfaction, produced with the expertise of a true professional, and presented at the table. A toasted muffin piled with spinach and smoked eel with a poached egg resting on top; smoked haddock chowder, rich and creamy; roast halibut and mussel fricassée. The aromas are mouth-wateringly wonderful and each dish looks good enough to eat, but temptation must be resisted. The finale from Jonathan's menu du matin is French toast with caramelised apple and sweet, crispy bacon, a dish in which every ingredient has been sourced locally. Jonathan chats happily as he cooks. He is loyal to his local suppliers: "I trust them and it's important to me to have top quality ingredients," he maintains, "it's fundamental to good cooking." Happily, Suffolk is not short of good, artisan products of every description, and over the years Jonathan has built up a network of reliable producers who share his values and keep him stocked with the best they can offer.

At Maple Farm, Kelsale, we visit the aforementioned contented hens. The home of William Kendall, Maple Farm is testament to its owner's commitment to organic, sustainable food production. Vegetables, fruit and seasonal salads are grown organically, and sold, as they come, to local stores and from the on-site farm shop. Maple Farm also produces honey from hives on the farm, special home-milled flours and a small range of organic meat that feeds the growing public desire for food from ethical sources.

Past the old-fashioned orchards, in a large field, the hens amble about, pecking and picking as they go. They cluster in groups as William and Jonathan approach and scurry this way and that, clucking loudly as some make a dash for their hen-house. Following them to collect enough eggs to fill a tray, William admits that sometimes it's hard to keep up with demand, but his hens don't lay to order and so much depends on the vagaries of their natural lifestyle.

His chosen breeds, Black Rocks, Light Sussex and Marans, have a variety of grasses to eat in their fields, a diet that is supplemented with home-milled feed made from peas and wheat grown at Maple Farm. The hens live in small flocks of a couple of hundred birds and, as with everything William does here, they are kept to the highest standards. Officially approved by the Soil Association, all the eggs are graded and sorted before leaving the farm for retail customers, with the not-so-perfect eggs kept for grateful friends and family.

William is obviously proud of his flocks, and as he and Jonathan wander among them they discuss the benefits of natural, organic production, the joys of delicious food, and the link to health and well-being. Surrounded by chickens, Jonathan relates his morning's menu with its eggy theme, and you could be forgiven for thinking that the Maple Farm hens are listening in, approving of it fully.

SUFFOLK FEAST

THE SAIL LOFT JONATHAN NICHOLSON

Smoked mackerel scotch egg with piccalilli

A simple light lunch or rustic starter, this is a little different from the familiar pork sausagemeat recipe. It uses the best of local Suffolk smoked fish and organic eggs with a country garnish of mustard-pickled vegetables. (serves 4)

Piccalilli
- 450g each of pickling onions, cauliflower florets, cucumber and green beans, all in bite-sized pieces
- 340g coarse rock salt
- 750ml distilled white malt vinegar
- 1 tbsp each of English mustard powder, ground ginger, ground turmeric and whole yellow mustard seeds
- 2 cloves garlic, peeled and chopped
- 175g light muscovado sugar
- 2-3 tbsp cornflour

Sterilise sufficient pickling jars, such as kilner flip top with seals.

Sprinkle the vegetables with salt in a glass bowl, toss, cover and chill for 12 hours.

Rinse well under a running tap for several minutes. Simmer the vinegar with the mustard, spices and garlic before adding the drained vegetables. Cook over a low heat until tender, about 20-25 minutes. Stir in the sugar and simmer for another few minutes.

Whisk a little water into 2 tbsp of cornflour to form a single cream texture, then stir well into the vegetables and cook for a further minute, leaving the mixture glossy and slightly thickened. If too thin, mix the remaining cornflour with a little more water and stir in similarly.

Leave to cool off the heat for 15 minutes and then carefully decant into the jars before sealing.

Store somewhere cool and dark for a month before using.

Forcemeat
- 4 smoked mackerel fillets, skinned
- 100g raw salmon fillet, boneless and skinned
- 100ml double cream
- 1 egg, beaten
- 1 small bunch of dill, chopped
- Zest of half a lemon
- 1 tbsp capers, chopped

Pulse all the ingredients in a food processor until just blended into a coarse but combined texture. Chill for 20 minutes.

Scotch eggs
- 4 large eggs
- Plain flour
- 2 eggs, beaten
- 200g day-old white breadcrumbs

Boil the eggs for 5 minutes, then submerge in iced water. Once cold, peel and dry on a clean tea towel.

Divide the forcemeat into four and flatten each piece out between oiled clingfilm into round patty shapes, sized to suit the circumference of the eggs.

Dust the eggs with plain flour, place one on each patty and carefully encase with the forcemeat. Place in the fridge to set for one hour.

Place the flour, beaten eggs and breadcrumbs into separate wide bowls. Dip one of the eggs through each bowl, covering well as you go, knocking off the excess crumbs. Shape carefully before setting aside on a floured tray and repeating with the remaining eggs. Chill for 20 minutes.

To serve
Deep-fry the scotch eggs for a few minutes in vegetable oil at 180c until golden, crispy and cooked through. Drain and lay on kitchen paper. To finish, season the warm eggs with sea salt and serve alongside the piccalilli.

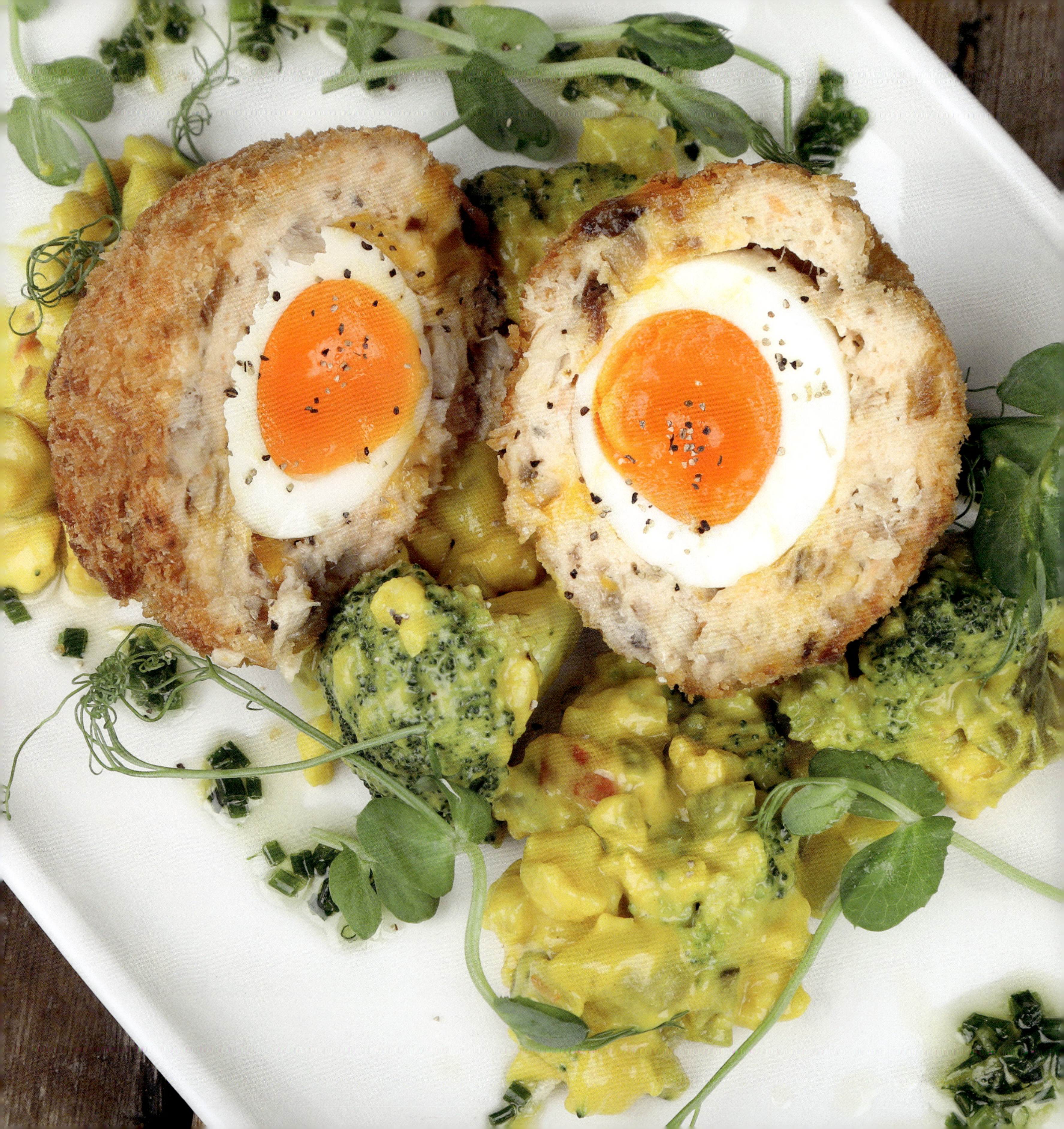

THE SAIL LOFT JONATHAN NICHOLSON

Eggs benedict with smoked eel and spinach

A brunch classic with a difference, replacing the crispy bacon with perhaps the best type of smoked fish you can buy. Cold or hot smoked salmon or trout works well too. (serves 2)

Salted butter
150ml milk
20g plain flour
2 tbsp wholegrain mustard
1 large handful baby spinach
4 eggs
2 English muffins
150g smoked eel fillet, shredded

Melt 20g of butter in the milk, add the flour and whisk together to a smooth sauce. Stir in the mustard and seasoning to taste.

Wash and drain the spinach before wilting down in a hot pan with a little butter and seasoning.

Poach the eggs and toast the muffins. Split the muffins and butter before topping with the spinach, smoked eel and an egg, finally coating with the mustard sauce.

Seafood fricassée

A flexible fishy main course for a simple lunch or a party appetiser. It works well with all firm, boneless, white fish and shellfish, just adapt the cooking time. I use halibut, smoothhound, cod or sea bream. Pictured, it is served with wilted kale and pea shoots. (serves 4)

1 small onion, chopped
1 garlic clove, finely sliced
Dry white vermouth or white wine
100ml good light stock
24 live closed mussels, cleaned
75ml double cream
4 white fish portions
Few sprigs of tarragon, leaves shredded, or pea shoots

Fry the onion and garlic together until softened, then add the vermouth and stock. Reduce to a few tablespoons. Add the mussels on a high heat, cover and turn down when simmering. Cook for a few minutes, stir and cover again. After another minute or two, check the mussels and discard any that haven't opened.

Strain the mussels, catching the liquor in a clean pan. Add the cream to the pan, simmer and season to taste. Keep warm.

Heat a frying pan and fry the oiled and seasoned fish fillets skinside down on a medium-hot heat. After a few minutes, turn over carefully and cook for 3-5 minutes until flaking. Remove and keep warm.

Bring the sauce back to a simmer, adding more cream if needed, and stir in the mussels. Serve up with the fish and dress with herbs or pea shoots.

French toast with apple and maple syrup

Another Sunday morning staple in our house, also known as eggy bread or 'pain perdu', it is delicious for kids of all ages. Best to use slightly stale brioche or to dry it out in a cool oven first. Smoky bacon and ripe strawberries eat well with the dish as pictured. (serves 2)

50ml full fat milk
2 eggs
2 thick slices of brioche
2 knobs unsalted butter
1 tbsp caster sugar, plus extra to caramelise
Pinch ground cinnamon
1 apple
Maple syrup

Whisk together the milk and eggs and dip in the brioche until well soaked.

Fry the brioche slices in a medium-hot frying pan with a knob of butter until golden-brown and crisp, about two minutes on each side. Keep warm.

Combine the caster sugar and cinnamon in a small bowl and set aside.

Peel, core and thinly slice the apple. Melt a knob of butter in a frying pan and toss the fruit in it for a few minutes, turning regularly and sprinkling in a little sugar to help the fruit caramelise.

Serve the French toast with the caramelised apples, a sprinkle of the cinnamon sugar and a good drizzle of maple syrup.

JONATHAN ON HIS...

LAST SUPPER?

On the menu – eggs Benedict with smoked salmon and crusty sourdough; aged Red Poll sirloin steak, Café de Paris butter, dripping chips, all the trimmings; Roquefort, apple and oatcakes with lots of port; toffee apple bread & butter pudding, whisky custard.

BEST DISHES EVER EATEN?

Marco's chicken liver and foie gras parfait at Harveys, it was perfect; oysters in San Fran' off the barbecue in a seaside seafood shack, somewhere off the beaten track; Mark Jordan's white chocolate mousse when we worked together at Congham Hall.

UNFULFILLED DREAM JOB?

Food producer, probably a goat farmer making dairy products and cheeses, and charcuterie.

TOOLS OF THE TRADE?

A dishwasher, human or machine; decent steel for sharp knives, essential; heavy chopping boards, wood is best at home; thick-bottomed saucepans.

FOODIE NOSTALGIA?

Marmite, on toast, eaten it since I was knee high, especially as soldiers into dippy eggs; fish and chips growing up in lovely Hunny (Hunstanton in North Norfolk).

COOK'S CHEAT

Speedy mayonnaise in a food processor- mix the egg yolk, mustard and garlic well first, then on maximum speed, blend in a fast trickle of oil at the beginning for a few seconds and then the rest at normal pouring speed from the bottle, no standing around taking ages, just finish with lemon juice when thickened, job done!

LUCKY DAY OFF?

On Southwold beach, down towards the dunes, fun for the kids, swimming, burying me in the sand, boogie boarding in the waves.

SIGNATURE DISHES

Starters

Seared cod cheeks, chorizo chilli jam, crème fraîche & pickled fennel

Our Sail Loft Bloody Mary prawn cocktail with crunchy gem salad

Sticky BBQ chicken wings, American blue cheese sauce

Mains

Roast sea bass with Deben mussels and pea chowder

Crispy confit lamb shoulder, champ potato, savoy cabbage, bacon and rosemary gravy

Reuben steak burger, pulled salt beef, Swiss cheese, sauerkraut, thick chips & slaw

Puddings

Sticky toffee banana pudding with salted caramel ice cream

Vanilla pannacotta, raspberry compote and lemon shortbread

Double chocolate brownie, pistachio ice cream and chocolate sauce

MIDNIGHT FEAST?

After work, lots of my favourite local cheeses, some of our home-made chutney or even Branston, forget the biscuits! Or a big bowl of steamed marinière mussels or one of our burgers, we do make rather special ones at both The Sail Loft and The Bell. I will also admit to an occasional kebab from up the street in Sax'. Pete at Zorba's uses the same great butchers as us, Jeremy at Clarke's of Bramfield, so I know it'll always be good!

SUFFOLK FEAST

A man with two missions

Jonathan Nicholson has had a very varied career in the food industry. Working in London in his younger days he quickly decided that he wanted to be his own boss, and settled on a pub well away from the capital in Long Melford.

His next move was to The Bell at Sax', the hotel-restaurant in Saxmundham that he bought in 2013. However, in 2017, not content with running just one place, the energetic Jonathan took on The Sail Loft, a bar/café/restaurant tucked between Southwold's grassy marshes and the beach on the road out of town that heads towards the harbour; he calls it 'Southwold's beachside hideaway'.

The property had been rebuilt and redecorated by Jonathan's predecessors and has a modern yet rustic look with reclaimed wood used for tables, old wine crates for shelves and bare wooden floors to cope with dogs and muddy boots. It's the perfect, no-fuss backdrop for Jonathan's no-nonsense, all-day menu; 'casual and fun' is how he puts it.

He supplements the food offer with regular themed evenings and live music, and the five en suite bedrooms upstairs provide good reason to extend a stay.

Jonathan relies on a team of ten chefs and near enough 50 employees to run The Sail Loft and The Bell at Sax'. He likes to make sure everything operates smoothly and, most importantly for a successful business, to keep his customers happy and coming back for more.

The Sail Loft
53 Ferry Road, Southwold IP18 6HQ
W: sailloftsouthwold.uk
T: 01502 725713
E: info@sailloftsouthwold.uk
- /TheSaiLloftSouthwold
- @TheSailLoftSW
- /thesailloftsw

Accolades and listings: winner, Family Dining Award, *EAT* Suffolk Food and Drink Awards 2018; 8 out of 10 hotel rating, *The Daily Telegraph*; recommended by Fiona Duncan's The Hotel Guru and by Cool Places

Food served: all week Mon-Sat 9.30-9; Sun B 9.30-12, L 12-6

Cost: starters from £5; mains from £13; desserts from £5; wine from £16.95; pint from £4

Details: 80 seats; al fresco tables; live music every Thursday; 5 en suite bedrooms; accessible; dogs welcome

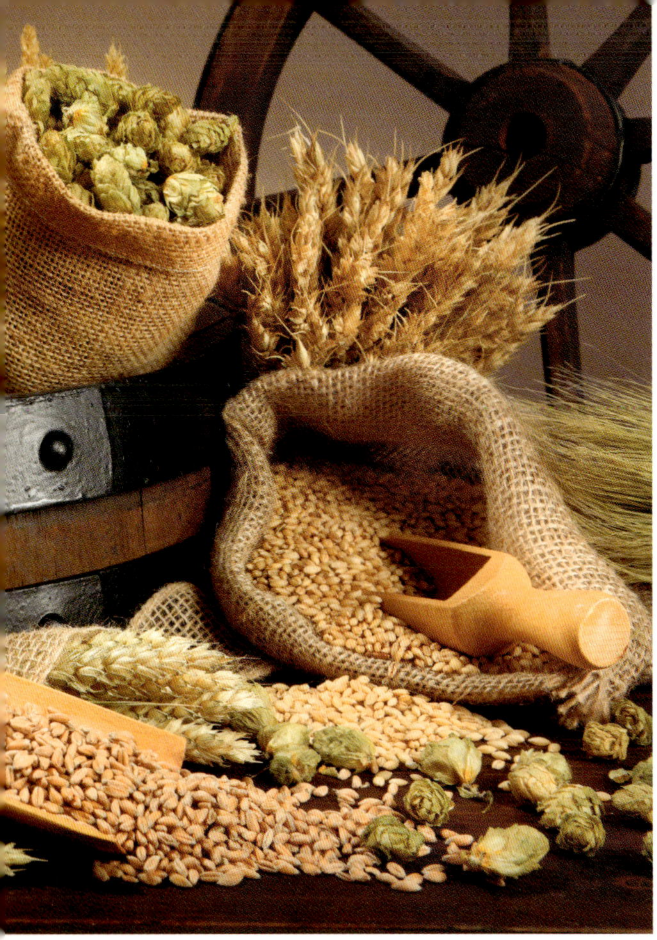
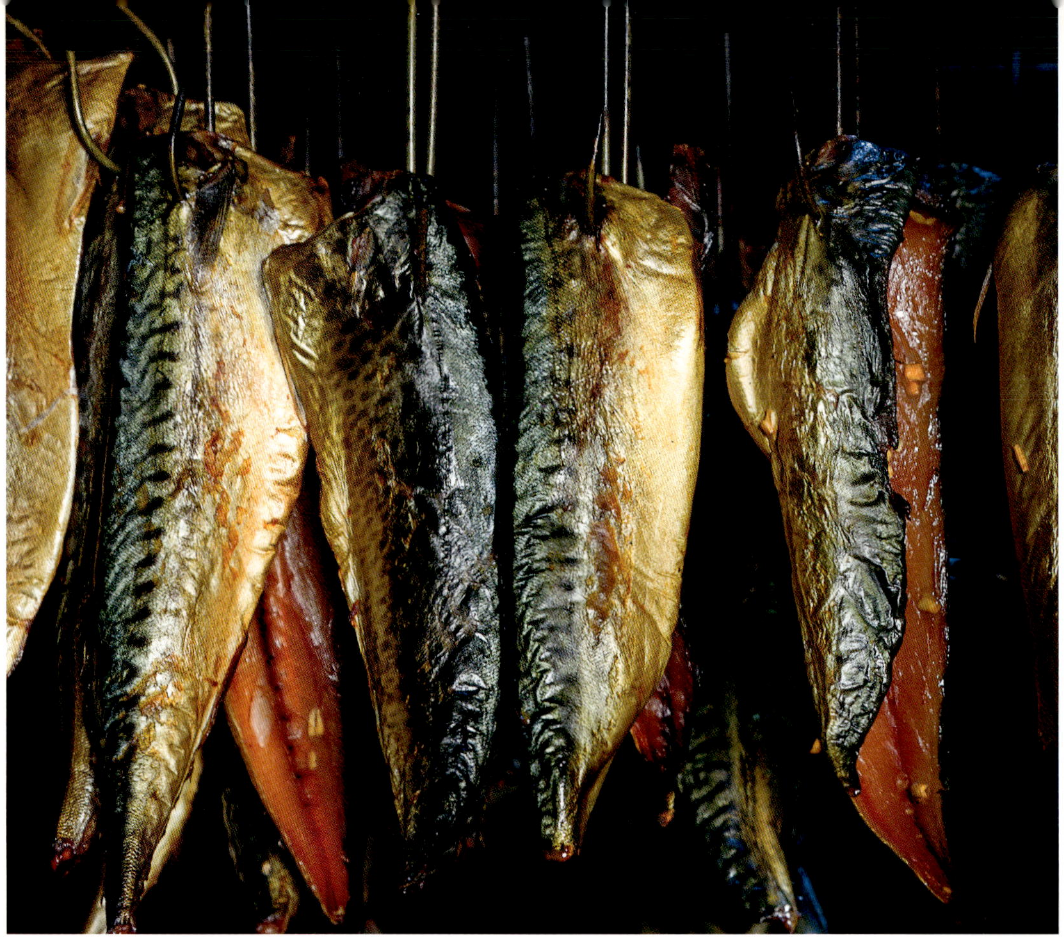
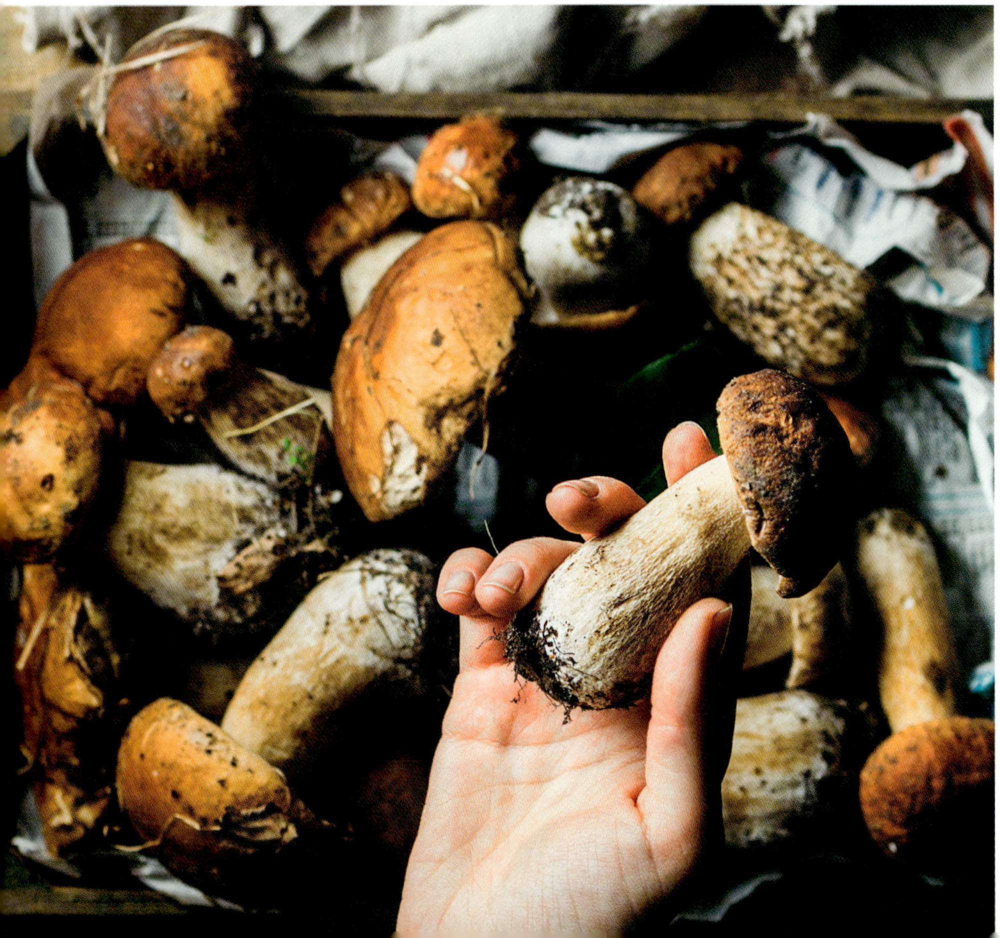
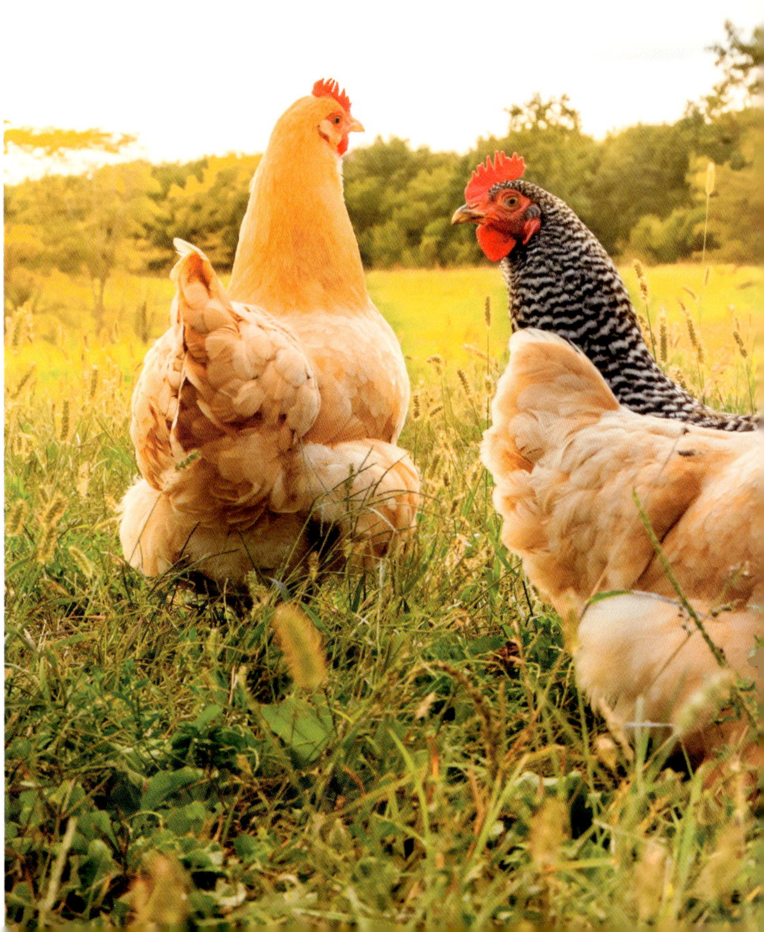

SUFFOLK FEAST

FOOD LOVERS' GUIDE

Welcome to our 'little black book', a guide to everything that is tasty about the lovely county of Suffolk that we are lucky enough to call home.

Whether you are exploring this wonderful corner of Britain as a first-time visitor, or are blessed enough to live here, we hope the following pages will open your eyes to some of the most delicious things about Suffolk, maybe tempt you to try some less familiar local foods or drinks, or discover places and foodie businesses that are off the beaten track, as well as visiting ones already firmly on the map.

OTB indicates that an entry is from 'over the border', because food lovers don't follow county boundaries...

If there's anything you feel we should have included, do let us know. Share the knowledge on our Facebook page, or drop us a note on Twitter @feastpublishing. We'd love to hear from you!

We hope you find our guide a perfect starting point to this delicious county, and that it helps you enjoy the Suffolk good life that little bit more.

FOOD LOVERS' GUIDE
Your deliciously indispensable companion to enjoying Suffolk, edible and otherwise

WHAT TO DRINK

BEER
Centuries of brewing tradition and modern techniques mean Suffolk's beers and ales need little introduction. From notable brands to small microbreweries, we get the best of grain.

Adnams Brewery
Sole Bay Brewery, East Green,
Southwold IP18 6JW
T: 01502 727200
W: adnams.co.uk/beers

Calvors Suffolk Lagers and Ales
T: 01449 711055
W: calvors.co.uk

Green Jack Brewery
Argyle Place, Love Road, Lowestoft NR32 2RF
T: 01502 562863
W: green-jack.com

Old Cannon Street Brewery
86 Cannon Street, Bury St Edmunds IP33 1JR
T: 01284 768769
W: oldcannonbrewery.co.uk

St Peter's Brewery
St Peter's Hall, St. Peter South Elmham,
near Bungay NR35 1NQ
T: 01986 782322
W: stpetersbrewery.co.uk

Nethergate Brewery
Rodbridge Corner, Long Melford CO10 9HJ
T: 01787 377087
W: nethergate.co.uk

St. Jude's Tavern and Microbrewery
(beers only sold at Tavern)
69 St. Matthew's Street, Ipswich IP1 3EW
T: 07879 360879
W: stjudestavern.com

Mauldon's The Black Adder Brewery
also at The Brewery Tap, 21 East Street,
Sudbury CO10 2TP
T: 01787 311055
W: mauldons.co.uk

Greene King
T: 01284 763222
W: greeneking.co.uk

CIDER AND PERRY
Perhaps more familiar to the West Country, our few cidermakers more than make up for their rarity with the quality of their produce.

Aspall Cyder
T: 01728 860510
W: aspall.co.uk

Shawsgate Vineyard *cider and still perry*
Badingham Road B1120, Framlingham IP13 9HZ
T: 01728 724060
W: shawsgate.co.uk

The Cider Place and Suffolk Apple Juice
Cherry Tree Farm, Halesworth Road,
Ilketshall St. Lawrence, near Bungay NR34 8LB
T: 01986 781353
W: suffolkapplejuice.co.uk

Harleston Cider Company *OTB*
T: 07886 940746
W: harlestoncider.co.uk

WINES
East Anglia's award-winning wines take more trophies than any other region of the UK.

Giffords Hall Vineyard
Shimpling Road, Hartest IP29 4EX
T: 01284 830799
W: giffordshall.co.uk

Wyken Vineyards
Wyken Road, Stanton IP31 2DW
T: 01359 250287
W: wykenvineyards.co.uk

Shawsgate Vineyard
Badingham Road B1120, Framlingham IP13 9HZ
T: 01728 724060
W: shawsgate.co.uk

Valley Farm Vineyards
Rumburgh Road, Wissett, near Halesworth IP19 0JJ
T: 07867 009967
W: valleyfarmvineyards.co.uk

Flint Vineyard, Earsham *OTB*
Camphill Farm, Middle Road, Earsham NR35 2AH
T: 01986 893209
W: flintvineyard.com

Dedham Vale Vineyard *OTB*
Green Lane, Boxted CO4 5TS
T: 01206 271136
W: dedhamvalevineyard.com

SPIRITS
Suffolk's enthusiasm for distilling is creating interesting and delicious bottlings.

Adnams Distillery
gins, whiskies, vodkas, liqueurs etc
Southwold Store (full store list under
Wine Merchants and Cookshops)
4 Drayman Square, Victoria Street,
Southwold IP18 6GB
T: 01502 725612
W: adnams.co.uk/spirits

Heart of Suffolk Distillery *gins*
4 Finbows Yard, Station Road, Bacton IP14 4NH
T: 07740 597331
W: heartofsuffolkdistillery.co.uk

Fishers Gin
W: fishersgin.com

Carpenter's Distillery *gins*
W: carpentersdistillery.co.uk

COLD DRINKS
Our fertile earth and history of mixed farming make orchards and soft fruit plantations a familiar part of our horticultural landscape.

James White Drinks
T: 01473 890111
W: jameswhite.co.uk

High House Fruit Farm
Off Ferry Road, Sudbourne IP12 2BL
T: 01394 450263
W: high-house.co.uk

Maynard House Orchards
T: 01284 388680
W: maynardhouse.co.uk

Hedgerow Cordials
T: 07950 248263
W: hedgerowcordials.co.uk

Suffolk Apple Juice and The Cider Place
Cherry Tree Farm, Halesworth Road, Ilketshall St.
Lawrence, near Bungay NR34 8LB
T: 01986 781353
W: suffolkapplejuice.co.uk

LA Kombucha *cold fermented teas*
W: labrewery.co.uk

COFFEE AND TEA

Morning coffee and afternoon tea are a great British tradition. These expert roasters and merchants have Suffolk passion and taste.

Paddy and Scott's *coffees*
The Bean Barn, Moat Park, Framlingham Road, Earl Soham IP13 7SR
T: 08444 778586
W: paddyandscotts.co.uk

The Suffolk Coffee Company
T: 07720 844016
W: thesuffolkcoffeecompany.co.uk

Fire Station Coffee Roasters & Café
21a Thoroughfare, Woodbridge IP12 1AA
T: 01394 383253
W: firestationcoffee.co.uk

Thistledown Cottage Coffee
T: 07818 813028
W: thistledowncottagecoffee.co.uk

Deepmills Coffee
T: 07549 999481
W: deepmills.co.uk

Butterworth and Son *coffees and teas*
T: 01284 767969
butterworthandson.co.uk

WHAT TO EAT

FARMYARD MEATS

Suffolk farmers' hard graft and rich pasture result in well-fed, well-bred livestock and poultry; discover these and other fine meats at your local independent butcher's shops.

Blythburgh Free Range Pork
T: 01986 873298
W: freerangepork.co.uk

Alde Valley Lamb via Salter & King, Aldeburgh
107-109 High Street, Aldeburgh IP15 5AR
T: 01728 452758
W: salterandking.co.uk

Peakhill Farm *grass-fed beef*
T: 01728 602248
W: peakhillfarm.co.uk

The Culford Flock
Jacob lamb and Highland/Angus beef
T: 07846 862037
W: club-noticeboard.co.uk/culfordflock

Cratfield Beef *traditional breed beef*
T: 01986 798099
W: cratfieldbeef.co.uk

Kenton Hall Estate *Longhorn beef*
T: 01728 862062
W: kentonhallestate.co.uk

Hundred River Farm *Hereford beef*
T: 01502 476063
W: hundredriverfarm.co.uk

Worlingworth Hall *Suffolk Red Poll beef*
The Grange, Tannington, Woodbridge IP13 7EL
T: 01728 628762
W: worlingworthhall.co.uk

Stackyard Nursery
Suffolk Horn lamb and Berkshire cross pork
Old Station Road, Mendlesham IP14 5RS
T: 01449 768078
W: stackyard-nursery.co.uk

Dingley Dell Pork
T: 01728 748097
W: dingleydell.com

Shimpling Park Farm *organic NZ Romney lamb*
T: 01284 827317
W: shimplingpark.com

Denham Estate *lamb*
T: 01284 810231
W: denhamestate.co.uk

Sutton Hoo Chicken
T: 01394 386797
W: suttonhoochicken.co.uk

Gressingham Foods *ducks and other poultry*
T: 01473 735456
W: gressinghamduck.co.uk

PA Mobbs and Sons *turkeys and guinea fowl*
T: 01986 798340
W: pamobbs.co.uk

GAME MEATS

The landscape of field, hedgerow and wood provides essential habitat for our flora 'n' fauna, and of course tasty, great value meat from fur and feather.

The Wild Meat Company *oven-ready game*
T: 01728 687627
W: wildmeat.co.uk

Truly Traceable *game pies and savouries*
T: 01986 835980
W: trulytraceable.com

New England Boar Company
T: 01440 763258
W: thenewenglandboarcompany.co.uk

Long Melford and Lavenham Game
T: 07812 580765
W: facebook.com/gamesmeatslml

Discover Venison
T: 07545 477693
W: discovervenison.co.uk

Bluebell Woods Wild Venison and Deer Control
T: 01502 733501
W: wildvenison.co.uk

Denham Estate Venison
T: 01284 810231
W: denhamestate.co.uk

MEAT PRODUCE

Great Suffolk meat gives us wonderful hams, bacon, sausages and other meat delicacies for a proper breakfast or hearty lunchtime snack.

Emmett's Ham
The Street, Peasenhall IP17 2HJ
T: 01728 660250
W: emmettsham.co.uk

Lane Farm Country Foods *hams*
Suffolk Salami Co.
T: 01379 384593
W: lanefarm.co.uk
suffolksalami.co.uk

Musk's of Newmarket *sausages*
T: 01638 662626
W: musks.com

Powters of Newmarket *sausages*
T: 01638 662418
W: powters.co.uk

FOOD LOVERS' GUIDE
Your deliciously indispensable companion to enjoying Suffolk, edible and otherwise

Procter's Sausages
T: 01473 281191
W: procters-sausages.co.uk

Truly Traceable *game pies and savouries*
T: 01986 835980
W: trulytraceable.com

The Pie Kitchen
T: 07846 953340
W: facebook.com/thepiekitchen

Curry Pie
T: 07948 387117
W: currypie.co.uk

Suffolk Pâté Company
T: 01449 760629
W: thesuffolkpatecompany.co.uk

Marsh Pig *salami & chorizo OTB*
T: 01508 480560
W: marshpig.co.uk

EGGS
A proper full English breakfast and good baking call for freshly laid, free-range eggs.

Maple Farm, Kelsale *organic eggs*
East Green, Kelsale, Saxmundham IP17 2PL
T: 01728 652000
W: maplefarmkelsale.co.uk

Worlingworth Hall *free-range eggs*
The Grange, Tannington, Woodbridge IP13 7EL
T: 01728 628762
W: worlingworthhall.co.uk

Havensfield Happy Hens *free-range eggs*
T: 01379 669039
W: havensfieldeggs.co.uk

Gate Farm, Flowton *free-range eggs*
Flowton Road, Flowton near Ipswich IP8 4LH
T: 01473 658394

FISH AND SEAFOOD
Our protected coastal reserves and rich, tidal waters provide a delicious, bountiful harvest.

Sole Bay Fish Co., Southwold
Shed 22e, Blackshore Harbour,
Southwold IP18 6ND
T: 01502 724241
W: solebayfishco.co.uk

Pinney's of Orford
The Old Warehouse, Quay Street, Orford IP12 2NU
T: 01394 459183
W: pinneysoforford.co.uk

Simpers of Ramsholt *home deliveries*
T: 01394 411025
W: simpersoframsholt.co.uk

SMOKEHOUSES
Curing and smoking to transform foods has been a long heritage tradition.

Suffolk Smokehouse and Deli
T: 01728 768263
W: suffolksmokehouse.net

Artisan Smokehouse, Café and Deli, Falkenham
Goose Barn, Back Road, Falkenham IP10 0QR
T: 01394 448414
W: artisansmokehouse.co.uk

Anchor Smokehouse, Lowestoft
Katwijk Way, Lowestoft NR32 1QZ
T: 01502 515744
W: facebook.com/anchorsmokehouse

Waveney Valley Smokehouse
T: 01502 589856
W: smoka.co.uk

CHEESE
Cheesemaking is enjoying a resurgence in Suffolk and our passionate farmers are producing a tasty variety of styles.

Suffolk Farmhouse Cheeses
Suffolk Gold & Suffolk Blue
Whitegate Farm, A140 Norwich Road,
Creeting St. Mary IP6 8PG
T: 01449 710458
W: suffolkcheese.co.uk

Rodwell Farm Dairy *Shipcord and Hawkston*
T: 01473 830192
W: rodwellfarmdairy.co.uk

Fen Farm Dairy *Baron Bigod brie*
Flixton Road, Bungay NR35 1PD
T: 01986 892350
W: fenfarmdairy.co.uk

White Wood Dairy *St. Jude*
T: 07771 618385
W: whitewooddairy.co.uk

Slate Cheese and Provisions,
Aldeburgh and Southwold
138 High Street, Aldeburgh IP15 5AQ
T: 01728 454052
6 Victoria Street, Southwold IP18 6HZ
T: 01502 724318
W: slatecheese.co.uk

Hamish Johnston Fine Cheeses
T: 01394 388127
W: hamishjohnston.com

DAIRY AND ICE CREAM
Our strength in livestock farming and milk production gives a wide and delicious range.

Alder Tree Fruit Cream Ices
T: 01449 721220
W: alder-tree.co.uk

Suffolk Meadow Ice Cream
T: 01986 899320
W: suffolkmeadow.co.uk

Hadley's of Lavenham *ice cream parlour*
91 High St, Lavenham CO10 9PZ
T: 01787 249001
W: handmadebyhadleys.co.uk

Criterion Ices
T: 01359 230208
W: criterion-ices.co.uk

Parravanis Ice Creams
T: 01502 715970
W: parravanis.co.uk

Marybelle Dairy *milk and dairy produce*
T: 01986 784658
W: marybelle.co.uk

Hundred River Farm *ice cream and dairy produce*
T: 01502 476063
W: hundredriverfarm.co.uk

The Calf At Foot Dairy, Somerleyton
raw Jersey milk
Home Farm, B1074 Somerleyton NR32 5PR
T: 07787 103508
W: the-calf-at-foot-dairy.co.uk

Old Hall Farm, Woodton *dairy produce OTB*
Norwich Road, Woodton NR35 2LP
T: 07900 814252
W: oldhallfarm.co.uk

Lickety Ice *gourmet frozen lollies*
T: 07737 229041
W: licketyice.co.uk

SUFFOLK FEAST

CAKES, BREADS AND PASTRIES

The best of grain gives bakers and cakemakers the finest raw ingredient in flour, delicious when combined with our beet sugar (Silver Spoon), rich dairy and free range eggs.

Pump Street Bakery *artisan breads*
1 Pump Street, Orford IP12 2LZ
T: 01394 459829
W: pumpstreetbakery.com

Maple Farm Kelsale *flours*
East Green, Kelsale near Saxmundham IP17 2PL
T: 01728 652000
W: maplefarmkelsale.co.uk

Wooster's, Bardwell *artisan breads and bakery*
The Windmill, School Lane, Bardwell IP31 1AD
T: 01359 408409
W: woostersbakery.co.uk

Simply Home Bake *cakes and sponges*
T: 01473 829348
W: suffolkmarketevents.co.uk

Farmhouse Cooking *cakes and savouries*
T: 01728 746344
W: farmhousecooking.co.uk

Harrisons Bakery *cakes*
T: 07714 662424
W: harrisonsbakery.com

The Penny Ben Bakehouse *artisan breads*
T: 07737 537880
W: thepennybunbakehouse.co.uk

The Cake Shop Bakery *breads and cakes*
19 Thoroughfare, Woodbridge IP12 1AA
T: 01394 382515
W: cakeshopbakery.com

Moo Moo Cakes
T: 07400 967799
W: moomoocakes.co.uk

The Friendly Loaf Bakery *breads and quiches*
T: 01284 754252
W: thefriendlyloaf.co.uk

The Wheaten Mill *cakes*
T: 01473 827010
W: wheatenmill.co.uk

Two Magpies Bakery *breads and cakes*
88 High Street, Southwold IP18 6DP
T: 01502 726120
W: twomagpiesbakery.co.uk

Earsham Street Café *cakes*
11-13 Earsham Street, Bungay NR35 1AE
T: 01986 893103
W: earshamstreetcafe.co.uk

Cakes To Celebrate
T: 01986 781382
W: cakes-to-celebrate.co.uk

Suffolk Cupcake Company
W: suffolkcupcakes.co.uk

Vanilla Pâtisserie
T: 01728 445000
W: vanillapatisserie.co.uk

Lady Bakewell-Park *cakes and iced biscuits*
T: 07841 922677
W: ladybakewellpark.com

SWEETS AND CHOCOLATES

Over coffee or any time of the day, an energy boost or simple luxury, sticky confectionery and chocolates hit the spot.

Pump Street Chocolate
1 Pump Street, Orford IP12 2LZ
T: 01394 459829
W: pumpstreetbakery.com

Tosier Chocolates
T: 07760 478724
W: tosier.co.uk

Ailsa's Country Cream Fudge
T: 01502 740365
W: aldeburghfoodanddrink.co.uk

B Chocolates
T: 07939 262001
W: bchocolates.co.uk

Petite and Sweet *chocolates and wedding favours*
T: 07908 200179
W: petiteandsweet.co.uk

Artistry in Cocoa *chocolate products*
T: 01638 660503
W: artistryincocoa.co.uk

VEGETABLES, HERBS AND SALADS

Farmers and market gardeners make great use of fertile soils and a perfect climate.

Humdinger Produce
T: 01394 421449
W: humdingerproduce.co.uk

Trimley Herbs
T: 07807 658689
W: trimleyherbs.co.uk

Waveney Mushrooms
T: 01986 782571
W: waveneymushrooms.co.uk

Home Farm Nacton
T: 01473 659280
W: homefarmnacton.co.uk

Clinks Care Farm, Toft Monks *OTB veg boxes and farm shop*
Church Road, Toft Monks NR34 0ET
T: 01502 679134
W: clinkscarefarm.org.uk

Moyns Park Organics *garden produce OTB*
T: 07772 457063
W: moynsparkorganics.co.uk

ORGANIC, DIETARY AND FREE-FROM FOODS

Special or selective diets and chemical-free production can bring benefits for health and nature.

Food By Lizzi *vegetarian & vegan foods*
T: 07724 004171
W: foodbylizzi.com

Organics for All at Longwood Organic Farm
The Green, Tuddenham St. Mary IP28 6TB
T: 01638 717120
W: organicsforall.co.uk

Swallow Organics, Saxmundham
High Marsh, Brussels Green, Darsham IP17 3RN
T: 01728 668201

KITCHEN ESSENTIALS AND SUNDRIES

The simpler things and the kitchen basics are often the foundation for good food.

Hillfarm Oils *virgin rapeseed oil and mayonnaises*
T: 01986 798660
W: hillfarmoils.com

Aspall *vinegars*
T: 01728 860510
W: aspall.co.uk

Hodmedod's *pulses and grains*
T: 01986 467567
W: hodmedods.co.uk

FOOD LOVERS' GUIDE
Your deliciously indispensable companion to enjoying Suffolk, edible and otherwise

Pakenham Water Mill *flours*
Mill Road, Pakenham,
Bury St. Edmunds IP31 2NB
T: 01359 230275
W: pakenhamwatermill.org.uk

Woodbridge Tide Mill *flours*
Tide Mill Way, Woodbridge IP12 1BY
T: 01394 388202
W: woodbridgetidemill.org.uk

Badu's Indian Feast *masala curry kits*
T: 07824 345521
W: badusindianfeast.co.uk

Curry With Love *spice boxes*
21 High Street, Ixworth IP31 2HH
T: 01359 408941
W: curry-with-love.co.uk

Red Chilli Kitchen *Vietnamese spice products*
T: 07977 218169
W: redchillikitchen.co.uk

Red Hot Chilli Fella *chilli Products*
T: 07807 555570
W: redhotchillifella.co.uk

Munchy Seeds
T: 01728 833004
W: munchyseeds.co.uk

Newlands Cheese Straws
T: 07850 072061
W: newlandscheesestraws.com

Barbecube *charcoal*
T: 01449 721220
W: facebook.com/barbecubeuk

CountryCare Charcoal
T: 01728 747474
W: countrycare.co.uk

Barkers of Suffolk *gourmet pet treats*
T: 01473 597598
W: barkersofsuffolk.co.uk

The Prior's Flour, Swaffham Prior *OTB*
T: 01638 741009
W: priorsflour.co.uk

PICKLES, PRESERVES AND HONEY
Picked in season and conserved in style, condiments should be consumed with relish.

Mr Bees Honey
T: 07503 773630
W: mrbees.co.uk

The Apple Butter Company
T: 07985 411289
W: applebuttercompany.co.uk

Fruits of Suffolk
T: 01449 760629
W: fruitsofsuffolk.co.uk

Mrs Bennett's Pickles
T: 01473 822650
W: mrsbennetts.co.uk

Scarlett and Mustard *dressings*
T: 01728 685210
W: scarlettandmustard.co.uk

Stokes Sauces *table sauces*
T: 01394 462150
W: stokessauces.co.uk

Hillfarm *virgin rapeseed oil and mayonnaises*
T: 01986 798660
W: hillfarmoils.com

Salubrious Sauce Company
T: 01394 548709
W: salubrioussauceco.co.uk

East Coast Chilli Company *chilli sauces*
T: 07563 360703
W: eastcoastchillicompany.co.uk

Sym's Pantry *bacon condiments*
T: 07933 710185
W: symspantry.com

Bee House Honey Company *OTB*
T: 07975 591617
W: facebook.com/bhhoneycompany

PLACES TO BUY

FARMERS' MARKETS
Perhaps a true expression of our historic family farms and artisan food and drink production, the best farmers' markets thrive as an essential part of our Suffolk food scene.

Wyken Vineyards Farmers' Market, Stanton
every Saturday 9-1
Wyken Road, Stanton IP31 2DW
T: 01359 250287
W: wykenvineyards.co.uk

Woodbridge Farmers' Market
2nd & 4th Saturdays monthly 9-12.30
Woodbridge Community Hall,
Station Road, Woodbridge IP12 4AU
T: 01394 383128
W: woodbridgefarmersmarket.co.uk

Lavenham Farmers' Market
4th Sunday monthly 10-1.30
Lavenham Village Hall, Church St,
Lavenham CO10 9QT
T: 07704 627973
W: suffolkmarketevents.co.uk

Sudbury Farmers' Market
last Friday monthly 9.30-2
St. Peter's Sudbury, Market Hill,
Sudbury CO10 2EA
T: 07704 627973
W: suffolkmarketevents.co.uk

Bury St Edmunds Farmers' Market
2nd Sunday monthly 10-4
The Traverse, Bury St Edmunds IP33 1BJ
T: 07704 627973
W: suffolkmarketevents.co.uk

Snape Maltings Farmers' Market
1st Saturday monthly 9.30-1
Snape Bridge B1069, Snape IP17 1SP
T: 01728 688303
W: snapemaltings.co.uk

Beccles Farmers Market
1st and 3rd Saturday monthly 9-1
Ellough Airfield, Ellough, near Beccles
T: 01502 476240
W: beccllesfarmersmarket.co.uk

DELIS AND FOOD HALLS
While we love local fresh seasonal produce, we get ever more fascinated with globe-trotting cuisines and flavours to add interest to our food. Well-stocked knowledgeable purveyors are a joy to explore.

Food Hall & Pantry at Snape Maltings
Snape Bridge B1069, Snape IP17 1SP
T: 01728 688303
W: snapemaltings.co.uk

The Courtyard, Elveden Estate
Brandon Road, Elveden IP24 3TJ
T: 01842 898068
W: elvedencourtyard.com

SUFFOLK FEAST

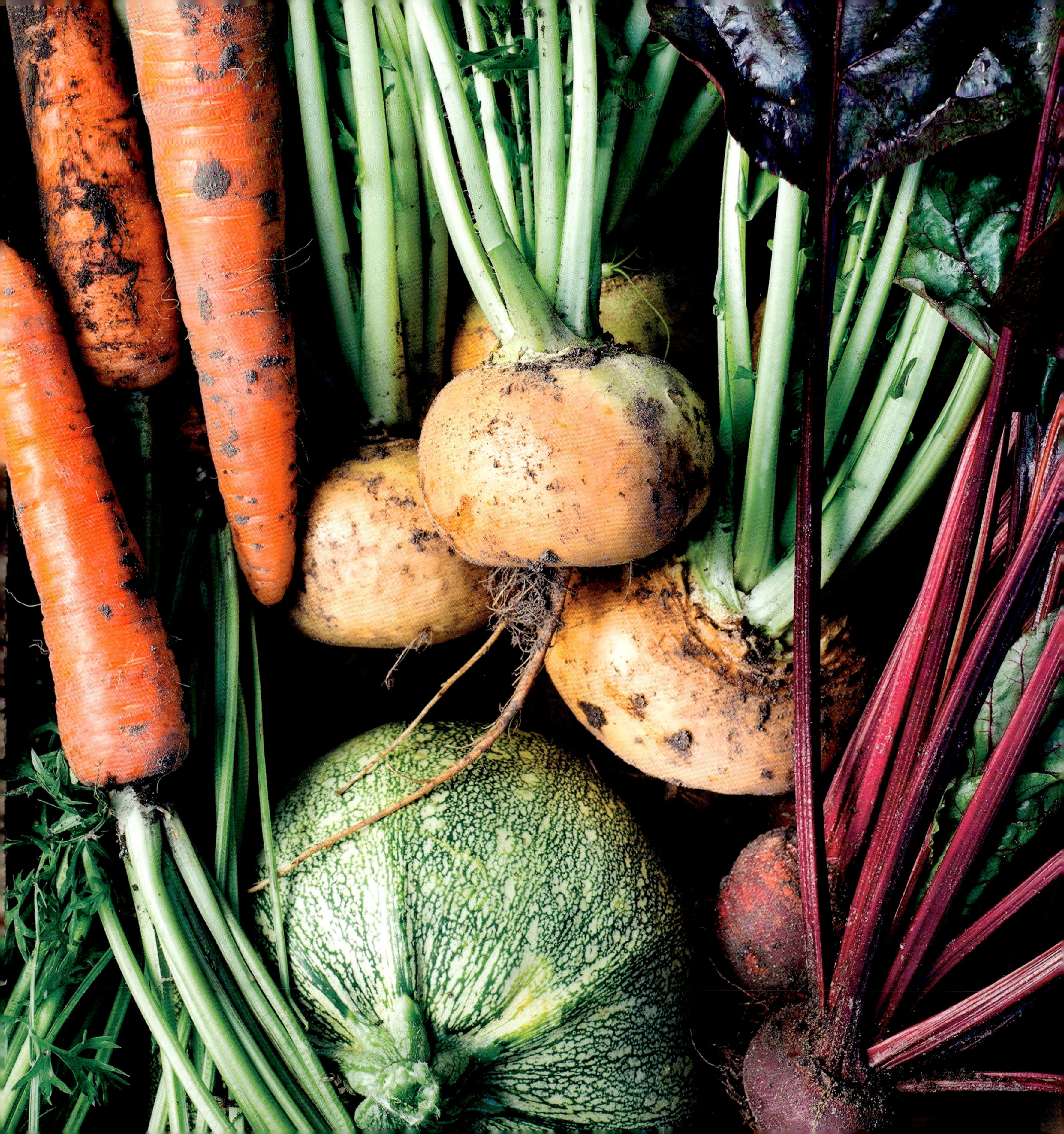

FOOD LOVERS' GUIDE

Your deliciously indispensable companion to enjoying Suffolk, edible and otherwise

Emmett's Stores, Peasenhall
The Street, Peasenhall IP17 2HJ
T: 01728 660250
W: emmettsham.co.uk

Suffolk Food Hall, Wherstead
B1456 Wherstead, near Ipswich IP9 2AB
T: 01473 786610
W: suffolkfoodhall.co.uk

Farm Café + Shop, Marlesford
Main Road A12, Marlesford,
near Wickham Market IP13 0AG
T: 01728 747717
W: farmcafe.co.uk

Slate Cheese and Provisions,
Aldeburgh and Southwold
138 High Street, Aldeburgh IP15 5AQ
T: 01728 454052
6 Victoria Street, Southwold IP18 6HZ
T: 01502 724318
W: slatecheese.co.uk

Artisan Smokehouse, Café and Deli, Falkenham
Goose Barn, Back Road, Falkenham IP10 0QR
T: 01394 448414
W: artisansmokehouse.co.uk

Leo's Deli, Framlingham
17 Market Hill, Framlingham IP13 9AN
T: 01728 724059
W: leosdeli.co.uk

Earsham Street Delicatessen, Bungay
51 Earsham St, Bungay NR35 1AF
T: 01986 894754
W: earshamstreetdeli.co.uk

The Black Dog Deli, Walberswick
The Street, Walberswick IP18 6UG
T: 01502 723925
W: blackdogdeliwalberswick.com

DeliCafé at The Chilli Farm, Mendlesham
Norwich Road A140, Mendlesham IP14 5NQ
T: 01449 766344
W: delicafeatchillifarm.co.uk

The Pantry, Newmarket
17-18 The Guineas, Newmarket CB8 8EQ
T: 01638 661181
W: thepantryfinefoods.com

Bailey's Deli, Beccles
2 Hungate, Beccles NR34 9TL
T: 01502 710609
W: upstairsatbaileys.co.uk

Focus Organic, Halesworth
14 Thoroughfare, Halesworth IP19 8AH
T: 01986 872899
W: focusorganic.co.uk

Chilli and Chives Deli-Café, Lavenham
16A High St, Lavenham CO10 9PT
T: 01787 249028

Juniper Barn, Rendham
Bridge Street, Rendham IP17 2AZ
T: 01728 663773
W: juniperbarnsuffolk.co.uk

Thoroughfare Delicatessen, Halesworth
4 Thoroughfare, Halesworth IP19 8AH
T: 01986 872000

Thorpeness Village Stores
Peace Place, Old Homes Road, Thorpeness IP16 4NA
T: 01728 451930
W: thorpenessdolphin.com

Fergusons Delicatessen
48 High Street, Hadleigh IP7 5AL
T: 01473 824665
W: fergusonsdelicatessen.co.uk

FARM SHOPS

Agricultural diversification has become vital in recent years. Selling produce direct has saved many farmers and enabled communities to understand where their food comes from. Support your local farmer!

Hollow Trees Farm Shop, Semer
Semer, near Hadleigh IP7 6HX
T: 01449 741247
W: hollowtrees.co.uk

Maple Farm Kelsale
East Green, Kelsale near Saxmundham IP17 2PL
T: 01728 652000
W: maplefarmkelsale.co.uk

Friday Street Farm Shop
Friday Street A1094 near Snape IP17 1JX
T: 01728 602783
W: fridaystfarm.co.uk

Alder Carr Farm Shop, Creeting St. Mary
off St. Mary's Road, Creeting St. Mary,
near Needham Market IP6 8LX
T: 01449 720820
W: aldercarrfarm.co.uk

Jimmy's Farm, Wherstead
Pannington Hall Lane, Wherstead,
near Ipswich IP9 2AR
T: 01473 604206
W: jimmysfarm.com

Emmerdale Farm Shop, Darsham
Westleton Road, Darsham,
near Yoxford IP17 3BP
T: 01728 668648
W: emmerdalefarmshop.co.uk

High House Fruit Farm
Sudbourne, Woodbridge IP12 2BL
T: 01394 450263
W: high-house.co.uk

Willow Tree Farm Shop, Glemsford
Lower Road, Glemsford, Sudbury CO10 7QU
T: 01787 280341
W: willowtreefarmshop.co.uk

Maisebrooke Farm, Shipmeadow
Shipmeadow B1062 near Beccles NR34 8HJ
T: 01502 711018

Wangford Farm Shop
Church Street, Wangford,
near Southwold NR34 8AS
T: 01502 578246
W: wangfordfarmshop.co.uk

Market Fields Farm Shop, Halesworth
Holton Road Garden Centre, 36 Holton Road,
Halesworth IP19 8HG
T: 01986 872134

Railway Farm Shop, Benhall
Main Road, Benhall Green,
near Saxmundham IP17 1NA
T: 01728 605793

Wheldon's Fruit Farm Shop, Newton Leys
Joes Road, Newton Leys,
Sudbury CO10 0QE
T: 01787 374322
W: wheldonsfruitfarm.co.uk

Garnetts Gardens, Hacheston
The Street, Hacheston,
near Woodbridge IP13 0DT
T: 01728 724589
W: garnettsgardens.co.uk

Bloomsberries Café and Deli, Lakenheath
Christmas Hill Farm, Station Road,
Lakenheath IP27 9AB
T: 01842 861144
W: christmashill.co.uk

Mr Allard's Farm Shop and Butchery, Stowupland
Rendall Lane, Stowupland,
near Stowmarket IP14 4BD
T: 01449 678650
W: mrallardsfarmbutchery.com

Assington Farm Shop
Assington Barn, The Street, Assington CO10 5LW
T: 01787 211610
W: thebarnassington.co.uk

North Green Farm Shop
London Road, Shadingfield NR34 8DF
T: 07717 075312
W: facebook.com/thenorthgreenfarmshop

Heath Farm, Hessett
off The Green, Hessett
near Bury St Edmunds IP30 9BE
T: 07788 428109
W: heathfarmsuffolk.co.uk

Laurel Farm Garden Centre, Ipswich
Henley Road, Ipswich IP1 6TE
T: 01473 215984
W: laurelfarmgardencentre.co.uk

Victoria Nurseries, Ipswich
1 Kettlebaston Way,
Westerfield Road, Ipswich IP4 2XX
T: 01473 253980
W: victorianurseriesipswich.co.uk

La Hogue Farm Shop, Chippenham *OTB*
La Hogue Road, Chippenham,
near Newmarket CB7 5PZ
T: 01638 751128
W: lahogue.co.uk

Hall Farm Shop & Café *OTB*
Hall Farm, Church Road, Stratford St. Mary,
near Colchester, Essex CO7 6LS
T: 01206 322572
W: hallfarmshop.com

Clinks Care Farm, Toft Monks *OTB*
Church Road, Toft Monks NR34 0ET
T: 01502 679134
W: clinkscarefarm.org.uk

Old Hall Farm, Woodton *OTB*
Norwich Road, Woodton NR35 2LP
T: 07900 814252
W: oldhallfarm.co.uk

BUTCHERS
Well-bred, well-hung farmyard meats are what our foodie county is well known for. Befriend your local independent butcher.

Mills and Sons, Southwold
23 Market Place, Southwold IP18 6ED
T: 01502 722104
W: twitter.com/mills_and_sons

Salter & King, Aldeburgh
107-109 High Street, Aldeburgh IP15 5AR
T: 01728 452758
W: salterandking.co.uk

John Hutton Butchers, Earl Soham
The Street, Earl Soham IP13 7SA
T: 01728 685259
W: johnhuttonbutcher.co.uk

E W Revett and Son Butcher, Wickham Market
81 High St, Wickham Market IP13 0RA
T: 01728 746263
W: revett.co.uk

Lavenham Butchers
1 High Street, Lavenham CO10 9PX
T: 01787 247226
W: lavenhambutchers.com

Eric Tennant Butchers, Newmarket
11 The Guineas Centre, Newmarket CB8 8EQ
T: 01638 661530
W: erictennantbutcher.co.uk

Ruse and Son Family Butchers, Long Melford
Hall Street, Long Melford CO10 9JF
T: 01787 378227
W: rusebutchers.co.uk

Mr Allard's Farm Shop and Butchery, Stowupland
Rendall Lane, Stowupland, near Stowmarket IP14 4BD
T: 01449 678650
W: mrallardsfarmbutchery.com

Maisebrooke Farm Meats, Shipmeadow
Shipmeadow B1062 near Beccles NR34 8HJ
T: 01502 711018

Procter's Sausages, Ipswich
12, The Walk, Ipswich IP1 1EE
T: 01473 281191
W: procters-sausages.co.uk

Powters Butchers' and Newmarket Sausages
Wellington St, Newmarket CB8 0HT
T: 01638 662418
W: powters.co.uk

Clarke's of Bramfield
Low Road, Bramfield, near Halesworth IP19 9JH
T: 01986 784244
W: clarkesofbramfield.co.uk

Creaseys of Peasenhall
The Causeway, Peasenhall, near Yoxford IP17 2HU
T: 01728 660219
W: creaseysofpeasenhall.co.uk

Emmerdale Farm Shop, Darsham
Westleton Road, Darsham near Yoxford IP17 3BP
T: 01728 668648
W: emmerdalefarmshop.co.uk

Rolfe's Butchers, Walsham le Willows and Elmswell
The Street, Walsham le Willows IP31 3AZ
T: 01359 259225
Station Road, Elmswell IP30 9HD
T: 01359 241181
W: rolfesbutchers.co.uk

J R Creasey, Woodbridge
6 Turban Centre, Hamblin Walk, Woodbridge IP12 1DE
T: 01394 386739

BAKERS
Perfect loaves and plump cakes are always best from an artisan baker's shop.

Pump Street Bakery, Orford
1 Pump Street, Orford IP12 2LZ
T: 01394 459829
W: pumpstreetbakery.com

The Cake Shop Bakery, Woodbridge
19 Thoroughfare, Woodbridge IP12 1AA
T: 01394 382515
W: cakeshopbakery.com

Two Magpies Bakery, Southwold
88 High Street, Southwold IP18 6DP
T: 01502 726120
W: twomagpiesbakery.co.uk

Wooster's, Bardwell
The Windmill, School Lane, Bardwell IP31 1AD
T: 01359 408409
W: woostersbakery.co.uk

Sparling and Faiers, Lavenham
11 Market Place, Lavenham CO10 9QZ
T: 01787 247297

Tudor Bakehouse, Eye
11 Broad Street, Eye IP23 7AF
T: 01379 870974
W: tudorbakehouse.co.uk

FOOD LOVERS' GUIDE
Your deliciously indispensable companion to enjoying Suffolk, edible and otherwise

FISHMONGERS
With deep river estuaries and a long coastline, fresh fish continues to be a delicious treat, especially from our small in-shore day boats.

Pinneys of Orford
The Old Warehouse, Quay St, Orford IP12 2NU
T: 01394 459183
W: pinneysoforford.co.uk

Paul's Fishbox, Woodbridge
The Kiosk, Turban Centre, Hamblin Road,
Woodbridge IP12 1DE
T: 01394 384939
W: twitter.com/paulsfishbox

Maximus Fish at Friday Street Farm Shop
Friday Street A1094 near Snape IP17 1JX
T: 01728 607554
W: maximusfish.co.uk

Turners Fishmongers' Van
West Suffolk – various locations
T: 01787 377768 / 07971 811947
W: turners-fishmongers.business.site

Springtide Fish, Felixstowe
Ferry Road, Felixstowe Ferry IP11 9RZ
T: 01394 284582

GREENGROCERS
Market gardeners and farmers grace the shelves with their fresh, seasonal produce.

Giddens and Thompson, Bungay
36b Earsham Street, Bungay NR35 1AQ
T: 01986 897944
W: facebook.com/giddensandthompson

Crab Apple, Southwold
21 Market Place, Southwold IP18 6ED
T: 01502 722329

Market Garden Produce, Woodbridge
10 Hamblin Rd, Woodbridge IP12 1DE
T: 01394 386298

Melons, Halesworth
50 Thoroughfare, Halesworth IP19 8AR
T: 01986 874562
W: melonshalesworth.co.uk

Rose's Fruit Fare, Southwold
3 Market Place, Southwold IP18 6DX
T: 01502 723232

ORGANIC AND HEALTH FOOD STORES
Specialist food stores cater for those seeking specific diets and wholesome ingredients.

Hungate Health Store, Beccles
4 Hungate, Beccles NR34 9TL
T: 01502 715009
W: facebook.com/hungatehealthstore

Focus Organic, Halesworth
14 Thoroughfare, Halesworth IP19 8AH
T: 01986 872899
W: focusorganic.co.uk

The Bodhi Tree, Bury St Edmunds
9 The Traverse, Bury St Edmunds IP33 1BJ
T: 01284 755410

WINE MERCHANTS AND DRINK STORES
For most, great food would be missing a link without something good in the glass.

Adnams Stores all over Suffolk
Victoria Street, Southwold IP18 6GB
T: 01502 725612
Station Road, Woodbridge IP12 4AU
T: 01394 386594
43a Cornhill, Bury St Edmunds IP33 1DX
T: 01284 705746
179b High Street, Aldeburgh IP15 5AN
T: 01728 454520
73-75 High Street, Hadleigh IP7 5DY
T: 01473 827796
Old Auction Rooms, 1 Market Street,
Saffron Walden CB10 1HZ *OTB*
T: 01799 527281
Behind the Cardinal's Hat, 23 The Thoroughfare,
Harleston IP20 9AS *OTB*
T: 01379 854788

Richard Kihl Fine Wines
140-144 High Street, Aldeburgh IP15 5AQ
T: 01728 454455
W: richardkihl.ltd.uk

DJ Wines *fruit wines and liqueurs*
T: 07882 649833
W: dj-wines.com

Trevor Hughes Wines
5 Station Way, Brandon IP27 0BH
T: 01842 814414
W: trevorhugheswines.com

The Wine Store, Chippenham *OTB*
La Hogue Road, Chippenham,
near Newmarket CB7 5PZ
T: 01638 555190
W: winetasting.co.uk

COOKWARE
Good chefs, amateur or pro', need the best cooks' toys, both traditional tools and the latest kitchen wizardry.

Adnams Stores throughout Suffolk and beyond
Victoria Street, Southwold IP18 6GB
T: 01502 725612
Station Road, Woodbridge IP12 4AU
T: 01394 386594
43a Cornhill, Bury St Edmunds IP33 1DX
T: 01284 705746
179b High Street, Aldeburgh IP15 5AN
T: 01728 454520
73-75 High Street, Hadleigh IP7 5DY
T: 01473 827796
Old Auction Rooms, 1 Market Street,
Saffron Walden CB10 1HZ *OTB*
T: 01799 527281
Behind the Cardinal's Hat, 23 The Thoroughfare,
Harleston IP20 9AS *OTB*
T: 01379 854788

House & Garden at Snape Maltings
Snape Bridge B1069, Snape IP17 1SP
T: 01728 688303
W: snapemaltings.co.uk

The Woodbridge Kitchen Company
7 Thoroughfare, Woodbridge IP12 1AA
T: 01394 382091
W: woodbridgekitchencompany.co.uk

The Steamer Trading Cook Shop
79 St. John's St, Bury St Edmunds IP33 1SQ
T: 01284 705636
W: steamer.co.uk

Henry Watson Potteries
Pottery Hill, Wattisfield IP22 1NH
T: 01359 251239
W: henrywatson.com

Winch and Blatch, Sudbury
22 King St, Sudbury CO10 2EH
T: 01787 373737
W: winchblatch.co.uk

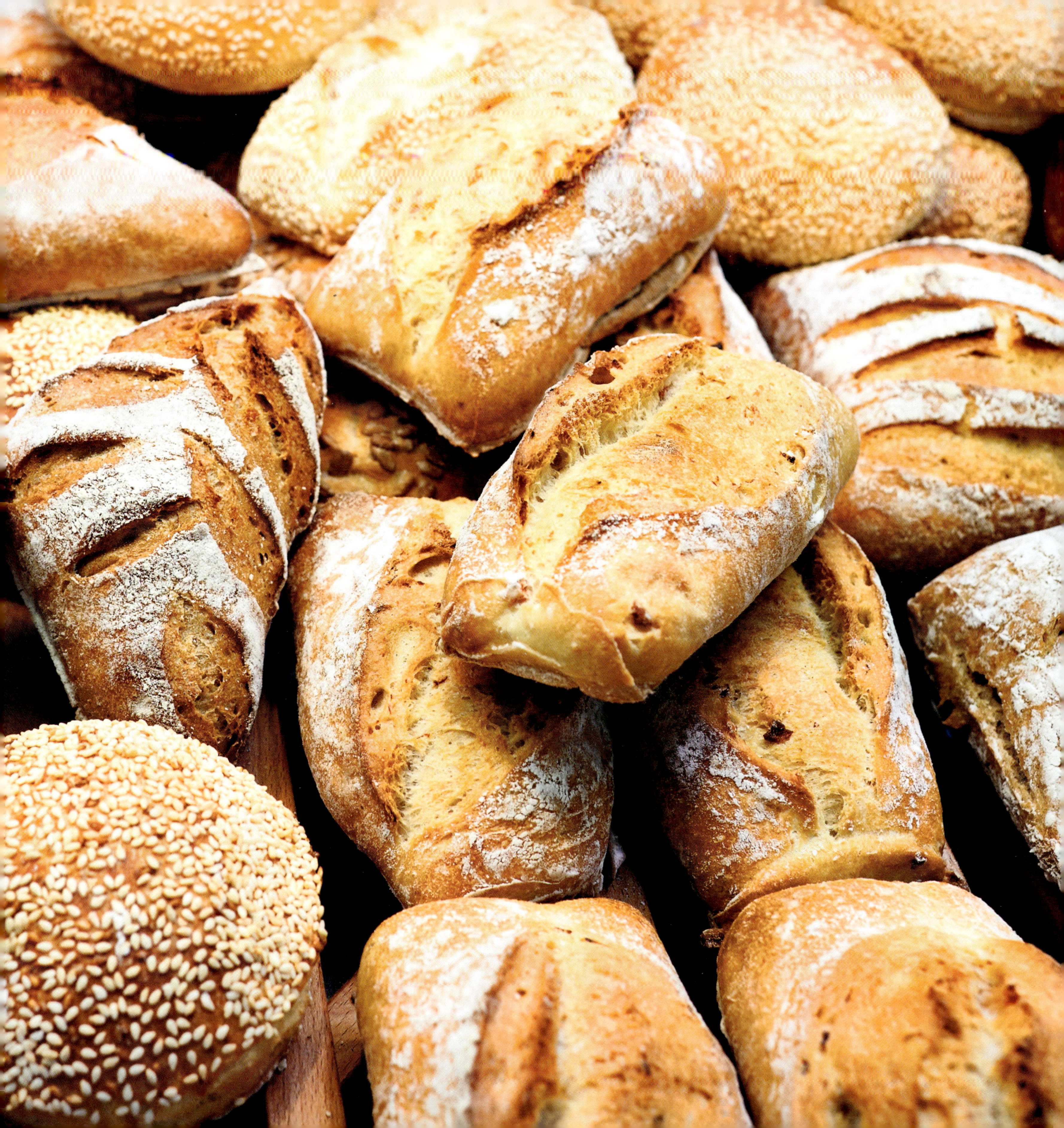

FOOD LOVERS' GUIDE
Your deliciously indispensable companion to enjoying Suffolk, edible and otherwise

Ruby and Scarlet, Felixstowe
48-50 Hamilton Road, Felixstowe IP11 7AJ
T: 01394 285378
W: rubyandscarlet.com

ICE Cook Shop, Bury St. Edmunds
2 Lundy Court, Bury St. Edmunds IP30 9ND
T: 01359 272577
W: icecookschool.co.uk

Tea and Kate, Felixstowe
10a Victoria Street, Felixstowe IP11 7ER
T: 01394 276189
W: teaandkate.co.uk

Partridges of Hadleigh
60 High Street, Hadleigh IP7 5EE
T: 01473 822333
W: partridgeshadleigh.co.uk

The Kitchen Range & Cookshop, Framlingham
3 Well Close Square, Framlingham IP13 9DT
T: 01728 723757
W: krcookshop.com

Elmers of Kesgrave
59-61 Edmonton Road, Kesgrave, Ipswich IP5 1EQ
T: 01473 623381
W: elmershardware.co.uk

The Galley Cookshop, Beccles
41-43 Smallgate, Beccles NR34 9AE
T: 01502 217075
W: facebook.com/thegalleycookshop

Lakeland, Ipswich
The Ancient House, 30 Buttermarket,
Ipswich IP1 1BT
T: 01473 214144
W: lakeland.co.uk

Castang's Kitchen
66a St. John's Street, Bury St Edmunds IP331SJ
T: 07497 105036
W: castangskitchen.com

PLACES TO DRINK

PUBS AND INNS
Suffolk is blessed with too many great pubs to list. Seek out a few of our favourites, which have something unique beyond being just very fine hostelries.

Arcade Street Tavern, Ipswich
artisan gins, craft beers and street food
1 Arcade Street, Ipswich IP1 1EX
T: 01473 805454
W: arcadetavern.co.uk

The Lord Nelson, Southwold
Some would say the perfect local to sup Suffolk's best beers
42 East Street, Southwold IP18 6EJ
T: 01502 722079
W: thelordnelsonsouthwold.co.uk

The Geldeston Locks Inn
Historic riverside setting to enjoy heritage music and folk dance
Lock's Lane, Geldeston, near Beccles NR34 0HS
T: 01508 518414
W: geldestonlocks.co.uk

The White Horse Inn, Sweffling
Proper tap room with perfectly limited pub fare
Low Road, Sweffling IP17 2BB
T: 01728 664178
W: swefflingwhitehorse.co.uk

The Kings Head (aka The Low House), Laxfield
Community-owned traditional alehouse pouring straight from the barrel
Gorams Mill Lane, Laxfield IP13 8DW
T: 01986 798395
W: facebook.com/kingsheadlaxfield

The Bell, Walberswick
Supposedly haunted, delightfully quaint and hugely popular Adnams inn
Ferry Rd, Walberswick IP18 6TN
T: 01502 723109
W: bellinnwalberswick.co.uk

The Crown Inn, Snape
Smallholding meets pub-restaurant, this is field-to-fork at its best
Bridge Road, Snape IP17 1SL
T: 01728 688324
W: snape-crown.co.uk

The Eels Foot, Eastbridge
The soul of Suffolk folk music, the impromptu Thursday 'squit night' is a must-hear
Eastbridge near Leiston IP16 4SN
T: 01728 830154
W: theeelsfootinn.co.uk

The Nutshell, Bury St Edmunds
Allegedly the tiniest in Britain and at the heart of the town. Breathe in as you enter
The Traverse, Bury St Edmunds IP33 1BJ
T: 01284 764867
W: thenutshellpub.co.uk

The Queen's Head, Hawkedon
The epitome of a country pub, thatched, pretty and a warm welcome
Rede Road, Hawkedon, Bury St Edmunds IP29 4NN
T: 01284 789218
W: hawkedonqueen.co.uk

The Old Cannon, Bury St Edmunds
Unique town centre inn and brewery
86 Cannon Street, Bury St Edmunds IP33 1JR
T: 01284 768769
W: oldcannonbrewery.co.uk

The Oyster Inn, Butley
Once a smugglers' inn, now complete with micro brewery, community shop and tiny cinema
Woodbridge Road, Butley, Woodbridge IP12 3NZ
T: 01394 459722
W: butleyoyster.com

The Swan, Stratford St. Mary
Riverside hostelry in Constable country plus home-brewed ales, flavoured from the hop garden
Lower Street, Stratford St. Mary CO7 6JR
T: 01206 321244
W: stratfordswan.com

The Ship Inn, Dunwich
At the heart of a quintessential medieval Suffolk village surrounded by a nature reserve and the stuff of myriad legends
St. James' Street, Dunwich IP17 3DT
T: 01728 648219
W: shipatdunwich.co.uk

PLACES TO EAT

TEAROOMS

A great British institution, whether bone china, crusts off and pinkies raised or not, do make time for tea.

Granary Tea Shop at Snape Maltings
Snape Bridge B1069, Snape IP17 1SP
T: 01728 688303
W: snapemaltings.co.uk

The Courtyard, Elveden Estate
Brandon Road, Elveden IP24 3TJ
T: 01842 898068
W: elvedencourtyard.com

Cragg Sisters Tearoom, Aldeburgh
110 High Street, Aldeburgh IP15 5AB
T: 07813 552181
W: craggsisters.co.uk

The Copper Kettle, Kersey
Kersey Mill, off A1141, Kersey IP7 6DP
T: 01473 827001
W: thecopperkettleatkerseymill.co.uk

Thorpeness Meare Shop and Tearooms
Thorpeness Meare, Thorpeness IP16 4NW
T: 01728 452156

Riverside Tearoom, Orford
Orford Quay, Orford IP12 2NU
T: 01394 459797

Mill Tea Room at Pakenham Water Mill
Mill Road, Pakenham,
Bury St. Edmunds IP31 2NB
T: 01359 230275
W: pakenhamwatermill.org.uk

Baileys 2, Bury St Edmunds
5 Whiting St, Bury St Edmunds IP33 1NX
T: 01284 706198
W: baileys2.co.uk

Harriets Café Tearooms, Bury St. Edmunds
57 Cornhill Buildings, Bury St. Edmunds IP33 1BT
T: 01284 756256
W: harrietscafetearooms.co.uk

Earsham Street Café, Bungay
11-13 Earsham Street, Bungay NR35 1AE
T: 01986 893103
W: earshamstreetcafe.co.uk

Really Rather Good, Bury St Edmunds
31A Abbeygate Street, Bury St Edmunds IP33 1LW
T: 01284 756181
W: rrgood.co.uk

The Secret Garden, Sudbury
21 Friars St, Sudbury CO10 2AA
T: 01787 372030
W: tsg.uk.net

The Tea Hut, Woodbridge
River Wall, Woodbridge IP12 4BB
T: 01394 384538
W: theteahut.co.uk

Weavers Tearoom, Peasenhall
2 The Knoll, Peasenhall, Saxmundham IP17 2JE
T: 01728 660548

CAFÉS AND COFFEE SHOPS

Smaller or simpler eating places can make for delicious escapes.

Café 1885 and Concert Hall Café at Snape Maltings
Snape Bridge B1069, Snape IP17 1SP
T: 01728 688303
W: snapemaltings.co.uk

The Courtyard, Elveden Estate
Brandon Road, Elveden IP24 3TJ
T: 01842 898068
W: elvedencourtyard.com

Farm Café and Shop, Marlesford
Main Road A12, Marlesford
IP13 0AG
T: 01728 747717
W: farmcafe.co.uk

Jimmy's Farm, Wherstead
Pannington Hall Lane, Wherstead IP9 2AR
T: 01473 604206
W: jimmysfarm.com

G & T's Café and Kitchen, Yoxford
The Old Post Office, High Street, Yoxford IP17 3EP
T: 01728 668009
W: facebook.com/GandTsCafe

Artisan Smokehouse, Café and Deli, Falkenham
Goose Barn, Back Road, Falkenham IP10 0QR
T: 01394 448414
W: artisansmokehouse.co.uk

Darsham Nurseries
Main Road A12, Darsham, Saxmundham IP17 3PW
T: 01728 667022
W: darshamnurseries.co.uk

The Aldeburgh Market
170-172 High St, Aldeburgh IP15 5AQ
T: 01728 452520
W: thealdeburghmarket.co.uk

Emmett's Stores, Peasenhall
The Street, Peasenhall IP17 2HJ
T: 01728 660250
W: emmettsham.co.uk

Juniper Barn, Rendham
B1119 Rendham IP17 2AZ
T: 01728 663773
W: juniperbarnsuffolk.co.uk

Coffee Shop at AG Lifestyle, Sudbury
38 Station Rd, Sudbury CO10 2SS
T: 01787 312126
W: aglifestyle.co.uk

Fire Station Coffee Roasters & Café, Woodbridge
21a Thoroughfare, Woodbridge IP12 1AA
T: 01394 389674
W: firestationcoffee.co.uk

Munchies, Aldeburgh
163 - 165 High Street, Aldeburgh IP15 5AN
T: 01728 454566
W: facebook.com/aldeburghmunchies

Butley-Orford Oysterage, Orford
Market Hill, Orford IP12 2LH
T: 01394 450277
W: pinneysoforford.co.uk

Pump Street Bakery Café, Orford
1 Pump Street Orford IP12 2LZ
T: 01394 459829
W: pumpstreetbakery.com

Lizzy's Coffee Shop, Risby
Risby Barn, South Street, Risby IP28 6QU
T: 01284 810022
W: risbybarn.co.uk

Suffolk Food Hall, Wherstead
Wherstead, near Ipswich IP9 2AB
T: 01473 786616
W: suffolkfoodhall.co.uk

Two Magpies Bakery Café, Southwold
88 High Street, Southwold IP18 6DP
T: 01502 726120
W: twomagpiesbakery.co.uk

Bloomsberries Café and Deli, Lakenheath
Christmas Hill Farm, Station Road,
Lakenheath IP27 9LN
T: 01842 861144
W: christmashill.co.uk

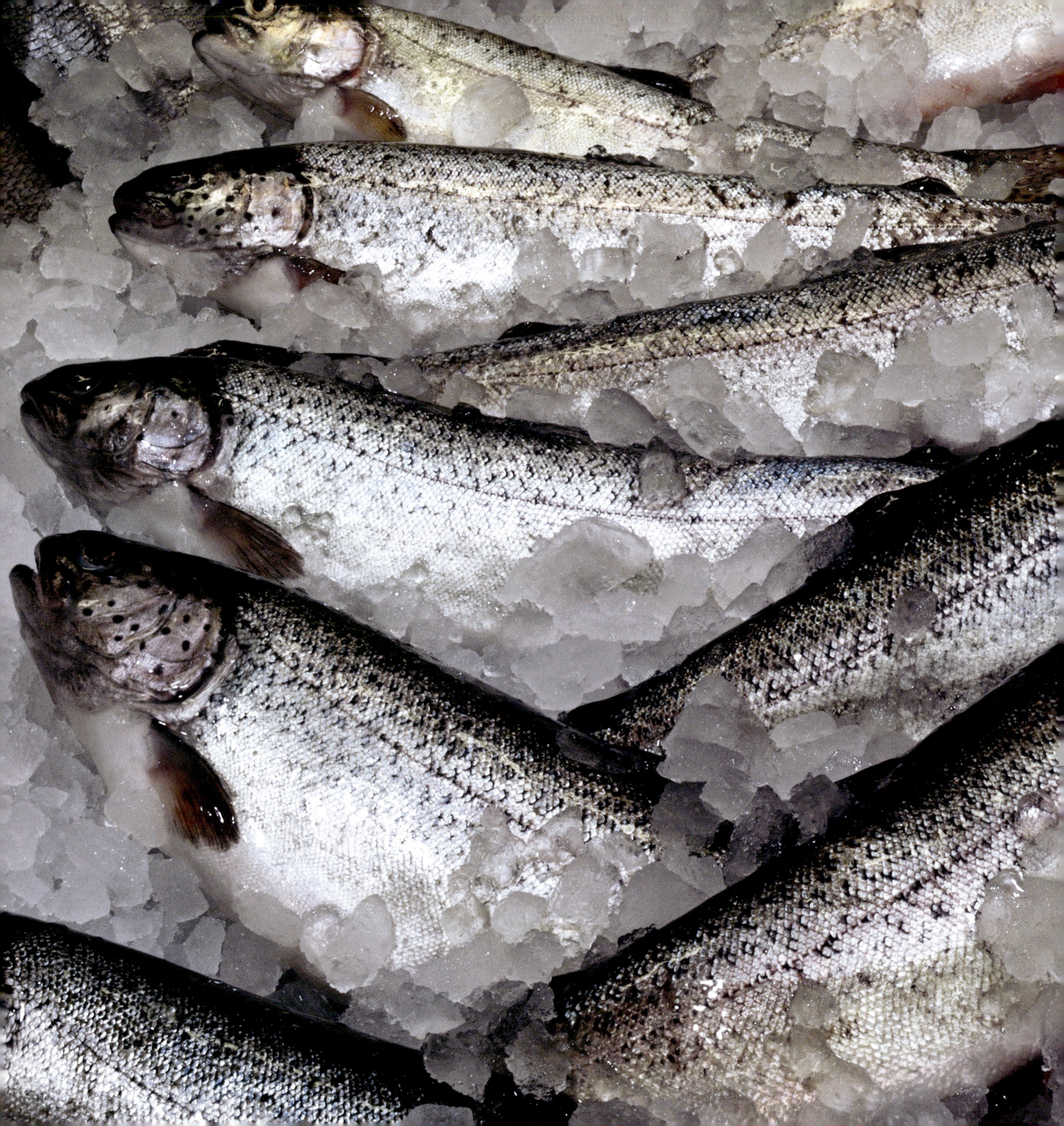

FOOD LOVERS' GUIDE

Your deliciously indispensable companion to enjoying Suffolk, edible and otherwise

Paddy and Scott's Cafés,
Bury St. Edmunds and Hadleigh
12 Abbeygate Street, Bury St. Edmunds IP33 1UN
T: 01284 760661
High Street, Hadleigh IP7 5EF
T: 01473 823601
W: paddyandscotts.co.uk

Sole Bay Fish Co., Southwold
Shed 22e, Blackshore Harbour,
Southwold IP18 6ND
T: 01502 724241
W: solebayfishco.co.uk

Mr Allard's Farm Shop Café, Stowupland
Rendall Lane, Stowupland,
near Stowmarket IP14 4BD
T: 01449 678650
W: mrallardsfarmbutchery.com

DeliCafé at The Chilli Farm, Mendlesham
Norwich Road, Mendlesham IP14 5NQ
T: 01449 766344
W: delicafeatchillifarm.co.uk

The Dancing Goat, Framlingham
33 Market Hill, Framlingham IP13 9BA
T: 01728 621434
W: thedancinggoatframlingham.wordpress.com

Focus Organic, Halesworth
14 Thoroughfare, Halesworth IP19 8AH
T: 01986 872899
W: focusorganic.co.uk

The Common Room Café, Framlingham
22 Bridge St, Framlingham IP13 9AH
T: 01728 768238
W: thecommonroomfram.com

Cafe Kottani, Bury St Edmunds
30 Buttermarket, Bury St Edmunds IP33 1DW
T: 01284 766551
W: facebook.com/cafekottani

No 4 Hatter Street at Abbeygate Cinema,
Bury St Edmunds
4 Hatter Street, Bury St Edmunds IP33 1LZ
T: 01284 754477
W: abbeygatecinema.co.uk/no4

Assington Country Kitchen
Assington Farm Shop
Assington Barn, The Street, Assington CO10 5LW
T: 01787 210242
W: assingtoncountrykitchen.com

Cradle Foods, Sudbury *vegan*
40 North Street, Sudbury CO10 1RD
T: 01787 464656
W: cradlefoods.co.uk

Applaud Coffee, Ipswich
19 St. Peter's Street, Ipswich IP1 1XF
T: 01473 808142
W: applaud-coffee.co.uk

Hollow Trees Farm Café, Semer
Semer, near Hadleigh IP7 6HX
T: 01449 741247
W: hollowtrees.co.uk

Twyfords, Beccles
Exchange Square, Beccles NR34 9HL
T: 01502 710614
W: twyfordscafe.co.uk

Gastrono-me, Bury St Edmunds
22 Abbeygate Street, Bury St Edmunds IP33 1UN
T: 01284 277980
W: gastrono-me.co.uk

Harris & James, Southwold and Aldeburgh
11 East Street, Southwold IP18 6EH
T: 01502 726061
159 High Street, Aldeburgh IP15 5AN
T: 01728 453676
W: facebook.com/madefromthebean

Café Jungle, Weston
Urban Jungle, London Road,
Weston near Beccles NR34 8TT
T: 01502 219110
W: urbanjungle.uk.com

ICE Café, Bury St. Edmunds
2 Lundy Court, Bury St. Edmunds IP30 9ND
T: 01359 272577
W: icecookschool.co.uk

Guat's Up!, Bury St Edmunds
7 Guildhall Street, Bury St Edmunds IP33 1PR
T: 01284 755612
W: guatsup.coffee

La Hogue Farm Shop Café, Chippenham *OTB*
La Hogue Road, Chippenham,
near Newmarket CB7 5PZ
T: 01638 751128
W: lahogue.co.uk

POP-UPS

A new wave of quirky pop-ups and innovative destinations are shaking up how we eat.

Shillingford's At The Quay, Sudbury
wild foods pop-up restaurant (Thu, Fri & Sat eve)
Top Floor, The Quay Theatre, Quay Lane
Sudbury CO10 2AN
T: 01787 211328
W: quaysudbury.com/shillingfords-quay

Peter Harrison, East Suffolk
pop-up artisan chef suppers
T: 07970 913312
W: peterharrisonchef.co.uk

FISH & CHIPS

Eating out for a quick treat can be really tasty at some of these better places.

Aldeburgh Fish and Chip Shop
226 High St, Aldeburgh IP15 5DB
T: 01728 452250
W: aldeburghfishandchips.co.uk

Seashell Fish & Chips, Halesworth
5 Bridge Street, Halesworth IP19 8AB
T: 01986 872293
W: seashell.business.site

Miller's Fish & Chips, Ipswich
137 London Road, Ipswich IP1 2HH
T: 01473 226678
W: facebook.com/millersfishandchips

The Codfather, Sudbury
37 King Street, Sudbury CO10 2EQ
T: 01787 882100

Regal Fish Bar, Felixstowe
Sea Road, Felixstowe IP11 2DH
T: 01394 273977
W: theregalrestaurant.com

Bury Chippy
64a St. Andrews Street South,
Bury St. Edmunds IP33 1SD
T: 01284 754589

Mrs T's Fish and Chips, Southwold Harbour
BlackShore Harbour, Southwold IP18 6TA
T: 01502 724709

The Little Fish and Chip Shop
2 East Street, Southwold IP18 6EH
T: 01502 218120
W: solebayfishco.co.uk

SUFFOLK FEAST

FOOD LOVERS' GUIDE
Your deliciously indispensable companion to enjoying Suffolk, edible and otherwise

PLACES TO STAY

B&Bs AND GUEST ACCOMMODATION
Whether the charm of a rural village, the buzz of a town or the peace of a farm, a comfortable bed and a hearty breakfast is one of the greatest simple pleasures.

Juniper Barn, Rendham
T: 01728 663773
W: juniperbarnsuffolk.co.uk

Valley Farm, Middleton
T: 01728 648217
W: valley-farm.co.uk

Sandpit Farm, Bruisyard
T: 01728 663445
W: aldevalleybreaks.co.uk

Rendham Hall
T: 01728 663440
W: rendhamhall.co.uk

Church Farm, Bradfield Combust
T: 01284 386333
W: churchfarm-bandb.co.uk

Flindor Cottage, Framsden
T: 01473 890058
W: flindorcottage.co.uk

Haughley House
T: 01449 673398
W: haughleyhouse.co.uk

The Old Rectory Country House, Great Waldingfield
T: 01787 372428
W: rectorymanorhouse.co.uk

West Stow Hall
T: 01787 728127
W: weststowhall.com

Holly Tree House B&B, Wingfield
T: 01379 384854
W: hollytreehousebandb.co.uk

HOLIDAY HOMES
Getting under the skin of Suffolk for a weekend or longer, staying as welcome guests in a local community and surrounded by family and friends are the stuff of happy life-long memories.

The Brewer's House, Southwold
T: 01502 722186
W: adnams.co.uk/hotels

High Lodge Luxury Holiday Lodges, Darsham
T: 01986 784347
W: highlodge.co.uk

Ore Valley Cottages, Little Glemham
T: 01728 602783
W: holidaycottagessuffolk-orevalley.co.uk

Valley Farm Cottages, Sudbourne
T: 01394 450979
W: valleyfarmcottages.co.uk

The Wash House Studio, Orford
T: 01394 450959
W: orfordwashhouse.co.uk

Woodfarm Barns, Stonham Aspal
T: 01449 710032
W: woodfarmbarns.com

Sweffling Hall Farm
T: 01728 664084
W: swefflinghallfarm.com

The Windmill, Cockfield
T: 01284 828458
W: thewindmillsuffolk.com

GLAMPING AND CAMPING
Whether you bring your own or enjoy the luxury of having it pitched for you, there is nothing quite like being at one with nature, under the stars and in the open air.

Suffolk Yurt Holidays, Bredfield
T: 07907 964890
W: suffolkyurtholidays.co.uk

Alde Garden, Sweffling
T: 01728 664178
W: aldegarden.co.uk

Kenton Hall Estate
T: 01728 862062
W: kentonhallestate.co.uk

Newbourne Woodland Campsite
T: 01473 736201
W: newbourne-campsite.co.uk

Secret Meadows Luxury Camping, Hasketon
T: 01394 382992
W: secretmeadows.co.uk

Dawn Chorus Glamping
Barsham
T: 01502 713152
W: dawnchorusholidays.com

Wardley Hill, Kirby Cane *OTB*
T: 07733 306543
W: wardleyhillcampsite.com

Ling's Meadow, Hepworth *OTB*
T: 01359 250594
W: lingsmeadow.co.uk

Lantern and Larks, Sweffling
T: 01638 563478
W: lanternandlarks.co.uk

West Stow Pods, near Bury St Edmunds
T: 01284 728136
W: weststowpods.co.uk

FUN STUFF

EVENT CATERING
Sometimes we just want to relax and host, leaving it in the hands of the professionals.

Mackenzie-David Events
Aldeburgh Yacht Club, Slaughden Road,
Aldeburgh IP15 5NA
T: 01986 893991 / 07460 400276
W: mackenzie-david.co.uk

The Duck Truck
T: 07919 160271
W: theducktruck.co.uk

My Kitchen Your Place
T: 07814 682903
W: mykitchenyourplace.co.uk

Peter Harrison
T: 07970 913312
W: peterharrisonchef.co.uk

The Suffolk Hog Roast Company
T: 01284 788757
W: thesuffolkhogroastcompany.co.uk

The Fish Hut *mobile seafood*
T: 07971 196626
W: facebook.com/thefishhut1

Gamekeeper's Daughter *OTB*
T: 01473 780402
W: gamekeepers-daughter.co.uk

WEDDINGS AND PARTIES
Try these for your truly individual Suffolk wedding or special celebration.

Mackenzie-David Events *catering*
Aldeburgh Yacht Club, Slaughden Road,
Aldeburgh IP15 5NA
T: 01986 893991 / 07460 400276
W: mackenzie-david.co.uk

Jimmy's Farm *venue*
Pannington Hall Lane, Wherstead,
near Ipswich IP9 2AR
T: 01473 604206
W: jimmysfarm.com

Vanilla Pâtisserie *wedding and celebration cakes*
T: 01728 445000
W: vanillapatisserie.co.uk

Shimpling Park Farm *venue*
T: 01284 827317
W: shimplingpark.com

Earsham Hall *venue*
T: 01986 893868
W: earshamhallevents.co.uk

Kenton Hall Estate *venue and glamping*
T: 01728 862062
W: kentonhallestate.co.uk

Alpheton Hall Barns
T: 01284 830200
W: alpheton-hall-barns.co.uk

COOKERY SCHOOLS
If inspired to do more than pick up a good recipe book, learn hands-on from a masterchef.

The Cooking Experience *cookery school*
The Chapel House, 9 High Street, Hadleigh IP7 5AP
T: 01473 827568
W: cookingexperience.co.uk

Suffolk Food Hall *cookery courses and demos*
Wherstead, near Ipswich IP9 2AR
T: 01473 786610
W: suffolkfoodhall.co.uk

The Food Hub *cookery school*
Kenton Hall Estate, Kenton, Stowmarket IP14 6JU
T: 01728 862062
W: kentonhallestate.co.uk

Emma Crowhurst
W: emmacrowhurst.co.uk

The Gamekeeper's Daughter *OTB*
game cookery courses
T: 01206 298089
W: gamekeepers-daughter.co.uk

ICE Cook School, Bury St. Edmunds
2 Lundy Court, Bury St. Edmunds IP30 9ND
T: 01359 272577
W: icecookschool.co.uk

Mistley Kitchen, Mistley *OTB*
High Street, Mistley near Manningtree,
Essex CO11 1HD
T: 01206 391024
W: mistleykitchen.com

FOODIE EXPERIENCES AND EDUCATION
Getting closer to ingredients, produce and harvest is all part of being a true foodie.

Foragers Feast *foraging with a chef and teacher*
T: 07704 627973
W: suffolkmarketevents.co.uk

Secret Meadows
rural workshops and therapies
T: 01394 382992
W: secretmeadows.co.uk

The Secret Garden *breadmaking courses*
T: 01787 372030
W: tsg.uk.net

Wild For Woods *foraging and bushcraft OTB*
T: 07896 678956
W: wildforwoods.co.uk

FESTIVALS AND EVENTS
No better advert for all that is great about tasty Suffolk, go explore the artisan vibe.

Aldeburgh Food and Drink Festival
last weekend of September
Snape Maltings, Snape IP17 1SR
T: 01728 688303
W: aldeburghfoodanddrink.co.uk

Alde Valley Spring Festival *April and May*
celebrating food, farming, landscape and the arts
White House Farm, Great Glemham IP17 1LS
T: 01728 663531
W: aldevalleyspringfestival.co.uk

Woodbridge Shuck Seafood Festival
first weekend of October
throughout Woodbridge
T: 01394 411025
W: woodbridgeshuck.co.uk

Bury St Edmunds Food & Drink Festival
last weekend of August
Buttermarket, Bury St. Edmunds
T: 01284 766258
W: burystedmundsfestivals.com

Jimmy's Farm Sausage & Beer Festival *late July*
Pannington Hall Lane, Wherstead, Ipswich IP9 2AR
T: 01473 604206
W: jimmysfarm.com

Suffolk Show *late May*
Suffolk Showground, Trinity Park,
Felixtowe Road, Ipswich IP3 8UH
T: 01473 707110
W: suffolkshow.co.uk

Suffolk Dog Day *late July*
Helmingham Hall, Helmingham IP14 6EF
T: 01473 786918
W: suffolkdogday.com

FolkEast Festival *late August*
Glemham Hall, Little Glemham,
near Wickham Market IP13 0BT
W: folkeast.co.uk

Latitude Festival *mid July*
Henham Park, Henham, near Southwold NR34 8AQ
T: 0207 009 3001
W: latitudefestival.com

Maui Waui Festival *late August*
Peakhill Farm, Theberton IP16 4TG
T: 07910 691483
W: mauiwauievents.co.uk

FOOD LOVERS' GUIDE

Your deliciously indispensable companion to enjoying Suffolk, edible and otherwise

OUT AND ABOUT
Feeding the soul is just as important as feasting. Fill up on eclectic, rustic, local entertainment.

Iken Canoe
Iken Cliff, Iken IP12 2EN
T: 07979 517186
W: ikencanoe.co.uk

Southwold Maize Maze
Halesworth Road, Reydon, Southwold IP18 6SG
T: 07801 065845
W: southwoldmaizemaze.co.uk

East Coast Mountain Bike Hire *pre-booked*
T: 07706 479965 *(text only)*
W: eastcoastmountainbiking.co.uk

High Lodge Sporting and Leisure
Haw Wood, Hinton, Darsham IP17 3QT
T: 01986 784347
W: highlodge.co.uk

Deben Cruises *pre-booked*
T: 01473 736 260
W: debencruises.co.uk

River Cruise Restaurants *pre-booked*
T: 01473 558712
W: lady-florence.co.uk

Easton Farm Park
off The Street, Easton IP13 0EQ
T: 01728 746475
W: eastonfarmpark.co.uk

Flatford Mill *National Trust*
Flatford near East Bergholt CO7 6UL
T: 01206 298260
W: nationaltrust.org.uk/flatford/

Go Ape! Forest Adventure
High Lodge Forest Centre,
Santon Downham near Brandon IP27 0AF
T: 08456 439215
W: goape.co.uk/days-out/thetford

RSPB Minsmere Nature Reserve
off Dunwich Road, Westleton IP17 3BY
T: 01728 648281
W: rspb.org.uk/minsmere

Helmingham Hall Gardens and Tearooms
B1077 Helmingham IP14 6EF
T: 01473 890799
W: helmingham.com

Jimmy's Farm
Pannington Hall Lane, Wherstead,
near Ipswich IP9 2AR
T: 01473 604206
W: jimmysfarm.com

Southwold Pier
North Parade, Southwold IP18 6BN
T: 01502 722105
W: southwoldpier.co.uk

Snape Maltings
Bridge Road, Snape IP17 1SR
T: 01728 688303
W: snapemaltings.co.uk

Stonham Barns and Suffolk Owl Sanctuary
Pettaugh Road, Stonham Aspal IP14 6AT
T: 01449 711111
W: stonham-barns.co.uk

Museum of East Anglian Life
Iliffe Way, Stowmarket IP14 1DL
T: 01449 612229
W: eastanglianlife.org.uk

Sutton Hoo *National Trust*
Tranmer House, Sutton Hoo,
near Woodbridge IP12 3DJ
T: 01394 389700
W: nationaltrust.org.uk/sutton-hoo

Baylham House Rare Breeds Farm
Mill Lane, Baylham IP6 8LG
T: 01473 830264
W: baylham-house-farm.co.uk

HEALTH SPAS
A proper detox can work wonders for over-indulgence, or for just a little 'me time'.

The Spa at Ickworth Hotel
Ickworth Estate, Horringer,
near Bury St Edmunds IP29 5QE
T: 01284 735350
W: ickworthhotel.co.uk

Weavers House Spa
High Street, Lavenham CO10 9QA
T: 01787 247477
W: theswanatlavenham.co.uk

Aqua Sana at Center Parcs Elveden
Elveden IP27 0YZ
T: 03448 266205
W: aquasana.co.uk

The Spa at Bedford Lodge
Bury Road, Newmarket CB8 7BX
T: 01638 676130
W: bedfordlodgehotelspa.co.uk

LIFESTYLE
Enhancing your home makes for a stylish dining experience.

House & Garden at Snape Maltings
Snape Bridge B1069, Snape IP17 1SP
T: 01728 688303
W: snapemaltings.co.uk

The Courtyard, Elveden Estate
Brandon Road, Elveden IP24 3TQ
T: 01842 898068
W: elvedencourtyard.com

AG Lifestyle, Sudbury
38 Station Rd, Sudbury CO10 2SS
T: 01787 312126
W: aglifestyle.co.uk

The Country Store at Wyken Vineyards
Wyken Road, Stanton IP31 2DW
T: 01359 250287
W: wykenvineyards.co.uk

GARDEN CENTRES
There is nothing like growing your own, plucking the first crop as it shoots from your own little piece of England. Be inspired at a local garden centre – and enjoy some delicious treats at their fabulous little cafés.

House & Garden at Snape Maltings
Snape Bridge B1069, Snape IP17 1SP
T: 01728 688303
W: snapemaltings.co.uk

Darsham Nurseries
Main Road A12, Darsham, Saxmundham IP17 3PW
T: 01728 667022
W: darshamnurseries.co.uk

The Walled Garden, Benhall
Park Rd, Benhall near Saxmundham IP17 1JB
T: 01728 602510
W: thewalledgarden.co.uk

The Place for Plants, East Bergholt
East Bergholt Place, Mill Road, East Bergholt CO7 6UP
T: 01206 299224
W: placeforplants.co.uk

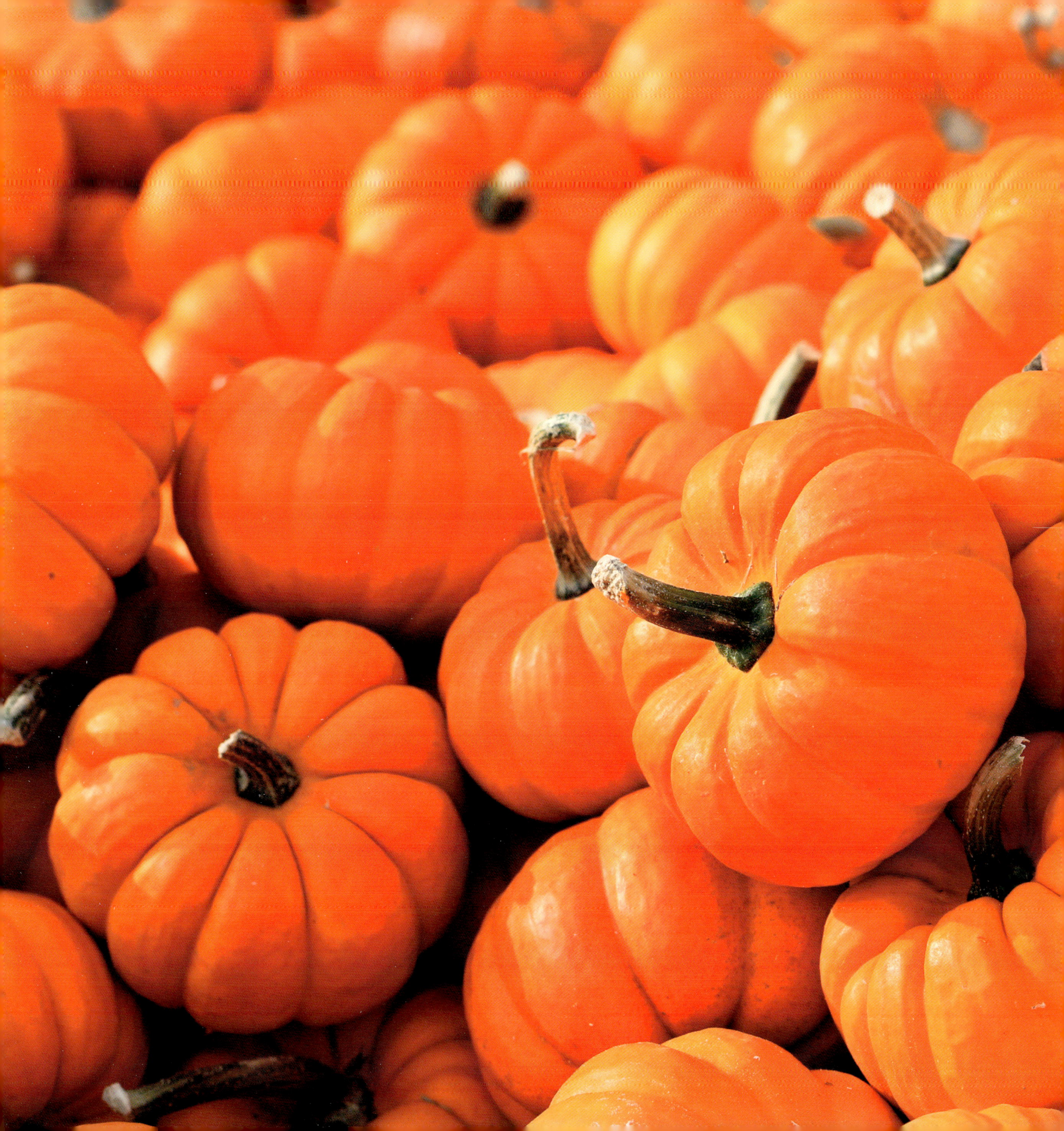

FOOD LOVERS' GUIDE
Your deliciously indispensable companion to enjoying Suffolk, edible and otherwise

Botanica, Campsea Ashe
Chantry Farm, Campsea Ashe, Woodbridge IP13 0PZ
T: 01728 747113
W: botanicaplantnursery.co.uk

Garnetts Gardens, Hacheston
The Street, Hacheston near Woodbridge IP13 0DT
T: 01728 724589
W: garnettsgardens.co.uk

Dogwood Garden Nursery, Risby
Risby Barn, South Street, Risby,
near Bury St Edmunds IP28 6QU
T: 01284 811055

Harveys Garden Plants, Thurston
Harveys Garden Plants, Great Green, Thurston,
near Bury St Edmunds IP31 3SJ
T: 01359 233363
W: harveysgardenplants.co.uk

Market Fields Farm Shop, Halesworth
Holton Road Garden Centre, 36 Holton Road,
Halesworth IP19 8HG
T: 01986 872761

Woottens of Wenhaston
The Iris Field, Hall Road, Wenhaston IP19 9HF
T: 01502 478258
W: woottensplants.com

Nareys Garden Centre, Stowmarket
Spikes Lane, Stowmarket IP14 3QD
T: 01449 612559
W: nareys.com

Bypass Nurseries, Capel St. Mary
London Road A12, Capel St.Mary IP9 2JR
T: 01473 310604
W: bypassnurseries.co.uk

Laurel Farm Garden Centre, Ipswich
Henley Road, Ipswich IP1 6TE
T: 01473 215984
W: laurelfarmgardencentre.co.uk

Urban Jungle, Beccles
London Road, Weston NR34 8TT
T: 01502 219110
W: urbanjungle.uk.com

Roots & Shoots Garden Centre, Badley
Stowmarket Road, Badley IP6 8RR
T: 01449 721965
W: rootsandshootsgc.co.uk

Marlows Home and Garden, Bury St Edmunds
Hollow Road, Bury St Edmunds IP32 7AP
T: 01284 763155
W: marlowsgardencentre.co.uk

Sturmer Nurseries, Haverhill
Church Walk, Sturmer, Haverhill CB9 7XD
T: 01440 706416
W: sturmernurseries.co.uk

Victoria Nurseries, Ipswich
1 Kettlebaston Way,
Westerfield Road, Ipswich IP4 2XX
T: 01473 253980
W: victorianurseriesipswich.co.uk

Three Willows Garden Centre, Bungay
Flixton Road, Bungay NR35 1PD
T: 01986 893834
W: threewillowsgardencentre.co.uk

Woolpit Nurseries, Woolpit
Old Stowmarket Rd, Woolpit IP30 9QS
T: 01359 240370
W: woolpitnurseries.co.uk

Bourne Garden Centre, Ipswich
578 Wherstead Rd, Ipswich IP2 8LS
T: 01473 691567
W: bournegardencentre.co.uk

The Exotic Garden Company, Aldeburgh
Hall Farm, Saxmundham Road,
Aldeburgh IP15 5GY
T: 01728 454456
W: theexoticgardencompany.com

KITCHEN DESIGNERS
A great cook and a good meal starts with the perfect culinary surroundings.

Plain English Cupboardmakers, Stowmarket
Stowupland Hall, Stowupland,
Stowmarket IP14 4BE
T: 01449 774028
W: plainenglishdesign.co.uk

Anglia Factors, Ipswich
34 Gloster Road, Martlesham Heath,
Ipswich IP5 3RD
T: 01473 610192
W: angliafactors.co.uk

Earsham Hall Kitchens & Interiors, Bungay
off Norwich Road, Earsham, Bungay NR35 2AN
T: 01986 893420
W: earshamhall.co.uk

Baker and Baker, Clare
Clare Hall Barn, Cavendish Road, Clare CO10 8PJ
T: 01787 279119
W: bakerandbaker.co.uk

Luxmoore & Co., Brandeston
Swallow Barn, Bridge Farm, Friday Street,
Brandeston IP13 7BP
T: 01728 685890
W: luxmooreandco.co.uk

Grahame R Bolton, Bungay
8 & 9 Willow Bus. Park, Southend Road, Bungay
NR35 1DP
T: 01986 895995
W: grbolton.co.uk

Mulberry Kitchen Studio, Beccles
31 Newgate, Beccles NR34 9QB
T: 01502 711210
W: mulberrykitchens.com

Orwells Furniture, Ipswich
Halifax House, 497 - 499 Wherstead Road,
Ipswich IP2 8LL
T: 01473 680091
W: orwellsfurniture.co.uk

Hadleigh Kitchens, Hadleigh
86 High Street, Hadleigh IP7 5EF
T: 01473 827666
W: hadleighkitchens.co.uk

Wood Farm Kitchens, Otley
Helmingham Road, Otley IP6 9NS
T: 01473 890122
W: woodfarmkitchens.co.uk

Kitchenology, Bury St Edmunds
The Bartons Retail Park, Barton Road,
Bury St Edmunds IP32 7BE
T: 01284 724723
W: kitchenologyltd.co.uk

Davonport, Colchester *OTB*
Peartree Road, Colchester, Essex CO3 0LQ
T: 0845 468 0025
W: davonport.com

Goddards Interiors, Saffron Walden *OTB*
Salaman House, Hill Street,
Saffron Walden, Essex CB10 1EH
T: 01799 522581
W: goddardsinteriors.co.uk

STOVES AND OVENS
Making the hearth and heart of the home.

Classic Stoves, Long Melford and Stowmarket
16 Charles Ind. Est. Stowupland Road,
Stowmarket IP14 5AH
T:01449 678659
Hall Street, Long Melford CO10 9JR
T: 01787 313699
W: classicstovesandfireplaces.co.uk

Suffolk Stoves, Middleton
Yoxford Road,
Middleton near Saxmundham IP17 3LU
T: 01728 648362
W: suffolkstoves.co.uk

Stove Solutions, Wrentham
6 High Street, Wrentham NR34 7HB
T: 01502 675544
W: stovesolutions.co.uk

The Kitchen Range & Cookshop, Framlingham
3 Well Close Square, Framlingham IP13 9DT
T: 01728 723757
W: krcookshop.com

Martin Melville, Martlesham
6 Bridge Business Park, Top Street,
Martlesham IP12 4RB
T: 01394 384175
W: martinmelville.com

The Fireplace, Framlingham
The Old Works, Crown & Anchor Lane,
Framlington IP13 3DL
T: 01728 621212
W: fireplaceframlingham.co.uk

Colne Stoves, Bury St Edmunds
Overland Park, Great Whelnetham,
Bury St Edmunds IP30 0UL
T: 01284 388188
W: colnestoves.com

Waveney Stoves and Fireplaces *OTB*
123 Old Yarmouth Rd, Ellingham,
Bungay NR35 2PG
T: 01508 518863
W: waveneystoves.co.uk

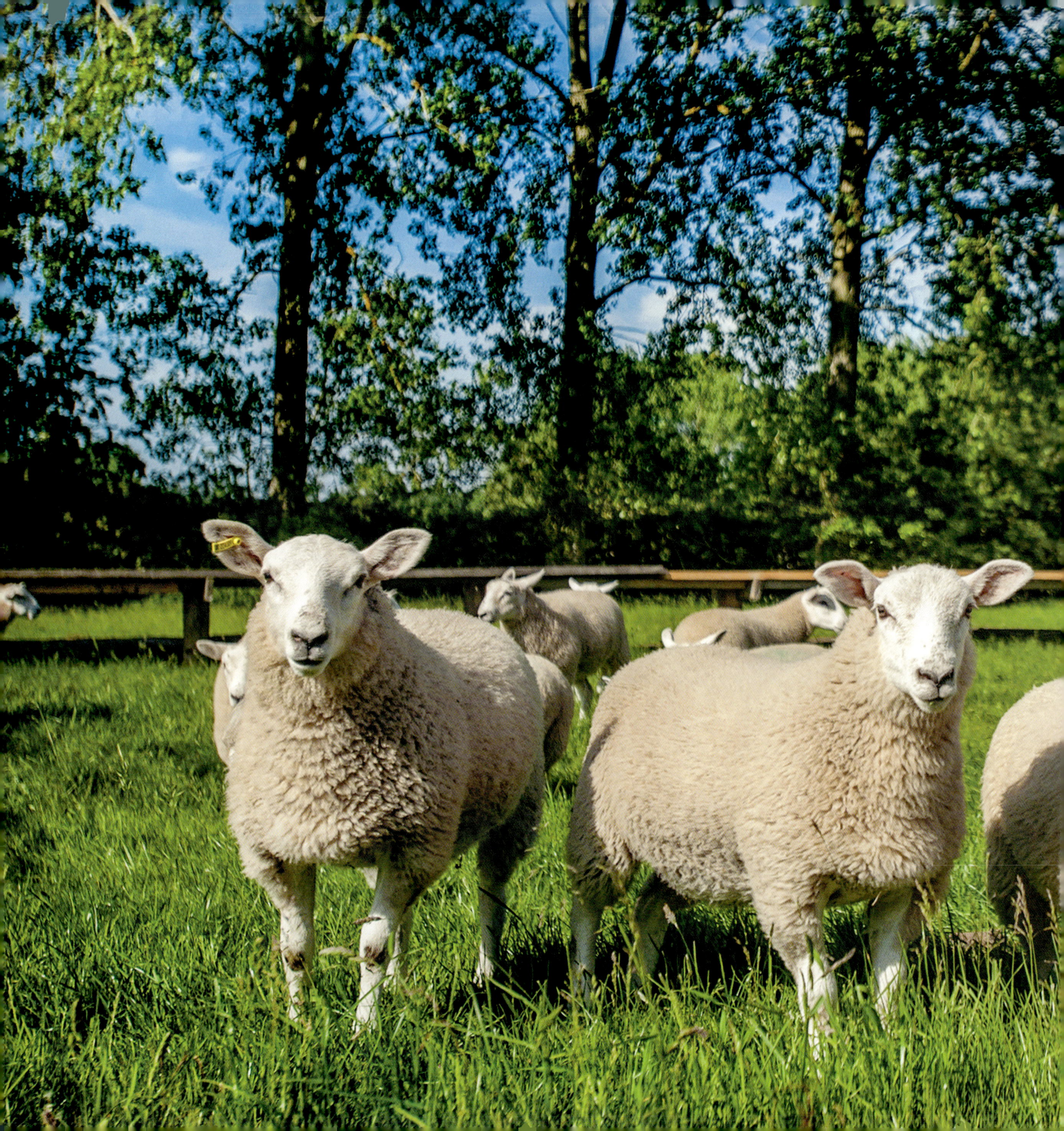

Recipe index

Starters, sides and light bites

Seared scallops and cauliflower	20
Smoked salmon with horseradish crème fraîche and beetroot	20
Parsley risotto	21
Sea trout tartare, horseradish crème fraîche	30
Beef tartare	40
Salt-baked celeriac soup, smoked mackerel and English mustard	40
Crab risotto	50
Salt cod tartare fishcakes	50
Citrus-marinated salmon mi-cuit	60
Finger lickin' partridge	70
Pork jowl, oyster mushroom and artichoke broth, cavolo nero	80
Carrots with honey, herbs and buttermilk	80
Zacuscă	90
Courgette carpaccio	90
Hummus	91
Wild alexanders with a foraged herb dressing	110
Warm salad of wood pigeon	120
Oyster tempura with seaweed salad cream and dill oil	130
Venison tartare with egg yolk dressing	131
Chorizo, brie and spicy 'nduja arancini	140
Oyster velouté	140
Buck rarebit	141
Venison scrumpets	150
Spiced pigs' cheek, black pudding and spinach	160
Sticky chicken wings and blue cheese dip	170
Heritage tomato, semi-dried olive and artichoke linguine	180
Beetroot-cured salmon, pickled beets and burnt orange	190
Tossed salad of crispy duck livers, smoked bacon and a cyder dressing	200
Smoked mackerel scotch egg with piccalilli	208
Eggs benedict with smoked eel and spinach	210

Mains

Partridge and duck liver wellington and terrine, boulangère potato	18
Chicken breast, leg croquette, leek, morels, tarragon, malted barley broth	28
Skillet-roasted Denham Estate venison haunch with turnips, confit potato and salted walnuts	38
Rabbit and roots stew with herb dumplings, greens, wild mushrooms and Suffolk cyder	48
Stuffed saddle of lamb, savoy cabbage and fondant potato	59
Buckwheat-crusted halibut steaks	61
Roast woodcock, wild mushroom risotto, root vegetables and balsamic onions	68
Pan-fried partridge breasts, parsnips three ways, English truffle oil	70
Lobster, oyster mayonnaise, alexanders butter, sea greens	78
Persian rice with kale, butternut squash, pumpkin seeds and turmeric aioli	88
Pink-poached loin and slow-roast leg of lamb, sweetbreads, roast onion and spring greens	98
Pheasant three ways	100
Lamb roly poly	101
Skate wing, caper and lemon butter sauce, new potatoes and purple sprouting broccoli	108
Smoked duck breast, sloe jelly and beetroot	110
Honey glazed pork tenderloin, Suffolk Blue cheese, black cabbage, Aspall cyder	118

SUFFOLK FEAST

Herb-crusted sea bass, crab, egg tagliatelle and vegetable ribbons	120
Rare-seared cutlets and ale-braised hogget breast	130
Blythburgh pork selection	148
Smoked haddock crumble, foraged samphire and tiger prawns	150
Celeriac and apple	160
Fillet of Longhorn beef, crispy bonbon, asparagus and wild garlic gnocchi	168
Pan-fried skate wing with prawn and cucumber butter	170
Roasted pheasant, chestnut gnocchi and truffle-scented wild mushroom fricassée	178
Rare-roasted venison steaks with heritage baby beets	180
Muntjac wellington, buttered heritage vegetables, butternut squash and red wine sauce	188
Cured pork ribeye, sweetheart cabbage, roast parsnips and a cyder and mushroom cream sauce	198
Pan-fried smoked mackerel, horseradish and potato salad	200
Seafood fricassée	210

Double-baked blackberry and pear soufflé	121
Wooster's sprouted rye sourdough and black treacle tart, buttermilk sorbet, blueberries, bee pollen and lemon verbena	128
Dark chocolate, campari, blood orange and honeycomb	139
Lemon curd	151
Apple crumble and custard	159
Strawberries and cream	161
Vanilla cheesecake and berry compote	171
White chocolate and vanilla pannacotta	181
Chocolate fondant puddings	190
Ginger crème brûlée	191
Apple and muscovado sugar parfait, walnuts and butterscotch	201
French toast with apple and maple syrup	211

Puddings

Elderflower gin pannacotta	30
Oat and whisky cranachan with raspberry sorbet	31
Roast apples with white chocolate and tarragon	41
Strawberry cheesecake	51
Risotto rice pudding and lemon ice cream	60
Cinnamon pannacotta with blackberry and apple	71
Baba au rhum	81
Apple parfait	101
Sticky toffee pudding	111

SUFFOLK FEAST: OUR FAVOURITE PLACES

Whether you're in the mood for elegant fine dining, or it's more a wet dog and muddy wellies sort of day, we've got it covered. From characterful town-centre neighbourhood restaurants to pubs with personality, some very classy hotels, and even a private chef, you need look no further than this line-up. We're not saying these are the only places in Suffolk to eat of course, but we are naturally particularly fond of them!

The Bildeston Crown
104 High Street, Bildeston IP7 7EB
W: thebildestoncrown.com
T: 01449 740510
12 bedrooms

The Swan Hotel
Market Place, Southwold IP18 6EG
W: theswansouthwold.co.uk
T: 01502 722186
35 bedrooms

The Packhorse Inn
Bridge Street, Moulton CB8 8SP
W: thepackhorseinn.com
T: 01638 751818
8 bedrooms

Mackenzie-David Events
Aldeburgh Yacht Club, Slaughden Road,
Aldeburgh IP15 5NA
W: mackenzie-david.co.uk
T: 01986 893991 / 07460 400276

Maison Bleue
Churchgate Street, Bury St Edmunds IP33 1RG
W: maisonbleue.co.uk
T: 01284 760623

The Froize
Chillesford, Woodbridge IP12 3PU
W: froize.co.uk
T: 01394 450282

Tuddenham Mill
High Street, Tuddenham,
Newmarket IP28 6SQ
W: tuddenhammill.co.uk
T: 01638 713552
15 bedrooms and 6 meadow nooks

The Anchor
The Street, Walberswick IP18 6UA
W: anchoratwalberswick.com
T: 01502 722112
10 bedrooms

Frederick's, The Ickworth
Horringer, Bury St Edmunds IP29 5QE
W: ickworthhotel.co.uk
T: 01284 735350
27 bedrooms plus apartments and lodges

The Table
3 Quay St, Woodbridge IP12 1BX
W: thetablewoodbridge.co.uk
T: 01394 382428

Hintlesham Hall
Hintlesham, Ipswich IP8 3NS
W: hintleshamhall.co.uk
T: 01473 652334
32 bedrooms

The Angel Hotel
Angel Hill, Bury St Edmunds IP33 1LT
W: theangel.co.uk
T: 01284 714000
77 bedrooms

The Unruly Pig
Orford Road, Bromeswell,
Woodbridge IP12 2PU
W: theunrulypig.co.uk
T: 01394 460310

The Boarding House Dining Rooms
10 Market Place, Halesworth IP19 8BA
W: boardinghousehalesworth.com
T: 01986 948306
new bedrooms opening soon

Stoke by Nayland Hotel, Golf & Spa
Keepers Lane, Leavenheath,
Colchester CO6 4PZ
W: stokebynayland.com
T: 01206 262836
80 bedrooms and 5 country lodges

The Plough & Sail
Snape Maltings, Snape IP17 1SR
W: theploughandsailsnape.com
T: 01728 688413
2 bedrooms (at The Golden Key, Snape)

The Weeping Willow
Bury Road, Barrow, Bury St Edmunds IP29 5AB
W: theweepingwillow.co.uk
T: 01284 771881

The Angel Inn
Polstead St, Stoke by Nayland CO6 4SA
W: angelinnsuffolk.co.uk
T: 01206 263245
6 bedrooms

The Kitchen@Thorpeness
Remembrance Road, Thorpeness IP16 4NW
W: thekitchenthorpeness.co.uk
T: 01728 453266
1 apartment for short breaks

The Sail Loft
53 Ferry Road, Southwold IP18 6HQ
W: sailloftsouthwold.uk
T: 01502 725713
5 bedrooms